Asian American Women

Asian American Women

◆

Issues, Concerns, and Responsive Human and Civil Rights Advocacy

Second Edition

Lora Jo Foo

iUniverse, Inc.
New York Lincoln Shanghai

Asian American Women
Issues, Concerns, and Responsive Human and Civil Rights Advocacy

iUniverse books may be ordered through booksellers or by contacting:

iUniverse
2021 Pine Lake Road, Suite 100
Lincoln, NE 68512
www.iuniverse.com
1-800-Authors (1-800-288-4677)

Because of the dynamic nature of the Internet, any Web addresses or links contained in this book may have changed since publication and may no longer be valid.

ISBN: 978-0-595-45299-6 (pbk)
ISBN: 978-0-595-90115-9 (cloth)
ISBN: 978-0-595-89613-4 (ebk)

Printed in the United States of America

Credits

Cover: Courtesy of Sweatshop Watch. Chinese American garment workers employed by Wins demonstrate for justice in San Francisco.

p.3 Courtesy of CAAAV: Organizing Asian Communities.

p.38 Courtesy of the Asian American Legal Defense and Education Fund (AALDEF). Design by Ramon Gil Art & Design.

p.59 Courtesy of Sweatshop Watch. Photographer: Robert Gumpert.

p.83 Courtesy of Service Employees International Union (SEIU), Local 616. Photographer: N'Sombi A. Mohammed.

p.121 Courtesy of Asian & Pacific Islanders for Reproductive Health (APIRH).

p.139 Courtesy of the Asian Women's Shelter. Design by Nancy Hom.

p.188 Thank you to Dr. Lawrence J. White for his statistical assistance with this pie chart.

p.203 Courtesy of National Asian Pacific American Women's Forum.

Contents

Part III   Special Focus

Preface to the Second Edition

Can a single report begin to fill the shameful void of data and research on Asian American women or to undo the harmful, mistaken view that they are a "model minority" and therefore have no social and economic needs or concerns?

This is exactly what *Asian American Women: Issues, Concerns, and Responsive Human and Civil Rights Advocacy* has taken on, with pioneering research, analysis and policy recommendations that take on the multiple influences of race, gender, class, age, language, immigrant status and other complexities. Five years after the original groundbreaking report was published in 2002, this updated edition reprises its broad network through groups like the National Asian Pacific American Women's Forum, Asian & Pacific Islander Institute on Domestic Violence, Southeast Asia Research Action Center and other knowledgeable community-based organizations to bring new understandings on the rapidly evolving landscape for Asian American women.

The Asian Americans has increased by 3 million since the first edition, to 14 million, now five percent of the U.S. population and growing. In spite of the significant growth, the damage resulting from long-standing ignorance and neglect is real: a study by the Asian Americans and Pacific Islanders in Philanthropy found that only 0.2 percent of foundation funding has gone to support Asian American and Pacific Islander communities, while few policy discussions on poverty, health, education, or other pressing issues include Asian Americans.

Asian American Women exposes the fallacies and policy traps that result when the 40+ Asian and Pacific Islander ethnic groups in the U.S. are lumped together. By disaggregating the data, author Lora Jo Foo and the many contributors are able to identify the segments of this population that are most at-risk and least considered. Their report brings a sorely-needed approach to these neglected populations.

Using meticulous research from survey data and scores of interviews, this report demonstrates how a disproportionate burden of budget cuts has fallen on Asian American immigrant women, for example; or how significant numbers of Asian women are pushed into dead-end workfare jobs where they learn no skills and are denied English-language training as an option; and that many immigrant welfare recipients lost or were denied benefits because the state failed to provide interpreters or to translate documents. The results fly in the face of prevailing stereotypes and assumptions about Asian Americans.

Without the sensationalism that accompanies news reports on trafficking, *Asian American Women* details the human rights battle of tens of thousands of women each year who are brought to the U.S. from the most impoverished countries of Asia. Lured by false promises of good jobs, they are enslaved, forced into prostitution, bonded sweatshop labor, and domestic servitude by criminal groups, wealthy émigrés and international bureaucrats alike.

Other chapters examine health and reproductive issues and the prevalence of domestic violence, sexual assault, or diseases like Hepatitis B; cervical cancer among Vietnamese American women; suicides of Chinese American women at rates that far exceed any other U.S. racial or ethnic group. The report also takes a close-up look at some of the least visible populations of all: Hmong Americans, Asian American lesbian, bisexual and transgender women, and the particular needs in the state of Hawai'i.

Besides offering a wealth of documentation, *Asian American Women* has a larger significance—it is a guide to advocacy and call for action. This updated edition of *Asian American Women* continues to set the benchmark for what is known—and what yet needs to be known—about the issues and concerns of women in these diverse communities. Here is a clear and compelling framework that removes ignorance as an excuse for political inertia, for doing nothing. By giving voice to these women, *Asian American Women* is a significant contribution and a must-read for all who work toward social justice and a stronger democracy.

Helen Zia is the author of
*Asian American Dreams: The
Emergence of An American People*

Preface to the First Edition

Fifty years ago, the United Nations adopted the Universal Declaration of Human Rights declaring that all human beings are born free and equal in dignity and rights, including the right to life, liberty, and security of person; the right to be free from hunger; and the right to have clothing, housing, and medical services. Yet, these fundamental human rights of Asian American women are denied every day. For example, they are trafficked into the US for sexual or severe labor exploitation, they work excessively long hours and earn poverty level wages as garment and domestic workers, they are slowly poisoned in high-tech jobs and endure degrading treatment when they try to access the US immigration, welfare and health care systems. In addition, prevailing racist and sexist stereotypes create a perception of Asian American women as the "other" and, as a result, their lives and issues are practically invisible to mainstream America. The Ford Foundation commissioned Lora Jo Foo to assist it in learning about the social and economic justice agenda of Asian American women.[1] Her report, Asian American Women: Issues, Concerns, and Responsive Human and Civil Rights Advocacy, illuminates the current situation of Asian American women in the United States.

This report builds on work done in 1997 and 1998 by the National Asian Pacific American Women's Forum (NAPAWF) to identify the issues facing Asian American women. NAPAWF held meetings with Asian American women in San Francisco, Seattle, Los Angeles, New York City, and Minneapolis, the results of which helped provide the framework for this report. The report "puts meat on the bones" of that framework, focusing on the two states with the largest Asian American populations, California and New York, and devoting special attention to the State of Hawai'i[2], which has the highest percentage of Asian Americans, and to Minnesota, the state with the second largest number of

---

1. The issues facing Pacific Islander women are not covered in this report. Not having sufficient familiarity with the Pacific Islander communities, Ms. Foo felt she could not write about or do justice to their issues. A report on Pacific Island women is more appropriately written by a Pacific Islander woman.
2. State residents prefer this punctuation.

Hmong Americans (after California). The first draft of this report was presented to a meeting convened by the Ford Foundation in June 2001 of longtime Asian American women activists from around the country who worked on the issues covered in this report. The final report incorporates their comments, critiques and invaluable contributions.

Only empowered Asian American women can make lasting changes in their communities and beyond. To achieve this, as the report shows, grassroots organizing and base-building efforts are crucial. An equally effective advocacy model has been the coalition work used by Asian American women. To build on what has been achieved, for Asian American women to move their social justice agenda and make the systemic changes needed to end the civil and human rights violations inflicted on them, a significant infusion of resources is needed to strengthen the capacity of the grassroots, base-building organizations and coalitions and to build regional and national infrastructure and institutions. The issues facing Asian American women are dire but the resources available to them are disproportionately low for the size of the population.

Although Asian American and Pacific Islander Americans (APA) are the fastest growing groups in the United States and significant numbers live well below poverty levels, very few resources are devoted to improving their situation. According to a study by Asian Americans/Pacific Islanders in Philanthropy, while Asian Americans represent 4% of the US population, only 0.2% of foundation funds were given to organizations working specifically on Asian American and Pacific Islander concerns. Unable to access major sources of foundation funding, Asian American communities have the weakest national infrastructure and institutions, and smallest budgets compared to their counterparts in other communities of color. There are only two small national Asian American women's advocacy organizations with paid staff[3], two fledgling national women's membership organizations without paid staff[4], and five national Asian American organizations[5] whose advocacy work, though not targeted at women's issues, has had an impact on Asian American women.

---

3.   The Asian and Pacific Islander Domestic Violence Institute and the National Asian Women's Health Organization.
4.   The National Asian Pacific American Women's Forum and the Asian Pacific, Lesbian, Bisexual and Transgender Network.
5.   The National Asian Pacific American Legal Consortium, the National Korean American Services and Education Consortium (NAKASEC), the Southeast Asia Resource Action Center, the Asian Pacific American Labor Alliance (AFL-CIO), and the Asian Pacific Islander Health Forum.

Despite the paucity of funding, beginning in the late 1960's, Asian American women organized against the civil and human rights violations inflicted against their sisters. Lacking strong national and women's organizations, the advocacy on behalf of Asian American women, then and now, and as reflected in this report, tends to be at the local level and through nongender specific organizations. However, the impact of these efforts has gone beyond the local level because Asian American women have worked with or led multiethnic coalitions in both joint advocacy and organizing efforts.[6] As this report explains, these groups have succeeded on many fronts including the legislative arena, in union organizing, and in consumer education campaigns, advocating for culturally and linguistically accessible services and breaking the silence on issues not previously considered appropriate for public discussion in many Asian communities. Asian American Women: Issues, Concerns, and Responsive Human and Civil Rights Advocacy speaks to foundations and charitable organizations; local, state, and federal level policy makers; advocates for social justice; universities and scholars; and members of the public committed to strengthening democracy. I hope the courage and integrity with which Asian American women speak through Lora Jo Foo's work on this report inspires and challenges institutions and individuals to join in this conversation and respond to this call to action.

Barbara Y. Phillips
Program Officer
Human Rights
Peace and Social Justice Program
The Ford Foundation

---

6. For instance, the San Francisco-based Asian Law Caucus led the successful statewide effort in the passage of the Sweatshop Accountability Bill, which will help women garment workers throughout California. The Caucus was also active in the effort to raise the minimum wage in California, which resulted in an increase in the federal minimum wage. For many years, the San Francisco-based Asian Women's Shelter and other local shelters engaged in advocacy in California for culturally and linguistically accessible domestic violence services that also had national impact.

Introduction

In 1999, as I was leaving the Asian Law Caucus after nine years as its Employ-ment/Labor attorney, Barbara Phillips was beginning her job as the program officer for the women's portfolio at the Ford Foundation. Barbara wanted to diversify her portfolio and begin funding women of color organizations. But she needed to learn about our communities. She asked me to write a think piece for her on the issues facing Asian American women.

I already had a clear idea about the priority issues for Asian American women. We had begun to identify our concerns in Beijing in 1995 at the Fourth World Women's Conference, where over 100 Asian American women met to discuss our issues. Upon returning to the United States, many of the women who were in Beijing founded the National Asian Pacific American Women's Forum (NAPAWF). I became its first national co-chair. The issues covered in this book were identified as priority issues for Asian American women at gatherings of NAPAWF held throughout 1997 and 1998 in cities around the country. I saw writing the think piece as an opportunity to "put meat on the bones," so to speak, of this framework of issues.

As I began my research, I was appalled by what I was finding. I began to understand the extent of the human and civil rights violations committed against Asian American women. I had already organized and advocated on behalf of Asian American women for close to 30 years, but outside of my area of expertise I was still fairly ignorant of the extent of the violations I was uncovering. I began writing not just for Barbara, but to educate our Asian American communities, advocates, organizers, service providers, policy mak-ers and funders. The think piece turned into a100 plus page report, then a book.

This book is divided into three parts and 10 chapters. Each chapter covers very different concerns of Asian American women. But a common thread runs through all the chapters: in the United States, race, gender and class oppressions converge to deny Asian American women their fundamental human rights. Racist and sexist stereotyping of Asian women turn us into the "other" so that society can turn a blind eye to the human rights violations we experience. The book is a call to action for Asian American women and our supporters to end these violations against us.

Part One covers Economic Justice, Part Two covers Health and Well-being, and Part Three looks at specific Asian American communities that receive very little attention. Each chapter of *Asian American Women: Issues, Concerns, and Responsive Human and Civil Rights Advocacy* places the issues Asian American women face in the broader economic, legal, political, and/or historical contexts of American society and describes specifically how Asian American women are affected. With the exception of domestic violence and issues of lesbian women that affect Asian American women across the socio-economic spectrum, the human and civil rights violations identified in this book affect primarily Asian immigrant women at the bottom of the economic ladder where poverty rates can be as high as 63% and limited English proficiency (LEP) is over 70% in certain Southeast Asian communities.

The chapters make assessments of the advocacy needed to address the issues and provide background information about some of the organizations that do the work. The book focuses on the grassroots and coalition efforts that have been the mainstay of the activism of Asian American women.

Part One, Economic Justice, looks at the class, race, and gender dynamics that work together to depress the socio-economic status of Asian American women. Chapter One deals with the new Welfare Reform system that discriminates against and denies equal access to public benefits to Asian immigrant women and their families. Chapter Two discusses the human rights violations suffered by Asian women who are trafficked into the United States and subjected to severe labor and sexual exploitation. Chapters Three and Four examine the various industries where the majority of poor Asian American women work and how they are trapped in the lowest paying jobs, laboring excessively long hours, often in unsafe workplaces, facing discrimination, and with little to no opportunity to move up the ladder.

Part Two, Health and Well-Being, examines the particular health concerns of Asian American women. The U.S. health care system is struggling to meet the needs of the U.S. citizen population, the majority of whom speak English; the needs of Asian American women are barely visible. There is very little data on the health status of Asian American women, and health care providers are guided instead by stereotypes and assumptions that can lead to misdiagnosis or worse. Chapter Five looks at the health care disparities between Asian American women and the general population and points to the urgent need to look at differences among Asian ethnic groups. Chapters Six and Seven address sexual and reproductive health and domestic violence; issues that have long been considered taboo subjects in Asian American communities. However, the consequences of silence around these issues can have fatal consequences and must be addressed.

Part Three, Special Focus, examines the needs of three particularly marginalized or invisible groups of Asian American women. These are Hmong women (Chapter Eight), Filipina and Native Hawai'ian women in Hawai'i (Chapter Nine) and lesbian, bisexual, and transgendered (LBT) Asian American women (Chapter Ten). Hmong American women are engaged in a powerful struggle to transform their patriarchal culture in a way that keeps the positive aspects but changes other aspects in order to fulfill the basic human right to be free from violence. Hawai'i has a predominantly Asian American population and the combination of race, class, and gender oppression play out very differently than it does on the mainland. Finally, Asian American LBTQs experience multiple forms of oppression based on race, gender, and sexual orientation making them perhaps the most marginalized of Asian American women.

PAUCITY OF DATA ON ASIAN AMERICA

Exacerbating the problems for Asian American women is the lack of data relating to their issues. Census 2000 counted about 11.9 million Asians/Asian Americans in the United States or 4 percent of the U.S. population. By 2007, the Asian American population increased by 3 million to 14.9 million or five percent of the U.S. population. Comprising only 5% of the U.S. population, Asian Americans' representation is "statistically insignificant" in most national studies, such as those on the impact of welfare reform, health, domestic violence, and low-wage workers. In certain key states such as California where 12% of the state's population is Asian American and a large enough population set for regional studies, the invisibility and perceived sameness has meant that little funding has been available from government or foundations for community specific studies. The studies that do include Asian American women have a tendency to focus on selected ethnic groups and/or do not disaggregate the data for the over 40 distinct ethnic groups that make up the Asian American community in the United States. The gap in data or failure to disaggregate can have dire consequences when, for example, it "hides" evidence about the distinct health needs of particular groups or fails to show how the impact of policies and programs varies from one Asian American community to another. The author and contributors to the second edition of this book made efforts to locate and review the relevant studies on Asian Americans. However, very little exists and in some places, they were forced to make use of anecdotal information. Clearly, there needs to be an increase in research, data collection, and statistical analysis relating to the issues raised in this book.

HISTORY OF ASIANS IN AMERICA[1]

The Asian presence in North America predates the 13 colonies' declaration of independence from Great Britain. The first Asians arrived in the Americas in the 1500's; they were reportedly conscripted sailors, primarily from what is now the Philippines, who jumped ship to seek freedom. Asians did not begin arriving in large numbers until the mid 1800's when the British ended the slave trade from Africa and started importing "coolies" from China and India to various parts of the Caribbean. Large numbers of Chinese laborers began arriving in the United States during the "Gold Rush" and during the construction of the Trans-Continental Railroad. But anti-Chinese sentiments against the influx of Chinese during the recessions of that period led, in 1882, to Congress passing the Chinese Exclusion Act. This was the first legislation passed on the basis of race and barred all Chinese from becoming U.S. citizens.

Other nations filled the gap created by the ban on Chinese labor. Workers from Japan, India, the Philippines, and Korea began arriving in the late 1880's. Most settled in the Western part of the United States with large concentrations of Japanese, as well as Koreans and Filipinos, in California and what is now the State of Hawai'i. By the turn of the century, several thousand Punjabi farmers were working on California farms. U.S. colonization of the Philippines meant that Filipinos had the status of U.S. nationals and were eligible for immigration to the U.S. However, this ended in 1934 when the Philippines was reclassified as a commonwealth which resulted in a change of status for Filipinos. They became aliens and hence, ineligible for citizenship.

---

1.   This section draws on Helen Zia, Asian American Dreams: The Emergence of an American People, Farrar, Straus and Giroux, 2000.

It is now well known that Japanese Americans were interned in camps during the xenophobic period of World War II.

By the early 1960's, approximately 500,000 Asians lived in the United States. Large numbers began arriving after repeal of anti-Asian exclusion laws and the passage of the 1965 Immigration Act lifted quotas based on national origin. The effect was immediate: between 1960 and 1970, immigration from Asia rose to above 10% of total immigration. The first wave of immigrants from the 1965 Act included large numbers of professionals from South and Southeast Asia, leading publications such as The New York Times and U.S. News and World Report to contrast their skill level and work ethics with those of African Americans. This was the birth of the "model minority" myth that endures to this day.

The Vietnam War was a turning point for Asian America on many levels. Outraged by U.S. action in Vietnam, Asian American students took part in antiwar protests. Influenced by parallel developments in the U.S. civil rights movement, these students also highlighted the racist overtones in the news coverage of events in Southeast Asia. It was at this time that the term "Asian American," created to replace the derogatory term "Oriental," came into parlance. During the civil rights movement and upheavals of the 1960's, Asian American women became politically active in large numbers. Second- and third- generation Chinese, Japanese, and Filipino women were involved in organizing against past and present injustices, indignities, and human rights violations against their communities and themselves. As a result of demands made during the militant student strikes of 1968, the first Asian American Studies centers were established and Asian American women's courses taught at San Francisco State University and the University of California, Berkeley.

In the early 1970's, large numbers of Cambodians, Laotians, and Vietnamese, displaced by the ravages of the Indo-China wars, began arriving in the United States. They were accepted as "boat people" but dispersed throughout the country with the hopes that they would soon blend in and assimilate. This wave of immigration included large numbers of women and children. In addition, significant number of middle class persons from all over Asia began arriving in 1970's with their working class counterparts arriving in large numbers in the 1980's. Once settled, the family members of immigrants also made the move from Asia. In all, some 4.5 million Asian immigrated to the US between 1970 and 1990.

DEMOGRAPHIC OVERVIEW [2]

Census 2000 reveals a nation in change and more diversified than 10 years earlier due in large part to immigration. From 1990 to 2000, the Asian American population increased by 52% from 6.6 million to 10 million, or 11.6 million when part-Asians are included. By comparison, the Hispanic population increased by 58% from 22 million to 35 million. Whites dropped from 76% in 1990 to 69% of the total U.S. population in 2000 while Hispanics increased to 13% and Asians to 4% of the U.S. population. (See Figure 1). By 2007, the U.S. Census Bureau estimates that Whites dropped to 66.6% while Asians increased to 5% of the U.S. population.

While the traditional entry points for Asians remain California where 36% and New York where 10% of the nation's Asian Americans live, the number of Asians in states like Indiana, Arkansas, and South Dakota doubled between 1990 and 2000. Half of all Asian Americans still live in the Western Region and 75% live in 10 states. (See Table 1). In 2000, half of all Asian Americans live in just three states—California (4.2 million), New York (1.2 million), and Hawai'i (0.7 million). By 2005, the state of Texas overtook Hawai'i as the state with the third largest Asian American population (726,027). In 2005, 922,978 Asians lived in New York City, 415,652 in Los Angeles, and about 250,000 in San Francisco, San Jose, and Honolulu.

In 2000, no racial or ethnic group is the majority in the State of California. (See Figure 2). Asians were the third largest group, making up from 11% to 12% (when part-Asians are included) of the state's population, with Hispanics at 32% and Whites at 47%. By 2005, Asians increased to 12.4% of California's population. Asian Americans are a larger percentage of certain counties and cities. In 2005, Asians make up 33.1% of San Francisco, 30.2% of Santa Clara, and 24.5% of Alameda counties. In Southern California, Los Angeles and Orange counties are 13.1% and 16.1% Asian, respectively. Six California cities are now majority Asian—Monterey Park (62%), Cerritos (58.4%), Walnut (55.6%), Milpitas (51.8%), Daly City (50.75%), and Rowland Hills (50.3%). In New York, the changes were also dramatic. Asian Americans increased to 10% of New York State's population. Asians are now

---

2.   The data in this section is drawn from U.S. Census 2000 and the Census Bureau's 2004 and 2005 American Community Survey Reports, found at http://www.census.gov/prod/2007pubs/acs-05.pdf and http://factfinder.census.gov.

10% of New York City as well. For the first time, New York City's White population make up less than half of the residents, at 45% of the city.

Census 2000 indicates that a wide gap remains between affluent Asians and those living in poverty. Though the Census Bureau has not released details, its March 1999 Current Population Reports states that while one-third of Asian families have incomes of $75,000 or more, one-fifth have incomes of less than $25,000. Asians are more likely than Whites to have earned a college degree and to have less than a ninth-grade education. Asian Americans occupy the extreme spectrums: from wealth to poverty, entrepreneurial success to marginal daily survival, advanced education to illiteracy. Research and data concerning Asian Americans often are not disaggregated for different subgroups. For example, when certain Asian ethnic subgroups have had poverty rates as high as 63%, Census 2000 reports an overall poverty rate of 10.7%. The Census Bureau's 2004 American Communities Survey disaggregated data for only six—Asian Indian, Chinese, Filipino, Japanese, Korean and Vietnamese—out of over 40 ethnic subgroups and reported an overall poverty rate of 12%, lower than the overall poverty rate of 13.1% for the U.S. population. The result is a picture that portrays Asian Americans as a "model minority" and hides the human and civil rights violations suffered by Asian American women at the bottom of the economic ladder.

▶ Table 1.

Ten States with Largest Asian and Pacific Islander American Populations in 2000

Rank (Highest Numbers of Asians)	State	Number Choosing Only Asian or Pacific Islander	Including Part Asians or Part APIs	Percent of State[2]		Percent of Asians/API Nationally (Minimum)
				Min	Max	
	All States	10,476,678	12,327,643			
1	California	3,752,596	4,321,585	11%	13%	36%
2	New York	1,041,156	1,167,226	5.5%	6%	10%
3	Hawaii	602,590	858,105	50%	71%	6%
4	Texas	565,202	644,087	2.7%	3%	5.4%
5	New Jersey	479,187	523,971	5.7%	6%	4.6%
6	Illinois	423,032	473,830	3.4%	3.8%	4%
7	Washington	342,180	427,328	5.8%	7%	3.3%
8	Florida	268,954	340,589	1.6%	2%	2.6%
9	Virginia	262,657	308,645	3.7%	4.4%	2.5%
10	Massachusetts	238,492	268,027	3.7%	4.2%	2.2%

Source: US Census Bureau and NY Times on The Web, http://nytime.com/2001/

[1] Census 2000 separated the Asian and Pacific Islander categories. Total Asian only population figures are 10,123,169 and Pacific Islander only population figures are 353,509. The figures listed in this table are combined Asian and Pacific Islander population figures, the only figures available to the author for these states as of this writing.

[2] Minimum percent represents percent of population who chose Asian or Pacific Islander only on Census 2000 and maximum percent includes those who chose Asians or API and another race.

▶ Figure 1.

A New Look at Race in America

Categories in 2000 are not directly comparable with those in 1990 because 2000 question-naire was the first that allowed people to choose more than one race.

Population	1990 Census	2000 Census	
		Number choosing just one race	Number choosing this race with other race(s)
Non-Hispanic			
White	188,128,296	194,552,774	198,177,900
Black	29,216,293	33,947,837	35,383,751
American Indian and Alaska Native	1,793,773	2,068,883	3,444,700
Asian	6,642,481	10,123,169	11,579,494
Native Hawai'ian and Other Pacific Islander	325,878	353,509	748,149
Other	249,093	467,770	
Hispanic			
(may be of any race)	22,354,059	35,305,818	1,770,645
Total Population	248,709,873	281,421,906	

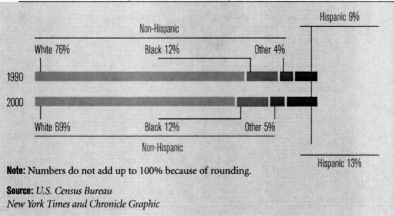

Note: Numbers do not add up to 100% because of rounding.

Source: *U.S. Census Bureau*
New York Times and Chronicle Graphic

▶ Figure 2.

California's Ethnic Pie

These pie charts reflect changes made in census breakdowns for race and ethnicity. In 2000, Asians and Pacific Islanders were counted as separate catergories and a mixed-race group was added. Hispanics have been subtracted from each racial category, so "black" shows non-Hispanic blacks, "white" shows non-Hispanic whites etc.

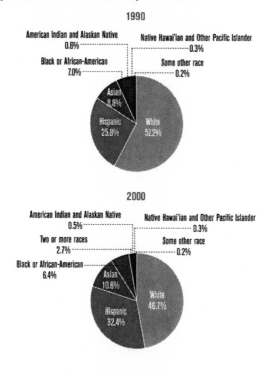

How Californians in major ethnic or racials groups identified themselves (Hispanics subtracted to create their own category):

White		Hispanic		Asian		Black	
1990	2000	1990	2000	1990	2000	1990	2000
57.2%	46.7%	25.8%	32.4%	8.8%	10.8%	7%	6.4%
17,029,126	15,816,790	7,687,938	10,966,556	2,613,599	3,648,860	2,092,446	2,181,926
Total for 2000 is 16,538,491 when counting people who listed more than one race.		In both 1990 and 2000, Hispanics could be of any race.		Total for 2000 is 4,030,025 when counting people who listed more than one race.		Total for 2000 is 2,370,367 when counting people who listed more than one race.	

Source: *U.S. Census Bureau*

NEW TO THE SECOND EDITION

Seven of the chapters of the second edition of this book were updated by Asian American women activists, advocates and/or organizers who have dedicated their lives to the elimination of the human and civil rights violations described in this book. Chapter 9, Hawai'i: A Different Paradigm remains unchanged because the author was unable to locate a local activist to update this chapter. Chapter 8, Hmong Women, was updated by a Hmong American woman so they could tell their story, that is, to provide a perspective that I, a non-Hmong, could not provide in the original chapter. This new chapter also includes the perspectives of Hmong men. Each of the updated chapters includes new statistics and facts drawn from studies and surveys conducted in the five years since the first edition. These studies, among other things, have confirmed the devastating results of Welfare Reform on Asian American women and their children. Another startling result is a focus on the higher prevalence of domestic violence in certain of our Asian American communities as well as the higher likelihood of Asian American domestic violence victims to die from domestic violence-related homicide than their white counterparts. Globalization continues to take its toll, resulting in the disappearance of jobs that Asian immigrant women relied on for their livelihoods, such as virtually all assembly line jobs in Silicon Valley and tens of thousands of jobs in the domestic garment industry. While these industries declined, Asian immigrant women found new jobs in the nail salon industry—which has led to increased health problems. Fortunately, Asian American grassroots and advocacy organizations have sprung up to address the problems these women face when exposed to the toxic chemicals found in the cosmetics that they use—chemicals that have been linked to miscarriages, infertility, and other reproductive harm.

On the positive side, the second edition highlights new and successful grassroots organizing efforts such as the struggle of Korean immigrant women restaurant workers for decent wages and working conditions in Los Angeles, and the defeat of parental notification ballot measures in California. In the intervening five years, a number of Asian American women's organizations have grown in strength and experience. For example, the National Asian Pacific American Women's Forum (NAPAWF) has grown from an organization run by volunteers to one with paid staff whose presence and voice is felt and heard in the national arena. The Asian & Pacific Islander Institute on Domestic Violence (APIDV) has conducted several major research projects that have added significantly to the knowledge of domestic violence in our communities. In addition, with seed funding from the Ford Foundation in 2005, the National Gender and Equity Campaign (the Campaign) was launched. Through grant-making, capacity-building, and the creation of learning communities, the Campaign seeks to build infrastructure in our communities and support social change work that lifts up and puts gender inequities on equal footing with other societal inequities, thereby addressing the underlying systemic problems that results in the perpetuation of the human and civil rights violations against Asian and Pacific Islander American women.

REFERENCES

Barnes, Jessica S. and Claudette E. Bennett, The Asian Population: 2000, Census 2000 Brief, US Census Bureau, C2KBR/01-16, February 2002

Chronicle News Service, New York City's Population Grows To 8 Million, Hispanics, African Americans in equal proportions, census says, San Francisco Chronicle, March 16, 2001

Fields, Robin, A Deepening Diversity, but a Growing Divide, Los Angeles Times, March 30, 2001

Hong, Peter Y., Daniel Yi, Fastest Growth of Any Ethnic Group in State, Los Angeles Times, March 30, 2001

Humes, Karen, and Jesse McKinnon, The Asian and Pacific Islander Population in the United States, Population Characteristics, US Census Bureau, March 1999 (issued September 2000)

Kim, Ryan, Census 2000, Who We Are, More Pacific Islanders Living In California Than in Hawai'i, San Francisco, Chronicle, March 31, 2001

La Ganga, Maria L., Shawn Hubler, California Grows to 33.9 Million, Reflecting Increased Diversity, Los Angeles Times, March 30, 2001

Los Angeles Times, Census 2000 Website, http://www.latimes.com/news/nation/reports/census/

Martelle, Scott, Phil Willon, Latinos and Asians Continue a Transformation, Los Angeles Times, March 30, 2001

Ness, Carol, and McCormick, Erin, Hispanics Now Make Up Third of Californians, San Francisco Chronicle, March 30, 2001

Ness, Carol, and Ryan Kim, Census Reveals Fast-Growing Diversity in U.S., San Francisco Chronicle, March 13, 2001

New York Times on the Web, http://nytime.com/2001/

Pimentel, Benjamin, Census 2000, Who We Are Area Grows More Diverse Census finds increase in Asians, Hispanics, San Francisco Chronicle, March 31, 2001

President's Advisory Commission on Asian Americans and Pacific Islanders, January 2001, A People Looking Forward, Action for Access and Partnership In the 21st Century, Interim Report to the President and Nation

The American Community—Asians: 2004, American Community Survey Reports, US Census Bureau, at http://www.census.gov/prod/2007pubs/acs-05.pdf

U.S. Census Bureau, Population Estimates, www.census.gov/popest/estimates/php

Acknowledgements

This book has been from its inception the joint product of many minds, hands and hearts.

First and foremost, I want to acknowledge and thank Barbara Phillips, because if not for her, the first edition of this book would not have been born. Barbara, then a program officer for the Ford Foundation, commissioned me to conduct research and write a think piece to educate her on the issues and concerns of Asian American women from a human and civil rights perspective. She also asked me to assist in convening a meeting of Asian American women activists to review the think piece before it was finalized. As she explained, she wanted "to spend a day in conversation creating collectively a prioritized human rights action agenda and strategies to implement over the next 5 years to meet the needs of Asian American women." I thank Barbara for the vision she had of the Ford Foundation supporting and fostering the building of our movement, an Asian American women's movement for social and economic justice.

When I began this project, I had no idea how challenging the research would be. There were practically no national studies on Asian Americans for most of the issue areas. I had to call on my "old girls' network" from around the country to find local studies and people whom I could interview to gather the facts and data I needed. This old girl's network was built over a 25-year period while I was an activist in the Asian American community and especially during the two years between 1996 and 1998 when I was national chair of the National Asian Pacific American Women's Forum (NAPAWP). To all those "old girls" who were part of my network, many of whom are listed as interviewees in the back of this book, very many thanks for taking time from your busy lives as activists to respond.

Many thanks also to Yin Ling Leung who assisted in the research, literature review, and/or interviews for Parts Two and Three of the first edition. I thank Laura Ho, friend and former colleague, who helped with the final editing of the first edition, often with very little notice and with demanding turnaround times.

The first edition was finalized after I had the benefit of comments, critique and insights from long-time Asian American women activists whom Barbara convened at the Ford Foundation in June 2001. They were: Jane Bai, Hae Jung Cho, Lisa Hasegawa, Lisa Ikemoto, Pacyinz Lyfoung, Becky Masaki, Trinity Ordona, Hina Shah, Peggy Saika, Xuan Nguyen Sutter, Doreena Wong, Jai Lee Wong and Ka YingYang.

Ford Foundation Deputy Directors Taryn Higashi and Urvashi Vaid attended that June 2001 meeting, as well as a March 2002 briefing session, and made helpful comments on the various chapters. In addition, Alan Jenkins, then Director of the Human Rights Unit, and Natalia Kanem, Deputy, Office of the Vice President, gave valuable insight on the overall report. My special thanks go to Mehlika Hoodbhoy, Editor and Publication Coordinator, whose editorial work was invaluable in turning the report into the first edition of this book.

The first edition of the book was published in September 2002. Believing that it could be both a powerful educational tool on the issues facing Asian American women and a call to action to our communities, the Ford Foundation funded a one-year book tour which brought me to nine cities and eight states where we held eighteen community, women's and funders' briefings on the book. We reached close to 1,000 women and men and distributed 5000 copies of the first edition. As Women's Studies and Ethnic Studies departments around the country began using the book, it became apparent that we needed to print more copies. The second printing of the first edition in 2003 by iUniverse, Inc. was made possible with the permission of the Ford Foundation.

Not only was the first edition being used in university classrooms, Asian American women activists were using the book in their public policy and other advocacy efforts. For the book to remain relevant and useful, it was clear that the book needed to be updated. In late 2005, I approached Kiran Ahuja, NAPAWF's executive director, and asked her organization to assist in updating the book and publishing the second edition. Kiran enthusiastically agreed. I want to acknowledge and thank NAPAWF and Kiran particularly for making this second edition possible.

Without the hard work of the NAPAWF staff, this second edition would not have been published. Janel George, then Women's Law and Public Policy Fellow, and Courtney Chappell, then Policy and Programs Director, took on the job of recruiting Asian American women activists who could update the chapters. They did an excellent job of recruiting women activists with the knowledge, expertise, and familiarity with developments over the last 5 years required to update the book.

Janel and Courtney coordinated the updating effort, including scheduling conference calls for me with the update writers, collecting proposed outlines, and acting as liaison between the writers and me throughout the year-long period it took to update the book. In addition, NAPAWF staff conducted research and/or wrote the updates for five chapters of the book. Janel conducted research for and wrote the first draft update of Chapter 7, "Domestic Violence"; Courtney conducted research for and updated Chapter 5, "Health" and Chapter 6, "Reproductive Justice"; and Gening Liao, a 2005 law clerk, assisted me in the research to update Chapter 3, "Garment Workers" and Chapter 4, "Other Low Wage Workers."

I especially want to thank the women who took time from their incredibly busy lives to update the other four chapters of this book: Jennet Sambour and Doua Thor, Chapter 1, "Welfare Reform"; Norma Timbang and Gabriela Villareal, Chapter 2, "Trafficking"; Mai Moua, Chapter 8, "Hmong Women"; and Rebecca Sawyer, Chapter 10, "Asian American LBTQ."

Staying true to the spirit of the first edition, we did not finalize the chapters until key activists in the field had the opportunity to review and comment. I want to thank the many women who reviewed and gave us their critique of the updated chapters. They were: Veronika Geronimo, Cary Sanders, Bo Thao, Dr. Sutapa Basu, Purvi Shah, Kavitha Sreeharsha, Pradeepta Upadhyay, Rini Chatraborty, Nikki Bas, Margaret Fung, Kim Kimerling, Andy Marra, CJ Jiang, Doreena Wong, and Ann Surapruik.

Thanks also to the women who conducted research for the various chapters, including Liezl Tomas Rebugio, Ruth Y. Kim and Eunsong (Angela) Kim.

Many thanks to Kim Van Eyck for her substantive editing of the updated chapters and to Jo Ellen Green Kaiser, copy editor, for her hard work.

Many thanks also to the Asian Americans and Pacific Islanders in Philanthropy (AAPIP) for providing the funding that made possible publication of this second edition.

Finally, I sincerely thank the Ford Foundation for its generosity in transferring copyright for this book to NAPAWF so that Asian American women activists can continue updating this book every three to four years to keep it a powerful tool for social change.

As the original author, I served as senior editor of the second edition to ensure that the updated chapters remained true to the spirit of the first edition. Thus, all errors and omissions are mine.

Lora Jo Foo
Castro Valley, California 2007

PART I
Economic Justice

Southeast Asian community members protesting 1996 Welfare
"Reform" measures.

1

Welfare Reform's Impact on Asian American Women

Updated by Jennet Sambour and Doua Thor[1]

INTRODUCTION

At age 49, Mai lives with her 58-year-old husband and four children in a crowded apartment in San Jose, California. She is the sole breadwinner, as her husband is disabled from arthritis compounded by the beatings he received in a Vietnamese re-education camp. Her job assembling electronics parts only yields about $200 per month on piece rates. Over half of Mai's income goes to pay the rent. To supplement her wages, Mai must rely on food stamps, Medi-Cal, cash assistance, and, as a last resort, a local church for free food. Mai wants a higher paying job, but she cannot read or write English and she has received only a few months of job training, ESL classes and job search assistance through Temporary Assistance for Needy Families (TANF). Mai says, "The five-year TANF limit is very rough. We've only been here a bit more than two years, and our lives are not stable. The fifth year will come and I'm afraid we won't be ready." (Equal Rights Advocates, 1999)

---

1. Jennet Sambour is a New Voices Fellow and the Women's Leadership Advocate at the Southeast Asia Resource Action Center, a national advocacy organization in Washington, D.C. Her family arrived in Providence, Rhode Island as refugees from Cambodia in 1981.

    Doua Thor is the Executive Director of the Southeast Asia Resource Action Center (SEARAC.) Ms. Thor is Hmong American. She and her family immigrated from Laos to Detroit, Michigan in 1979 as refugees.

Mai's statement was captured in 1999, but it is as true today as it was back then. Poverty affects a disproportionate number of Asian American women and their families. The 2003 U.S. Census Bureau found that 12% of Asian American women lived below the poverty level, compared to 12.4% of all women in the U.S. population. Asian American women over 65 were particularly vulnerable, with 16% living below poverty level, compared to approximately 12% of all US women over 65.[2] Among Asian Americans receiving some kind of welfare benefit (such as food stamps or Medicaid), more than 60% of recipients are women. The poverty Asian *immigrant* women face is often compounded by their tenuous immigrant status, anti-immigrant discrimination, language barriers, and the decreasing access to public assistance experienced by all welfare recipients since 1996.

In August 22, 1996, the Personal Responsibility and Work Opportunity Reconciliation Act (hereinafter referred to as "welfare reform") was signed into law. Immigrant women like Mai suffered twofold from the new reforms. First, welfare reform ended an entitlement program that existed as a safety net primarily for mothers with children, and replaced it with a program that limits assistance to a total of five years in a woman's lifetime (TANF). As Mai points out, it is difficult for immigrant families who are focused mainly on adjusting to life in the United States to make this five-year cut-off. Second, welfare reform excluded most immigrants from the right to receive federally funded food stamps and Supplemental Security Income (SSI) and left it within a state's discretion whether to provide TANF and Medicaid to immigrants. The result is that the burden of the welfare cuts that were made as part of the 1996 reforms fall disproportionately on immigrant women.

This chapter will describe in detail the changes that have occurred to various forms of government assistance and the ways in which these welfare reforms have disproportionately affected the Asian American community and women in particular.

---

2.   Asian Americans over 65 utilize public assistance at high rates. Within particular Asian American communities, the percent of seniors receiving assistance is very high: 67% of Hmong seniors, 57.8%, of Laotians, 53.2% of Cambodians, 51.1% of Vietnamese, 42.1% of Koreans, 37.5% of Thai, 29.3% of Filipino, 28.4% of South Asians, and 25.9% of Chinese.

PUBLIC WELFARE—THEN AND NOW

The landmark welfare reform legislation of 1996 ended Aid to Families with Dependent Children (AFDC), a federal program that had been in existence for 60 years, and replaced it with the Temporary Assistance for Needy Families (TANF), which gave fixed block grants to states so they could tailor programs to their welfare populations. The goals of the TANF program are ostensibly to assist needy families and to end dependence on welfare by promoting work over welfare. But many of the provisions of welfare reform, such as tying work requirements to receipt of benefits, and imposing sanctions and a five-year lifetime limit for federally-funded benefits, have negatively impacted low-income immigrant and refugee families who truly need the assistance. In addition, welfare reform has further reduced immigrants' access to public benefits by including a number of provisions specifically targeting immigrants. Among Asian American groups, Southeast Asian immigrants have been particularly hard hit by welfare reform. Cambodians, Hmongs and Laotians suffer the highest poverty rates of all communities of color, including African Americans and Latinos.[3]

From AFDC to TANF

Originally, the welfare program was intended as an income substitute for widows and "abandoned" mothers so that they could stay at home to care for their children. Over the years, however, the program has transformed into a transitional support system which forces poor mothers to work or participate in work-related activities in return for cash assistance and does not offer them a choice to be full-time caregivers to their children.

President Franklin D. Roosevelt began the programs we now know as welfare in response to the effects of the Great Depression. Adopted in 1935, the first welfare act, Aid to Dependent Children (ADC), focused on supporting poor children. The act was established as a federal financial aid program. The subsidy helped children in families with fathers who were deceased, absent or unable to work—mainly families headed by widows or what were at the time called "abandoned" mothers. Unlike mothers who were divorced, separated or unmarried, widows were deemed more "worthy" of government assistance.

---

3.   In California, 63% of Hmong, 51% of Laotians, and 47% of Cambodians live in poverty.

In 1939, following an amendment to the Social Security Act, the survivors' insurance system was created which allowed most widows to leave the welfare program and receive a monthly stipend from the government while caring full-time for their children. This shifted welfare caseloads from families headed by widows to families headed by divorced, separated or unmarried women. A vocal political concern that welfare "discouraged marriage" caused the government to subsequently modify the program. Welfare mothers who were divorced, separated or unmarried deviated from the dominant cultural family norms and were often viewed as morally suspect. Sometimes referred to as "lazy" or "looking for hand-outs," these mothers were rebuked for choosing to be a caregiver to their children full-time, rather than participating in the labor market. In addition, as large numbers of mothers entered the paid work-force during World War II and middle-class feminists championed the "rights" of women to work outside the home, they also challenged public assumptions of the merits of helping poor mothers stay at home to take care of their children.

In the 1960s, ADC was changed to Aid to Families with Dependent Children (AFDC), allowing states to assist other persons, such as an unemployed parent, a second parent in a family with an incapacitated or unemployed parent, and any other individual in the home deemed essential to the child. Under the AFDC program, families with unemployed parents who refused to accept work without "good cause" were denied assistance.

In 1968, Congress required states to set up a work and training program called Work Incentive (WIN) which emphasized work rather than welfare. Beginning in 1971, all AFDC parents were required to register for work or training with the WIN program except for mothers with children under age six. In 1988, the Job Opportunities and Basic Skills Training (JOBS) program replaced WIN and required states to engage most mothers without children below age three in education, work, or training.

From Full to Restricted Access for Immigrants

As demonstrated by the various work and training programs of the 1960s, welfare reform's concept of welfare-to-work, though inconsistent with what welfare first stood for, was hardly a new suggestion. Where the 1996 law differs most significantly from welfare reforms of the past, however, is in the government's treatment of immigrants. The 1996 law tied citizenship to receipt of benefits, which was not consistent with either previous U.S. policy or international standards. Most liberal democracies that accepted a large number of immigrants at the end of the 20th century provided both legal immigrants and citizens the same access to benefits. Previous U.S. policies recognized the rights of immigrants as well as their contributions to the country's social, economic and political spheres. For example, legal immigrants are required to pay taxes and can be drafted in time of war.

In 1996, for the first time in U.S. history, most legal immigrants became ineligible for federal benefits such as TANF, cash assistance, and public health insurance, and were, until partial restoration a year later, barred from Supplemental Security Income (SSI). The cuts to immigrants amounted to 40% of the savings in federal public assistance spending—despite the fact that, according to the Congressional Budget Office, in 1996 immigrants represented only 15% of all welfare recipients in the U.S.

Political forces constructing immigrants as "burdens" on society helped spur the new welfare restrictions. The political fervor surrounding the passage of Proposition 187 in California in 1994 (which denied almost all medical and social services to undocumented immigrants) prompted elected officials to propose eliminating public benefits to *all* immigrants, regardless of their status. This political trend ultimately led to the current TANF laws.

The 1996 welfare reform marked many turning points for U.S. immigration policy. For the first time, legal immigrants were eligible for fewer benefits than citizens. For the first time, a policy regarding treatment of immigrants once they were *in* the U.S. was being defined. And for the first time, the federal government handed over increasing control of immigration policy to the states. While the federal government continues to impose some standards, in providing block grants for states to implement TANF programs, states were allowed to determine whether and which legal immigrants should receive public benefits. Every state except Alabama opted to maintain TANF benefits for legal immigrants, and every state except Wyoming opted to maintain Medicaid eligibility for legal immigrants, at least for pre-enactment immigrants (those immigrants who were in the U.S. prior to welfare reform's passage on August 22, 1996). Of the 10 states with the largest number of Asian immigrants, all opted to provide TANF and Medicaid to pre-enactment immigrants.

To replace the federally funded TANF and SSI benefits for immigrants, over half the states provided at least one of four key substitute programs to immigrants: state-funded TANF programs and Medicaid to post-enactment immigrants and food stamps and SSI to pre- and/or post-enactment immigrants. Out of the seven largest immigrant-receiving states (CA, NY, TX, FL, IL, NJ, AZ), only California opted to provide all four state-funded substitute programs. New York opted to provide only food stamps and only to pre-enactment children, elderly, and the disabled. As **Table 2** shows, the safety net varies greatly state by state and the increasing restrictions and complexities of eligibility have caused many more immigrants to fall through the cracks.

▶ Table 2.

State Funded Substitute Programs as of August 1999 for Pre-and Post-enactment (August 22, 1996) Immigrants in states with largest numbers of Asian American population

STATE	TANF		SSI		Food Stamps		Medicaid	
	Pre-	Post-	Pre-	Post-	Pre	Post-	Pre-	Post-
California (no deeming)	x	x*	x	certain immigrants	x	certain immi-grants*	x	x
New York	x				children, elderly, dis-abled only		x	
Hawai'i	x	x*					x	x²
Texas	x				elderly, disabled only		x	
New Jersey	x				x*		x	
Illinois	x		x		x	certain immi-grants*	x	x
Washington	x	x*			x*	x*	x	x*
Florida	x						children, elderly, disabled	
Virginia	x						x	x
Massachu-setts	x	x			x	x	x	x
Minnesota	x	x*			x*	x*	x	x*

Source: Supplemental Report to "Patchwork Policies: State Assistance for Immigrants under Welfare Reform, The Urban Institute, August 1999

* Sponsor deeming: An immigrant is eligible only if the combined income of her and her sponsor (family member who sponsored her to US) does not exceed 50% to 80% of poverty.

¹ Most state funded substitute programs are not permanent and appropriations must be made each new legislative session. Some programs may have been added or ended since 1999.
² For children only, starting in 2000, with sponsor deeming.

Reauthorization of TANF

The original funding for TANF expired in September 2002 and operated on twelve temporary extensions because Congress was unable to agree on what provisions to keep in the reauthorization. On February 8, 2006, the Deficit Reduction Act (DRA) was signed into law, which reauthorized TANF until 2010. However, the DRA changes to TANF will make it even less likely to fulfill its goal of moving families from welfare to self-sufficiency. The new TANF establishes funding for "healthy marriage promotion" and "responsible fatherhood initiatives" (which have not been proven to lift families out of poverty) and also made significant changes to TANF work requirements. States are now required to engage more of their caseloads in work-related activities and/or reduce cash assistance caseloads.[4] Additional provisions require those families not participating in a work activity to be moved out of the federal TANF program into separate state programs.

By pushing even more welfare recipients off welfare and into low-wage jobs and further limiting educational and job training opportunities, DRA continues the 1996 welfare law's trend of rewarding states for decreasing their welfare rolls instead of rewarding them for alleviating the poverty and increasing self-sufficiency in poor communities.

IMPACT ON ASIAN AMERICAN WOMEN

In Los Angeles County, a city with one of the largest Asian populations in the country, 80% of Korean, 79% of Cambodian, 69% of Chinese, and 69% of Vietnamese adults who receive TANF are women (see **Table 3**), and 60% of SSI, 59% of food stamp, and 61% of Medicaid recipients are women (see **Table 4**). Asian immigrant women make up the majority of Asian welfare recipients and the cuts to public benefits will most severely hinder their ability to escape poverty.

---

4.   During debate of the bill, the Senate wanted to expand "work activities" to include participation in post-secondary education up to six months in a 24-month period and other education and activities to remove work barriers. However, the final legislation did not include this expanded definition.

▶ Table 3.

Asian TANF Recipients in Los Angeles County, June 2000

Adults	One Parent	% One Parent	Two Parent	% Two Parent	Total Adults	% Adults	Total House-holds	% One Parent	% Two Parent
All Races	114,058		43,697		157,755		136,578	84%	16%
Female	105,069	92%	22,520	52%	127,589	81%			
Male	8,989	8%	21,127	48%	30,116	19%			
All Asians	8,311		5,210		13,521		10,916	76%	24%
Female	7,646	92%	2,605	50%	10,251	76%			
Male	665	8%	2,605	50%	3,270	24%			
Cambodians	2,162		937		3,099		2,631	82%	19%
Female	1,989	92%	469	50%	2,458	79%			
Male	173	8%	468	50%	641	21%			
Chinese	771		969		1,740		1,256	61%	39%
Female	709	92%	485	50%	1,194	69%			
Male	62	8%	484	50%	546	31%			
Korean	144		55		199		172	84%	16%
Female	132	92%	28	50%	160	80%			
Male	12	8%	27	50%	39	20%			
Vietnamese	1,732		2,135		3,867		2,800	69%	31%
Female	1,593	92%	1,068	50%	2,661	69%			
Male	139	8%	1,067	50%	1,206	31%			

Note: The author determined the number and percent of females in one and two parent households assuming that 50% of the two parent and 92% (actual percent for all races) of one parent households were female.

Source: Los Angeles County Department of Public Social Services

▶ Table 4.

Adult Participation in Selected Programs, by Race/Ethnicity and by Sex, for the United States: 1996, 1997, 1998.

(in thousands) Program Participation of MHU Head/Spouse and Individual Race/Ethnicity	Adult Individuals					
	Women			Men		
	Total	Use	Use Rate	Total	Use	Use Rate
TANF						
Asian/Pacific Islander NH	128	86	67%	132	42	32%
Hispanic	779	588	76%	808	191	24%
Black NH	1,117	961	86% *	1,129	156	14% *
White	1,451	1,081	75%	1,394	369	27%
Total	3,530	2,757	78% *	3,530	773	22% *
SSI						
Asian/Pacific Islander NH	226	136	60%	229	90	39%
Hispanic	837	523	62%	869	314	36%
Black NH	1,516	925	61%	1,528	591	39%
White	3,275	1,930	59%	3,213	1,345	42%
Total	5,962	3,573	60%	5,962	2,389	40%
Food Stamps						
Asian/Pacific Islander NH	320	188	59%	331	132	40%
Hispanic	2,550	1,557	61%	2,636	993	38%
Black NH	3,716	2,568	69% *	3,741	1,148	31% *
White	5,704	3,555	62%	5,551	2,150	39%
Total	12,496	7,987	64%	12,496	4,509	36%
Medicaid						
Asian/Pacific Islander NH	747	454	61%	778	293	38%
Hispanic	3,801	2,321	61%	3,979	1,480	37%
Black NH	4,663	3,193	68% *	4,701	1,470	31% *
White	11,415	6,801	60%	11,106	4,613	42%
Total	20,978	12,967	62%	20,978	8,010	38%

Source: Urban Institute tabulations from edited March Supplements to the Current Population Surveys of 1997-1999. Table reflects an average of 1997, 1998 and 1999 data. See Fix and Passel (1999).

The unit of analysis is the "minimal household unit" or MHU; MHUs include married couples, either alone or with dependent children, and single adults. The MHUs approximate (continues on next page) nuclear families and, in many cases, welfare eligibility units better than either households, individuals, or CPS family units. See Van Hook, Glick, and Bean 1999.

Sex Difference	Intergroup Difference	
	Asian Women	Asian Men
Amt.	Amt.	Amt.
36% **		
52% **	-8%	8%
72% **	-19% *	18% *
48% **	-7%	5%
56% **	-11% *	10% *
21% **		
26% **	-2%	3%
22% **	-1%	1%
17% **	1%	-3%
20% **	0%	-1%
19% **		
23% **	-2%	2%
38% **	-10% *	9% *
24% **	-4%	1%
28% **	-5%	4%
23% **		
24% **	0%	1%
37% **	-8% *	6% *
18% **	1%	-4%
24% **	-1%	0%

American Indians are included in the total population count but do not appear in the table because of their small population size.

*   Difference as compared with Asian/Pacific Islander NH population is statistically significant at p < 0.10
** Difference between men and women is statistically significant at p < 0.10

TANF's Lifetime Limit

Under TANF, welfare recipients have up to a 5-year lifetime limit of receiving federal benefits. States have the option of limiting or extending the benefit, though to extend the benefit states must use state funds.[5] The result is that most welfare recipients are not allowed enough time to achieve self-sufficiency.

- In California, only 43% of former welfare recipients said they were better off financially than when they were receiving aid: 25% reported difficulties paying bills, and 62% still received other forms of public assistance.

- In Santa Clara County, California, 80% of residents who hit their lifetime limit in 2003 were Vietnamese refugees still struggling with English. Sixty-four percent were employed but earned too little to move off of welfare.

- In North Carolina, with a population of over 112,000 Asian residents, 24% of former welfare recipients reported they "sometimes" or "often" did not have enough to eat in the six months after they timed out, but "only 8% reported that they had experienced this hardship during their last six months on welfare."

A 2002 study on welfare time limits found that recipients who timed-out reported lower income and more material hardships *after* leaving welfare. The same study also reported that employment rates did not change after recipients were timed-out. Clearly, for the majority of welfare recipients, time limits have not facilitated a transition from welfare to work; instead, they have punished families even when they comply with program requirements.

State Flexibility

Under welfare reform, states ostensibly were given a certain amount of flexibility in designing their own welfare programs. However, the minimum levels of work participation rules imposed by TANF have in reality given states only

---

5.   A few states such as Arkansas, Connecticut, Idaho and Indiana have lifetime limits of 24 months or less. Other states, such as Minnesota and Washington, have extended the amount of time recipients can receive benefits. Pennsylvania and Maine, have adopted innovative programs, such as the Time Out Initiative, that provides a safety net period and help transition families off of TANF.

the flexibility to be _more_ not less restrictive with eligibility and benefit rules than under the prior federal law. Prior to 1996, states did have flexibility: they could apply for temporary welfare reform waivers under AFDC and adopt programs to extend or exempt time limits and/or include or exempt work-related activities. Programs implemented under these waivers have positively benefited Asian American women on welfare.

For example, the Minnesota Family Investment Program (MFIP) has focused on moving families out of poverty as they leave welfare by allowing a broad list of activities to count as work and by eliminating the participation time limit. English as a Second Language (ESL) classes were authorized as a "work activity" and long-term employment strategies were introduced to help move program participants into paid employment. A random assignment evaluation found a positive impact on employment and earnings among two-parent families, composed mainly of Hmong refugee families, involved with the MFIP program. Families in the MFIP program in Ramsey County, Minnesota had employment rates that were 19.1 percentage points higher and average earnings that were $1,742 higher than families in the control group.

A study undertaken by the U.S. Department of Health and Human Services (HHS) rated Portland, Oregon's TANF program, operated under a waiver, as one of the most successful in the nation, producing large increases in employment and earnings and large reductions in welfare receipt for a wide cross-section of welfare caseloads. Portland's program placed equal emphasis on encouraging welfare recipients to find employment quickly and helping recipients receive basic education and participate in skill-building activities.

Ironically, the states that exercised the temporary waivers and did _not_ comply with federal TANF rules were the ones that showed success in moving recipients from welfare to self-sufficiency. After 1996, states continued these programs while the waivers were in effect and had to end these programs once the waivers expired.

Discrimination in Work Participation

A major goal of welfare reform was to foster self-sufficiency through work. The 1996 law requires 50% of adult welfare recipients to be engaged in specific work-related activities. In addition, welfare recipients are required to find employment within two years or lose their benefits. During the two years, a recipient must agree to a welfare-to-work plan, conduct a job search, and engage in a work activity, such as unsubsidized employment, job training (limited to one year), education, or work for their welfare check.

Across the country, county-level welfare offices have not addressed the particular barriers Asian Americans, and in particular, Asian immigrant women face to attaining self-sufficiency through work, i.e., their limited-English proficiency (LEP) and lack of job skills. Certain states, including New York, have no mandate to require welfare offices to help recipients develop necessary job skills. Moreover, Asian immigrant women encounter discrimination at welfare offices and other hardships that often result in denial of access to job training and educational opportunities and result in dead-end, below poverty wage jobs.

1. Denial of Access to Job Training and Educational Opportunities

TANF did provide $3 billion to states over two years to pay for employment-related activities aimed largely at individuals with significant barriers to work. However, states deny immigrants equal access to vocational education and job training by offering classes only in English, failing to provide sufficient ESL classes and basic adult education, and steering them into Workfare programs.[6] This leaves many Asian immigrant women in dead-end, below poverty wage jobs.[7]

New York City's treatment of Asian American recipients is perhaps the most egregious. New York offers three ways for welfare recipients who cannot find unsubsidized employment to fulfill their work activities requirements: educational programs, job training, and Workfare. However, a 2000 survey of

---

6. Denied welfare-to-work services, non English-speaking Asian immigrant women often remain on welfare longer than English-speaking welfare recipients. In California, for example, English speakers are leaving welfare at a faster rate, dropping 14% from 1998-99, compared with 8% for LEPs. Caseworkers are able to find work for only one-fifth of welfare recipients who speak limited English, compared with about 60% of those who speak fluent English. Consequently, the proportion of LEP immigrants on TANF has increased while that of English speakers has decreased.

7. A study conducted by Ramsey County in Minnesota concluded that the single most important contributing factor to long-term dependence on public assistance is lack of education. Two separate studies of a training program serving mostly Hispanic immigrants with limited English skills in San Jose, California, found that integrating job training and English language skills had a large and lasting impact on earnings and employment.

100 Southeast Asian adults and 96 Southeast Asian youth in the Bronx conducted by the Committee Against Anti-Asian Violence (CAAAV) found that all 100 Southeast Asians surveyed were given only one option—Workfare. Not one survey participant was offered a job training or educational program. Eighty-one percent stated that caseworkers never even informed them of the job training option. Instead, as part of Workfare, these Asian American recipients cleaned parks or streets, often without proper equipment such as gloves and face masks. Because of language barriers, none of the survey participants could speak to their Workfare supervisors and Workfare never provided ESL training. Vocational ESL classes did not exist for Khmer or Vietnamese speaking recipients. As they wasted their days in Workfare, the five-year time limit on receipt of TANF benefits arrived before they were able to learn any transferable job skills.

Asian Americans in other states fare a little better, but not much. In a 1999 Wisconsin survey conducted by the Institute for Wisconsin's Future, 48% of Hmong report they lack job skills and 40% say language barriers prevented them from working. Nine out of 10 Hmong were placed in Workfare and of these, two-thirds were assigned to light assembly and cleaning jobs with little to no opportunity for skill development. Of the 137 Hmong interviewed, only 13 received job training as part of Workfare and only seven were taking ESL courses. The Applied Research Center's survey found that Asians were the least likely to be given job training. Looking at ethnic group participation in Workfare, only 28% of white respondents were enrolled in the Workfare program, compared to 33% of African Americans, 37% of Latinos, and 47% of Asians.

In a Santa Clara County, California study, only 38% of immigrant participants reported receiving any TANF services, including job search, English-language instruction, and job training, and only 7.3% of the participants said that TANF services had been helpful in finding them a job

2. Stuck in Dead-end, Below Poverty Wage Jobs

A 2000 Economic Roundtable study found that Southeast Asian women welfare workers fare worst of all welfare workers. Of these women, 63.8% earned below poverty wages as compared with 54.2% of Latinas and 53.3% of African American women. Southeast Asian women welfare workers have the highest poverty rate, at 97.2%, compared to Latinas at 88.8% and African American women at 81.6%. Eighty-five percent of Asian immigrant women on welfare work in low-wage industries. The niche industries for Southeast

Asian women are non-durable manufacturing (41%)—(primarily apparel jobs—where earnings are 40% of the Federal Poverty Level (FPL); 18% in other services where earnings are 44% of the FPL; and 10% in administrative positions where earnings are 49% of the FPL. Sixty-four percent of Southeast Asians are concentrated in a few low-wage niche industries compared to 38% of Latino immigrants who work in those industries.

Without job training, ESL, and vocational ESL classes, Asian immigrant women are tracked into minimum wage or below minimum wage jobs that lack health and other benefits. An Asian American woman, working full time at the federal minimum wage of $5.15 per hour or less, would have to work the equivalent of 60 to 80 hours a week (perhaps holding two or three jobs) just to move out of poverty.

Hungrier and Sicker Immigrant Women and Children

In 1997, when the first notices were sent advising recipients of SSI cut-offs, a number of desperate elderly immigrants in California, New York, and Wisconsin committed suicide because they did not want to become burdens to their families. These tragedies, along with intense pressure by advocates, led Congress to restore benefits to some 500,000 immigrants who were already receiving SSI as of August 22, 1996, and also to restore food stamps to immigrants under the age of 18, those 65 years or older on August 22, 1996, and those receiving disability assistance.

Congress divided immigrants between those who were in the U.S. prior to passage of welfare reform on August 22, 1996 (pre-enactment immigrants) and those who entered after that date (post-enactment immigrants). Despite the concessions made to the young, elderly, and disabled pre-enactment immigrants, most pre-enactment working age immigrants remained ineligible for food stamps. Most post-enactment immigrants, including the elderly and disabled, were excluded from eligibility for SSI and food stamps until they met the five-year residency requirement.[8] Since every year about 250,000 legal immigrants from Asia enter the U.S. to join their families, the number excluded from federal public benefits continues to grow.

1. Food Stamps

Welfare reform has increased food insecurity[9] for a significant number of Asian immigrant women. In 2003, an estimated 134,000 Asian women living in California were food insecure, but only 78,000 were receiving food stamps. In Los Angeles County, an estimated 100,000 Asian Americans who were eligible under the federal food stamps program were not receiving food stamps.

An August 2000 survey by Physicians for Human Rights examined the impact of food stamp cuts on Asian and Latino immigrants in California, Illinois, and Texas and found that 87% of the legal immigrant households living in poverty were food insecure—seven times the rate in the general population. In addition, 10% suffered from severe hunger, more than 10 times the rate of the general population. To pay rent and avoid having utilities turned off, the majority of adult immigrants surveyed ate only twice a day, making sure their children ate something. But even short-term periods of malnutrition can permanently affect a child's behavior, cognitive development, and future productivity. Food insecure pregnant women face high risks of low birth-weight infants and higher infant mortality rates.

---

8.   The Balanced Budget Act of 1997 restored SSI payments to pre- and post-enactment immigrants who are veterans and refugees, to pre-enactment immigrants who have worked 10 years or become citizens, and post-enactment immigrants in the U.S. for five years and who have worked 10 years. The Agricultural Research, Extension, and Education Act of 1998 restored eligibility for food stamps to immigrant children, and elderly and disabled immigrants who were residing in the US before August 1996, including veterans, refugees, and members of Hmong and Laotian tribes militarily assisting the U.S. during the Vietnam War but otherwise denied to most post-enactment immigrant for five years after entry. The veterans and 10-year work exceptions are biased against immigrant women, since most women are unlikely to have served in the armed forces. Asian immigrant women may find it difficult to meet the 10-year work requirement as so many work in the "informal economy" of sweatshops or as domestic workers where pay may be cash under the table or Social Security taxes are not paid on their behalf.
9.   Food insecure is defined as having limited or uncertain access to enough safe, nutritious food for an active and healthy life.

Hunger and illness are rising in immigrant communities, not just because welfare reform excluded large segments of the immigrant population from eligibility but also because of the barriers to access that welfare reform and government officials created for those who remained eligible.

A study commissioned by the U.S. Department of Agriculture found that non-citizens who were eligible for the food stamp program were significantly less likely to receive food stamps than all individuals who were eligible for the program. Forty-five percent of eligible non-citizens received food stamps compared to 59% of eligible individuals overall. Despite the fact that citizen children remained eligible for public benefits after welfare reform, an alarming number dropped out of the food stamp program. The CAAAV survey found that welfare centers were removing not only immigrant adults from the food stamps program but also their citizen children. Even though over three-quarters of children of immigrants are themselves citizens, only 34% of citizen children living with non-citizen adults participated in the food stamp program as opposed to 62% of all eligible individuals.

2. Medicaid and Health Insurance

Medicaid use and insurance coverage have declined significantly among immigrants. Immigrants who begin working become unqualified for Medicaid but often end up in industries that traditionally do not provide health insurance (e.g., agriculture, garment, and private households). In interviews conducted with immigrants soon after welfare reform, it was found that even qualified immigrants expressed fear that using Medicaid would prevent them from naturalizing or were misinformed that the new welfare changes made all immigrants ineligible. Thus, a higher percentage of immigrants (46%) are uninsured as compared to the 15% of U.S. citizens.

The Kaiser Commission on Medicaid and the Uninsured estimates that in 2004 over 2 million (18.5%) Asian and Pacific Islanders (API) under 65 were uninsured. For API women alone, the uninsured rate is even higher, at 24%, with only 6% of API women covered by Medicaid. Among the Asian subpopulations, Koreans and Southeast Asians are more likely to be uninsured than Chinese, Japanese, Filipinos and South Asians.

While there are no specific numbers on Asian Americans, according to the Latino Issues Forum, 70% or 420,000 California children eligible for Medicaid who live in families with immigrant parents are uninsured. The New York Immigrant Coalition estimates that 34,000 New York immigrants who were eligible in 2000 did not apply for Medicaid because of confusion over eligibility or fear that the U.S. Citizenship & Immigration Services (CIS, formerly INS) would deport them.

The health of immigrants has been harmed by the decrease in Medicaid coverage. Anecdotal evidence from doctors suggests that immigrants are generally sicker or in need of emergency care when they finally see a doctor. Uninsured immigrants postpone or forgo preventive and needed care due to expensive out-of-pocket costs and also because they do not have access to primary care. In fact, about 20% of the overall uninsured population, versus 3% of the insured population, said that the emergency room is their usual source of care.

BARRIERS TO EQUAL ACCESS

A number of factors prevent eligible Asian immigrant women from applying for benefits, even when they are ill or their children are hungry. In an August 2000 study by the Asian Pacific American Legal Center of Southern California (APALC) on the use of food stamps, organizations serving the Asian American community in Southern California identified the top barriers to benefits participation by the Asian immigrant community. These barriers included language, government and state intimidation,fear that using public benefits would make one an undesirable public charge, fear of causing liability to the immigrant's U.S. sponsor, fear that accepting benefits would cause the deportation of other family members, and confusion about which immigrants are eligible for which programs. Other barriers include the hostility of state and county government and caseworkers toward immigrants and intimidating government tactics that discourage immigrants from applying for benefits. The current hostile atmosphere towards immigrants has had a chilling effect on immigrants' use of public benefits.

Language barriers

On August 23, 2000, 50 young Vietnamese and Cambodian men and women from the Bronx held a rally to protest the lack of translators at welfare offices. Nine-year-old Maryanne Heam told the rally that she was tired of missing school to serve as a welfare interpreter. She did not speak much Cambodian and found it hard to translate for her mother. The demonstrators moved to a welfare office and demanded a meeting with officials. They got a pledge that welfare offices will stop using children to interpret, and at the very least provide an interpreter by phone.[10]

For immigrants one of the largest barriers to accessing public health and food benefits is language. Across the country, the lack of translated materials and interpreter services exacerbates the rampant confusion over immigrant eligibility and fear that use of public benefits could lead to one's or a family member's deportation. Asian immigrants, like other immigrants, who do manage to get approved for benefits, often get cut off or have benefits reduced when they cannot read or respond to English-only notices.

Federal law, Title VI of the Civil Rights Act of 1964, provides that no person shall be excluded from participation in, denied the benefits of, or be subjected to race, color, or national origin discrimination under any program or activity receiving federal financial assistance. California, New York, and other state laws require that LEP (Limited English Proficient) applicants and recipients be provided with written translations and interpreters to enable them to effectively communicate with caseworkers. Despite these laws, states routinely fail to provide language appropriate services to immigrants, thereby illegally denying them equal access to TANF benefits and services.

In New York City, 15,000 to 25,000 Southeast Asians, primarily from Vietnam and Cambodia, live in the Bronx. The 2000 CAAAV survey found that not one welfare center in the Bronx had Khmer or Vietnamese speaking translators even though 65% of the Southeast Asian population in the Bronx is on welfare. None of the adults surveyed were aware that the welfare centers were required by law to provide translation services. Although the city claims phone interpreters are available, 93 of the adults surveyed had never worked with a caseworker who made use of a phone interpreter. The children of Southeast Asian welfare recipients often find themselves translating for their parents at welfare centers. Of the youth surveyed, ranging from nine to twenty-one years old, 86% had missed school to translate for their parents. Most are not fluent in their parents' native tongues and report feeling uncomfortable translating but do so nonetheless in an attempt to preserve their families' welfare benefits.

Deprived of the right to interpreters, immigrants face personal indignities and financial penalties. Immigrants who are forced to rely on their children or complete strangers risk harming the parent/child relationship or embarrass-

---

10.   Wilson, Greg, "Translation Needs Voiced," *Daily News,* Aug. 23, 2000.

ment as their private lives are revealed to their children or a complete stranger. Financially, sanctions were imposed and benefits reduced for 48% of New York Southeast Asians surveyed by CAAAV, forcing many to spend rent money on food and finding themselves in debt or at the risk of eviction.

A Wisconsin study found that close to 70% of Hmong on TANF in Wisconsin were unable to communicate verbally with their caseworker. Close to 90% couldn't read the materials they received from the W-2 agency, Wisconsin's TANF program. One-third of Hmong welfare recipients lost or were denied benefits because the state failed to provide interpreters or translate documents, according to a 2000 federal investigation of the program. An Illinois study focusing exclusively on refugee women on welfare found that 83% do not speak English well or at all. While 81% had taken English classes, 74% still required translation assistance. A January 2001 Applied Research Center national study found that in New York City, problems were most pronounced for speakers of Asian languages. Eighty-four percent of Southeast Asians did not have access to translation when needed, compared to 50% of Latinos.

In Los Angeles County, 41% or about 94,000 welfare recipients speak languages other than English, including Armenian, Cambodian, Chinese, Spanish, and Vietnamese. Yet Los Angeles County routinely fails to provide written or verbal translations. In a complaint filed in December 1999 with the United States Department of Health and Human Services (HHS), Office for Civil Rights, by Asian and Latina TANF recipients, APALC, and other local legal organizations, plaintiffs allege that Los Angeles County fails to provide, in the immigrant's primary language, forms and program information, notice of mandatory appointments and notices of actions such as termination of aid, sanctions, approval or denial of various supportive services, appeal rights, and the right to participate in corrective action plans. The complaint also alleges that over 500 LEP households had their benefits terminated during the time English-only notices were used.

In November 2003, an historic agreement was reached between the Los Angeles County Department of Public Social Services (DPSS) and HHS. DPSS agreed that it will treat families on welfare who are limited English proficient fairly and that they will receive the same treatment as families on welfare who are fluent in English. Although this agreement is a huge step to ensuring that individuals who do not have English language ability have equal access to TANF benefits, advocates stress that this agreement is only the beginning of needed changes.

Oppressive Government Tactics

From 1994–99, the State of California funded a program at border points and airports to "catch" immigrant women who used prenatal care provided by Medicaid. Latina women were detained at the Mexican border by state and CIS agents. At the San Francisco and Los Angeles airports, 50% of those detained were Asian women, 25% were Latina, and 25% were of other nationalities. State and CIS agents specifically targeted women of childbearing age on flights from Asia and Mexico. Under questioning, if a woman indicated she had recently given birth and received public assistance at that time, the CIS agent on the spot decided whether she was a public charge and whether or not she received the assistance fraudulently. The state agent calculated how much she received. Women were intimidated into repaying the Medicaid benefits they received, even if they obtained the benefits legally, by the threat of imprisonment, deportation, or reduced chances for obtaining green cards or citizenship. In this way, California illegally collected $3.8 million from approximately 1,500 Asian and Latina women.[11]

The "Public Charge" Label

Being considered a public charge, i.e. someone who either has become or has the possibility of becoming dependent on government benefits by the CIS, is one of the primary barriers to immigrant women applying for public assistance. If the CIS considers a person likely to be a public charge, it can deny an immigrant's application for a green card, refuse immigrants reentry into the U.S., or deport the person.

In May 1999, the CIS issued guidelines making it clear that use of food stamps, nutritional assistance, Medicaid, and school lunches would not make an immigrant a public charge. However, one provision of the 1996 law explicitly states that state and local governments cannot restrict their employees from reporting any immigrants to CIS. Thus, immigrant families are not guaranteed confidentiality when providing personal information for receipt of benefits, even when applying for eligible family members, such as citizen children. More than a year after the CIS guidelines were issued, most Los Angeles area Asian American service providers surveyed in the APALC study stated

---

11. The program was challenged in court and settlements were reached that required the state to return the moneys unlawfully collected by the state. In April 1999, the state legislature de-funded the program.

they were reluctant to give assurances to immigrant women because they themselves were skeptical of the CIS guidelines. It is likely that thousands of Asian immigrant women will not apply for food stamps and Medicaid out of fear that they might jeopardize their chances of attaining citizenship or be deported.

The health consequences to women and their children who do not have Medicaid are already becoming manifest. The National Immigration Law Center reported that infant mortality rates climbed in immigrant communities such as New York City's Bedford-Stuyvesant, Harlem, and in part of Brooklyn and the Bronx since 1996, suggesting a correlation with the threat of the CIS public charge label.

Mandatory Reporting

Welfare reform requires that state agencies administering TANF, SSI, and food stamps programs report to the CIS any person the agency knows is not legally in the U.S. and allows voluntary reporting of any immigrant, even if she is here legally.

The CIS has not made it clear that reporting requirements apply to the individual seeking assistance and not to the whole family. State agencies typically ask about the immigration status of all family members. The vast majority, 85%, of immigrant families (those headed by a non-citizen parent) are "mixed status" families that include at least one U.S. citizen and may include undocumented family members. Fear of exposing undocumented family members to the CIS is the primary reason that immigrant women, Asian and Latina, do not apply for Medicaid or Food Stamps even if they are pregnant or have U.S. citizen children. Over seventy-five percent of the children in mixed status families are U.S. citizens and eligible for all forms of public assistance.

Sponsor Deeming

Under welfare reform, in determining an immigrant's eligibility for food stamps, Medicaid, TANF, and SSI, a state agency may count the income of the family member who sponsored the immigrant to the U.S. as part of the immigrant's income. In other words, the sponsor's income is "deemed" the applicant's income, usually resulting in a combined income that exceeds eligibility levels. If sponsors' incomes are low enough for applicants to be eligible for public assistance, the sponsors are financially liable for reimbursing for the use of Medicaid (except for emergency services) and food stamps. In order not to expose their sponsors to financial liability, immigrants often do not apply for benefits.

Inept or Hostile Caseworkers

Caseworkers sometimes create or compound problems Asian immigrants face in obtaining benefits.

If many Asian immigrants are unsure about their eligibility status, many of their caseworkers are also frequently confused. A myriad of immigrant categories were created by welfare reform (such as pre- and post-enactment, qualified and non-qualified, refugees, veterans, children, elderly, and disabled) and each group qualifies for different sets of benefits. Often, caseworkers assume that ineligibility for one type of benefit means ineligibility for all types of assistance, refusing to accept applications for particular services.

Immigrants also may face open hostility from many caseworkers, which often delays the receipt of benefits and sometimes create insurmountable barriers to applying for or receiving benefits. For example, one undocumented, pregnant, and battered Vietnamese women applied for Medicaid for her U.S. citizen child. Her caseworker told her, "You have no right to be having children here" and threatened to phone the CIS. The woman left the office without receiving any benefits. A Milwaukee widow was told that her benefits arrived only sporadically "because you're Hmong." An Oakland, California woman reported that a caseworker had torn her application form up in front of her because she could not understand the caseworker's English.

ADVOCACY NEEDED

The Reauthorization Fight

It is clear that TANF has failed in achieving its goal of moving welfare recipients, and particularly Asian American women from welfare to self-sufficiency. Advocacy efforts must include: 1) building a movement to demand an anti-poverty program that doesn't discriminate against immigrants when TANF comes up for reauthorization again in 2010—one which can truly achieve its goal of moving individuals from poverty into self-sufficiency; and 2) working with state governments to ensure that Asian immigrant women have equal access to existing TANF benefits and welfare to work services. An ideal safety net for Asian immigrant women and their families would include:

1. Access to all public benefits that citizens enjoy (TANF, food stamps, SSI, Medicaid)

Instead of marking a distinction between citizens and non-citizens for receipt of benefits, TANF policies should support all families who call the U.S. their home. The restrictions of the current welfare law have had a detrimental effect on low-income immigrant families, including Asian American women and their families.

2. Comprehensive employment services that include building sufficient English language skills, job training, job placement with opportunities for advancement, and educational opportunities

An ideal anti-poverty program would incorporate longer term educational (including language training) and job training programs (such as vocational trainings), rather than short-term job-preparation and training, which do not lift people out of poverty in the long run.

3. Increased funding for mental health services

Another barrier to employment is mental health, especially for Southeast Asian refugees who fled from traumatic situations. Southeast Asians refugees, who in California account for 90% of the Asian Pacific Islander TANF caseloads, often experience depression, post-traumatic stress, and flashbacks which impair their ability to work regularly. Increased resources for mental health services is crucial to removing these barriers to work.

4. Access to affordable childcare

In order for TANF recipients with young children to meet work requirements, they need access to affordable child care. Although DRA increased TANF funding for child care, the modest increases are insufficient to meet the needs of current and future recipients. The Congressional Budget Office estimated that just to *maintain* the current level of child care subsidies over the next five years and keep pace with inflation, a total of $4.8 billion in extra federal or state funds would be needed. However, President G.W. Bush only authorized an extra $1 billion over five years.[12]

Ensuring Equal Access

Ongoing advocacy must continue to ensure Asian immigrant women have equal access to TANF and other public benefits. Title VI complaints, in court and before HHS, have been filed in New York City, Los Angeles, Minneapolis, and the San Francisco Bay Area. These complaints claim that the failure to provide written translations and interpreters amounts to national origin discrimination and a denial of equal access to benefits to LEP immigrants. For immigrant women who were denied welfare-to-work services, the 60-month lifetime cap must be extended until they have received appropriate job training of ESL classes. To assuage eligible immigrants of their distrust of government and encourage use of food stamps and Medicaid programs, the CIS must be pressured to issue clearer guidelines. Caseworkers must be trained about immigrant eligibility rules so that immigrants are not wrongfully denied benefits. Immigrants need to know their eligibility rights and how to take action against illegal caseworker actions. Advocacy and litigation groups need to be funded to monitor and identify abuses, to take complaints from immigrants, and to counter systemic abuses.

Re-energizing Our Communities

Since the September 11th attacks, the welfare reform debate has taken a backseat to current debates about national security, the war on terrorism, and comprehensive immigration reform. The once passionate debate over poverty in America has lost tremendous momentum. Yet poverty persists and the gap between the rich and the poor is increasing in the U.S.

Most people in the U.S. are benefactors of some type of government support, whether it is tax breaks for homeowners or corporations, agricultural subsidies for farmers, or tax credits for education. Yet welfare is one of the only forms of government aid that has become deeply stigmatized. Such

---

12. Little data exists about whether Asian American families utilize TANF's child care option. The Asian and Pacific Islander Child Care Task Force of King County, Washington found that instead of putting them in formal care, more than 50% of Asian parents have family members or friends care for their children while they are working. More research is needed on Asian welfare recipients' use of child care subsidies and the reasons for their usage or lack of usage in order to properly assess whether Asian immigrant women are having trouble accessing the child care benefits of TANF.

stigma, in part, is rooted in stereotypes about welfare participants. In part, it also is due to changing public opinion about society's responsibility for new generations. The generations that supported the New Deal and Great Society saw the raising of children as both a private and public responsibility. They made sure that our tax dollars were sufficient to support universal K-12 education and that children from impoverished families did not go hungry and without housing and health care.

As advocates, our task is to bring about yet another paradigm shift in how the public views the role of government. Our task is to put an anti-poverty agenda back on the national agenda. The family-friendly policies of the European and other industrialized countries can be a model for the U.S. to emulate. These policies include: more generous parental leave policies, subsidized child care services, housing assistance and universal healthcare. In order to formulate more effective welfare reforms, we must re-frame welfare as an anti-poverty program. Instead of tinkering with piece-meal reforms, we must be more visionary about what's needed to lift communities out of poverty. We must renew our collective responsibility for ensuring economic justice for all Americans. As 2010 approaches, it is crucial to organize and unite voices demanding an anti-poverty program that will lift Asian American women and their children and all America's poor families out of poverty and into self-sufficiency.

REFERENCES

Administration for Children and Families, Temporary Assistance for Needy Families: *Fifth Annual Report to Congress* (Chapter 13: TANF Research and Evaluation), U.S. Department of Health and Human Services, Updated June 2006.
<http://www.acf.hhs.gov/programs/ofa/annualreport5/chap13.htm>

Administration for Children and Families, Temporary Assistance for Needy Families: *Sixth Annual Report to Congress* (Chapter 12: Specific Provisions of State Programs), U.S. Department of Health and Human Services, Updated April 2006.
<http://www.acf.hhs.gov/programs/ofa/annualreport6/chapter12/chap12.htm>

Albelda, Randy and Tilly, Chris, "Policies As If Families Really Mattered, A Reading" in *Women's Lives: Multicultural Perspectives*, Kirk, Gwen and Oka-zawa-Rey, Margo, McGraw-Hill, 2001.

Asian and Pacific Islander Child Care Task Force, "Steps to Improve the Quality of Care for Asian and Pacific Islander Children, Youth and Families," *Participatory Action Research Project Report*, King County Department of Community and Human Services, 2000.

Asian and Pacific Islander Institute on Domestic Violence and Asian and Pacific Islander American Health Forum, "TANF Reauthorization and its Effect on Asian and Pacific Islander Families," October 2002.

Asian Pacific American Legal Center of Southern California, "Barriers to Food Stamps for the Asian and Pacific Islander Community in Los Angeles County," Preliminary Report, August 31, 2000.

Asian Pacific American Legal Center of Southern California, Neighborhood Legal Services, and Legal Aid Foundation of Los Angeles, "Landmark Civil Rights Settlement Will Benefit Limited-English Proficient Welfare Families: Advocates Challenge Welfare Agency to Deliver on Promise of Equal Treatment for All," Press Release, November 20, 2003.

Auspos, Patricia, Miller, Cynthia, and Hunter, Jo Anna, *Final Report on the Implementation and Impacts of the Minnesota Family Investment Program in Ramsey County,* Manpower Demonstration Research Corporation, September 2000.

Blank, Susan, Blum, Barbara, "A Brief History of Work Expectations for Welfare Mothers," *The Future of Children,* V. 7, No. 1, Spring 1997.

Bloom, Dan, Farrell, Mary, and Fink, Barbara, "Welfare Time Limits: State Policies, Implementation, and Effects on Families," Manpower Demonstration Research Corporation, July 2002.

Bok, Marcia, "Education and Training for Low-Income Women: An Elusive Goal," *Affilia,* V. 19, No. 1, Spring 2004:39.

California Budget Project, "Timing Out: CalWORKs Recipients Face the State's Five-Year Time Limit," Welfare Reform Update, December 2002.

California Department of Social Services, "CalWORKs Leavers Survey: A Statewide Telephone Survey of Former CalWORKS Recipients," January 2000.

California Health Interview Survey, Information Database, A Collaborate Project of the UCLA Center for Health Policy Research, the California Department of Health Services, and the Public Health Institute. <http://www.chis.ucla.edu/main/default.asp>

Capps, Randy, Fix, Michael, Henderson, Everett, and Reardon-Anderson, Jane, "A Profile of Low-Income Working Immigrant Families," The Urban Institute, *Assessing the New Federalism,* Series B, No. b-67, June 2005.

Center for Third World Organizing, "Highlights from GROWL's Hear Our Voices Week of Action," March 2001.

Committee Against Anti-Asian Violence, "Eating Welfare: A Youth Conducted Report on the Impact of Welfare on the Southeast Asian Community," Report by the Southeast Asian Youth Leadership Project of the Summer 2000.

Congressional Budget Office, "Federal Budgetary Implications of The Personal Responsibility and Work Opportunity Reconciliation Act of 1996," December 1997.

de Sa, Karen, "California's Welfare Cutoffs Will Predominantly Impact Asian Americans," *San Jose Mercury News*, December 17, 2002.

Drayse, Mark, Flaming, Daniel, and Force, Peter, "The Cage of Poverty," *Economic Roundtable*, September 2002.

Equal Rights Advocates, "War on Poverty to War on Welfare: The Impact of Welfare Reform on the Lives of Immigrant Women," April 1999.

Falk, Gene, "TANF, Child Care, Marriage Promotion, and Responsible Fatherhood Provisions in the Deficit Reduction Act of 2005" (pp.. 109-171), *CRS Report for Congress*, February 17, 2006.

Falk, Gene, Gish, Melinda, and Solomon-Fears, Carmen, "Welfare Reauthorization: An Overview of the Issues," CRS Issue Brief for Congress, Feb. 14, 2006.

Farrell, Mary, et al., "Implementation, Participation Patterns, Costs, and Two-Year Impacts of the Portland (Oregon) Welfare-to-Work Program: Executive Summary," Manpower Demonstration Research Corporation, May 1998.

Feld, P., "Immigrants' Access to Health Care After Welfare Reform: Findings from Focus Groups in Four Cities," Kaiser Commission on Medicaid and the Uninsured, 2000.

Fix, Michael, and Laglagaron, Laureen, "Social Rights and Citizenship: An International Comparison," The Urban Institute, August 2002.

Fix, Michael, and Passel, Jeffrey, "The Scope and Impact of Welfare Reform's Immigrant Provisions," The Urban Institute, January 2002.

Fix, Michael, Zimmerman, Wendy, and Passel, Jeffrey, "The Integration of Immigrant Families in the United States," The Urban Institute, July 2001.

Flaming, Daniel, Drayse, Mark and Force, Peter, "On the Edge: A Progress Report on Welfare to Work in Los Angeles," Economic Roundtable, April 1999.

Fremstad, Shawn, "Immigrants, Persons with Limited Proficiency in English, and the TANF Program: What Do We Know?," Center on Budget and Policy Priorities, March 2003.

Fremstad, Shawn, et al., "Overcoming Barriers to Providing Health and Social Services to Immigrant Families," Center on Budget and Policy Priorities, March 2000.

Fujiwara, Lynn, "The Impact of Welfare Reform on Asian Immigrant Communities," *Social Justice*, V. 25, Spring 1998:82

Gayton, Celia, and Hernandez, Jose Atillo, "Beyond the Culture of Fear: How Welfare Reform Has Failed Immigrants and Public Health in California," Latino Issues Forum, January 1999.

Geronimo, Veronika, "The Impact of Welfare Reform on Asians and Pacific Islanders: Community Perspectives," Asian Pacific American Legal Center, September 2001.

Greenberg, Mark, and Laracy, Michael C., "Welfare Reform: Next Steps Offer New Opportunities, A Role for Philanthropy in Preparing for the Reauthorization of TANF in 2002," Neighborhood Funders Group, May 2000.

Hmong National Development, Inc., "TANF Reauthorization Priorities: HND Policy Recommendations" (no date). <http://www.hndlink.org/HND%20tanf%20recommendations.htm>

Hotz, V. Joseph, and Kilburn, M. Rebecca, "Regulating Child Care: Effects on Child Care Prices and Demand," *RAND, Labor and Population Program Working Paper Series*, 95-03, 1995

The Illinois Refugee Social Services Consortium and the Women's Bureau, DOL, "Moving from Welfare to Work: The Experience of Refugee Women in Illinois," August 1999.

Jang, Deeana, and Penserga, Luella, "Beyond the Safety Net: The Effect of Welfare Reform on the Self-Sufficiency of Asian and Pacific Islander Women in California," Asian and Pacific Islander American Health Forum, 1999.

Kaiser Commission on Medicaid and the Uninsured, "The Uninsured: A Primer, Key Facts about Americans Without Health Insurance," January 2006.

Kaiser Family Foundation, "Women's Health Policy Facts: Women's Health Insurance Coverage," July 2001.

Ku, Leighton, Fremstad, Shawn, and Broaddus, Matthew, "Noncitizens' Use of Public Benefits Has Declined Since 1996: Recent Report Paints Misleading Picture of Impact of Eligibility Restrictions on Immigrant Families," Center on Budget and Policy Priorities, April 2003.

Ku, Leighton, and Waidmann, Timothy, "How Race/Ethnicity, Immigration Status and Language Affect Health Insurance Coverage, Access to Care and Quality of Care Among the Low-Income Population," Kaiser Commission on Medicaid and the Uninsured, 2003.

Mink, Gwendolyn, *Welfare's End*, Cornell University Press, 1998.

Moore, Thomas, and Selkowe, Vicky, "The Impact of Welfare Reform on Wisconsin's Hmong Aid Recipients," Institute for Wisconsin's Future, December 1999.

National Immigration Law Center, "Immigrant Privacy Concerns Under Welfare Reform: The Need for Federal Guidance on 'The Communications Provisions,'" September 2000.

New York City Welfare Reform and Human Rights Documentation Project, "Hunger Is No Accident, New York and Federal Welfare Policies Violate the Human Right to Food," July 2000.

New York Immigrant Coalition, "Welfare Reform and Health Care: The Wrong Prescription for Immigrants," November 2000.

Office of the Assistant Secretary for Planning and Evaluation, "A Brief History of the AFDC Program," U.S. Department of Health and Human Services, (no date). <http://aspe.hhs.gov/hsp/AFDC/baseline/1history.pdf>

Park, Lisa Sun-Hee, et al., "Impact of Recent Welfare and Immigration Reform on Use of Medicaid for Prenatal Care on Immigrants in California," *Journal of Immigrant Health*, Vol. 2, No. 1, 2000.

Pimental, Benjamin, "From a Language of Work, Welfare and Opportunity," *San Francisco Chronicle*, December 3, 2000.

Physicians for Human Rights, "Hunger at Home: A Study of Food Insecurity and Hunger Among Legal Immigrants in the United States," August 2000.

Ribar, D., "Child Care and the Labor Supply of Married Women: Reduced Form Evidence," *Journal of Human Resources*, Winter 1992.

Schultze, Steve, "U.S. Criticizes W-2 Dealings with Hmong," *Milwaukee Journal Sentinel*, December 8, 2000.

Sen, Rinku, "The First Time was Tragedy, Will the Second be Farce? Fight Welfare 'Reform,'" *Color Lines*, Vol. 3, No. 3, Fall 2000.

Singer, Audrey, Welfare Reform and Immigrants: A Policy Review in *Immigrants, Welfare Reform, and the Poverty of Policy*, Kretsedemans, Philip and Aparicio, Ana (eds), Praeger Publishers, May 2004.

Southeast Asia Resource Action Center, "Welfare/Benefit Restoration Policies," September 2002. <http://www.searac.org/aawelandbfts-tanf.pdf>

Wilson, Greg, "Translation Needs Voiced," *Daily News*, August 23, 2000.

Wrigley, Heide, Richer, Elise, Martinson, Karin, Kubo, Hitomi, and Strawn, Julie, "The Language of Opportunity: Expanding Employment Prospects for Adults with Limited English Skills," Center for Law and Social Policy, *Workforce Development Series*, Brief No. 2, August 2003.

Zimmerman, Wendy, and Tumlin, Karen, "Patchwork Policies: State Assistance for Immigrants Under Welfare Reform," The Urban Institute, June 1999.

Jane Doe, et al. v. Los Angeles County Department of Public Social Services (DPSS), December 16, 1999, before the Office of Civil Rights, HHS, filed by the Asian Pacific American Legal Center, Legal Aide Foundation of Los Angeles, San Fernando Valley Neighborhood Legal Services and Western Center on Law and Poverty.

Neng Yang, et al. v. O'Keefe, Minnesota Department of Human Services, USDC, Class Action Complaint, Civil No. 99-2033, filed by Mid-Minnesota Legal Assistance.

From the Asian American Legal Defense and Education Fund (AAL-DEF) and the National Employment Law Project's jointly produced handbook "Rights Begin at Home: Protecting Yourself as a Domestic Worker" on employment laws in the New York City area.

2

The Trafficking of Asian Women

Updated by Gabriela Villareal and Norma Timbang[1]

Thonglim Khamphiranon, 41, and Somkhit Yindlphor, 57, two Thai women, were smuggled into the United States and enslaved for five years by Supawan Verapol, a Thai national living in the U.S. This employer forced them to work at her home and restaurant in Los Angeles. The women worked seven days a week, sometimes up to 18 to 20 hours a day, at Verapol's house and restaurant. They were forced to sleep on the floor outside the employer's door at night to be at her beck and call. They were denied medical and dental care. One of them was in such pain at one point that she resorted to pulling her own teeth with toenail clippers. The two women finally escaped in 1998 and found refuge at the Thai Community Development Center in Los Angeles.[2]

INTRODUCTION

Human trafficking and modern-day slavery are the most grievous of human rights violations. Although there are multiple definitions of human trafficking, it

---

1. Gabriela Villareal has advocated against human trafficking and modern day slavery for several years—first as a volunteer organizing an educational conference and currently as a coordinator for training and advocacy efforts through Safe Horizon's Anti-Trafficking Program. She lobbied with other Seattle activists for the passage of the first state anti-trafficking legislation and served as a member of the Washington State Human Trafficking Task Force.

    Norma Timbang is an at-large member of the National Asian Pacific American Women's Forum's national governing board and works as a community research, program evaluation, and organizational development consultant.
2. "2 reported in poverty after fleeing employer," *Daily News*, Kathryn McMahon, in *Trafficking of Women: A Report from Los Angeles*, April 3, 1998.

most commonly is defined as the recruitment, harboring, movement, or obtaining of a person by force, fraud, or coercion for the purposes of involuntary servitude, debt bondage, or slavery. Each year, an estimated 700,000 to 2,000,000 people are trafficked globally. The U.S. Department of State estimates that 80% of those trafficked are women and girls.[3] While men and boys are also trafficked into involuntary servitude, for women socioeconomic class, race, and gender oppression intersect to create harm of a different—and worse—nature and degree than for male victims. Women and girls are trafficked for sex, as well as labor deemed to be "women's work." Or they are forced into marriages and/or child reproduction while men and boys are not. Girls are most often trafficked into marriage and sexual servitude while boys are most often trafficked into sweatshop or other similar labor.

Of those trafficked globally, about 14,500 to 17,500 people are brought each year to the United States. Most of these trafficked persons originate from the East Asia-Pacific region. The primary Asian source countries for trafficked persons brought to the U.S. are China and Vietnam, but women have also been trafficked to the U.S. from every poor country of Asia. Trafficking of women has been reported in almost every state, with most cases occurring in New York, California, Texas, and Florida.

CAUSES OF TRAFFICKING

Recent technological advances, rising levels of poverty and inequality, a growing demand for cheap labor, and increasingly restrictive immigration and migration laws have all contributed to a rise in human trafficking, slavery, and the forced movement of people across borders for involuntary servitude. Trafficking in women flourishes in direct proportion to the growing economic inequity between the developing countries of the South and the industrialized countries of the North.[4] Traffickers recruit women in countries where poverty

---

3. While the federal government does not have statistics related to the approximate ages of trafficked persons and research is just beginning on the trafficking of Asian girls into the U.S., advocates have recently reported several cases of Asian girls forced into commercial sexual exploitation and domestic servitude. For example, according to a report, "Care for Trafficked Children" issued by the U.S. Conference of Catholic Bishops in April 2006, three Chinese girls who were placed in the federal Unaccompanied Refugee Minor Program in May 2005 were determined to be child victims of trafficking.

and unemployment are high, women have unequal access to employment and academic opportunities, safety nets are nonexistent, and social networks are disintegrating.

Following the introduction of International Monetary Fund imposed structural reforms mandating cuts to public services and programs, these countries struggle with diminished resources and offer few to no opportunities for education and employment for women. Denied access to the formal economy, yet faced with the obligation to contribute to their family's economic survival, poor women increasingly migrate alone across international borders. They are often coerced or deceived into traveling with traffickers, only to find themselves toiling in factories,[5] private homes, or in the sex industry.

Enticements and Deception

> *As soon as we landed our passports were confiscated. At a Daewoosa shop, I had to work from 7am to 2am and sometimes to 7am the next day, and also Saturday and Sunday[s] without being paid. We had no money to buy food, amenities or soap ... there was no air ventilation. Workers slept right next to each other. The temperature in the room sometime[s] went up to over 100 degrees. We were not allowed to step out for fresh air.*[6]

Traffickers frequently lure women from impoverished countries to the U.S. by making false promises of jobs as waitresses, nannies, models, and factory workers with high wages and good working conditions. Recruiters often say they will front the money for travel documents, transportation, and other services, often loaning women as much as $25,000 to $30,000. Repayments on the loans are then secured through garnished wages.

In addition to debt bondage, traffickers commonly employ other illegal and oppressive labor practices including isolation, denial of outside medical attention, the confiscation of identity documents, and the restriction of workers' physical movements by means of violence, or threats of violence to

---

4. The income gap between the richest and poorest countries has increased from 30 to 1 in 1960 to 74 to 1 in 1997. The worldwide flow of migrants looking for work increased from 85 million people per year in 1975 to 145 million in 2000.
5. Trafficking for the sweatshop industries will be covered in Chapters Three.
6. Testimony of Vi, a Vietnamese woman trafficked to American Samoa, before the U.S. House Committee on International Relations, 2001.

women or their families. Survivors of trafficking have also reported extreme physical and mental abuse, including rape, imprisonment, and forced abortions. Traffickers also commonly use psychological intimidation, threatening victims with deportation or arrest if they abandon their contracts.

Enormous Profits/Minimal Risks

The selling of vulnerable women and girls into bondage has become one of the fastest growing criminal enterprises in the global economy. Trafficking in persons is now more lucrative than the international trade in drug and arms. The FBI estimates that trafficking generates over 9 billion a year in profit. In one case involving Thai women and men garment workers, the Thai traffickers had profits estimated in the $8 million range over a six-year period.[7]

Criminal groups make big profits with little risk for the trafficking of human beings; the punishment is minimal. Until HR 3244 created stiffer penalties in the U.S., the statutory maximum for sale of a person into involuntary servitude was only 10 years per count. Sentences for traffickers of human beings ranged from 7 months to 9 years. By contrast, the punishment for distributing a kilo of heroin is a life sentence.

Demand to Meet the Supply

In receiving countries, such as the United States, economic inequity has increased, giving rise to an informal and underground economy that provides an environment favorable to trafficking and slavery. Across economic sectors—including the garment, domestic service, agricultural, and restaurant industries—multiple violations of minimum wage, overtime pay, health and safety, workers' compensation, and other labor laws occur. Trafficking often exacerbates the exploitation of women, migrants and workers of color in the informal and underground economy.

Yet labor law enforcement has been on the decline. For example, in the 1980s, the federal Department of Labor (DOL) had 1,600 wage and hour inspectors to police ninety million workers. Under President Reagan, the number was slashed to 700, and was increased only to 800 under President Clinton's tenure. The U.S. workforce continued to increase, yet the number of DOL inspectors have not increased significantly. Both New York and Cali-

---

7.   International Trafficking in Women to the United States 1999 CIA Report.

fornia states labor agencies are similarly under-funded and understaffed. Lack of law enforcement allows employers to violate labor laws with impunity, paving the way for trafficking to spread.

CURRENT U.S. LAWS ON HUMAN TRAFFICKING

One day, I fell for their trap. I had a little dream of my own. It was to make some money and to buy my house. I arrived in [America] with such hopes and dreams. Who would have known what would be waiting for me there instead? Since the day I arrived, I had to live like an animal. [The karaoke bar] was a prison that was filled with nothing but curses, threats, and beatings.[8]

Asian women are trafficked into the U.S. in different ways and for various purposes. Whether a person is considered to be trafficked depends on the definition adopted by a country. In 2000, advocates in the U.S. successfully lobbied for passage of the Victims of Trafficking and Violence Protection Act (TVPA), a comprehensive law with a broad definition of human trafficking, stiffer penalties for traffickers, and protections and services for victims.[9] The new definition is broad enough for prosecutors to establish the crime of trafficking where only psychological, rather than physical, coercion is used. The TVPA allows prosecutors to bring cases to court even when victims had agreed to migrate voluntarily to work as a domestic worker or in the sex industry, but are as a result of fraud find themselves in peonage, debt bondage, slavery, or involuntary servitude.

There have been two reauthorizations of the TVPA—the Trafficking Victims Protection Reauthorization Act (TVPRA) of 2003 and 2005. The 2003 Reauthorization allowed for additional funds for trafficking prevention initiatives in other countries and extra assistance to trafficked persons in the U.S. and abroad. Eligibility for benefits and services were extended to a trafficked

8. "Ms. Kim", a woman from China, was forced to work in the Northern Mariana Islands. U.S. Department of Justice Report on Activities to Combat HumanTrafficking Fiscal Years 2001-2005.
9. Penalties range from 10 to 20 years per count and life sentences if death, kidnapping, sexual abuse, or attempted murder are involved.

person's minor dependent children. The TVPRA of 2003 placed an emphasis on safety promotion and family reunification for unmarried siblings under the age of 18. The law requires that U.S. government contracts relating to international affairs contain clauses to authorize termination if the contractor engages in human trafficking, procures commercial sexual services, or is found to have used forced labor.

The TVPRA of 2005 gives U.S. courts jurisdiction over federal government employees and contractors accused of trafficking offenses committed abroad and strengthens the use of money laundering, racketeering, and civil and criminal forfeiture statutes against traffickers. U.S. assistance programs for post-conflict and humanitarian emergencies are now required to include anti-trafficking measures. In addition, new monies were also approved for additional investigations and prevention programs.

States have also addressed the crime of human trafficking by enacting a variety of laws. Washington State was the first of these, with a law that came about through the earnest advocacy and activism of Asian American women in the Seattle area. Multiple states have followed suit with legislation of their own to regulate international marriage brokers, criminalize human trafficking, provide civil remedies, and/or create task forces to study human trafficking. To date, 25 states have passed such legislation.[10]

THE TRAFFICKERS

In the popular imagination, traffickers are part of vast conspiracies. There may be some large criminal networks, but a significant amount of trafficking comes through smaller criminal networks, marriage brokers, wealthy private families, and even diplomatic officials.

Criminal Networks

In 2004, Florita and Nel Tolentino, owners of Omni Consortium, an international recruitment firm, were indicted for trafficking. The company had charged 273 Filipino teachers $10,000 each and promised them well-paying teaching jobs in the United States ... The teachers had been held in debt

---

10. These state statutes can be found at http://www. centerwomenpolicy.org/programs/trafficking/map/default_flash.asp.

bondage and were subsequently found to qualify as victims of trafficking by the federal government.[11]

The CIA believes that traffickers of Asian women into the United States are not typically part of highly organized crime syndicates, but operate primarily as smaller, loosely connected criminal networks.[12] Nevertheless, such groups are highly effective in setting up businesses in the United States, concealing the criminal nature of their activities, and deceiving women workers into accepting them as legitimate recruiters or employers. Employment or staffing agencies may serve as "front" businesses for traffickers. A joint venture between recruiters and "employers" may exist only temporarily for a given opportunity. Traffickers may subcontract out parts of their operation to groups such as street gangs or off-duty prison guards.

Marriage Brokers

A retired police officer divorced his wife to sponsor immigration for a woman from the Philippines. She came to the U.S. believing she would have a bona fide marriage with him. Upon her arrival, she found that the police officer and his "ex-wife" were still living together and the woman was forced into domestic service by the couple, who threatened her with deportation and imprisonment if she complained. She eventually escaped, the couple reported her to the immigration authorities, and she was placed in detention. In exchange for immunity, the couple testified against her and she has been fighting her case now for several years. During this time, she fell in love, married, and had two children. If deported, she will be separated from her children and husband indefinitely.[13]

On any given day, international marriage brokers advertise from 100,000 to 150,000 women from around the globe as "available for marriage" in "mail-order" catalogues, email "pen-pal" clubs, internet web pages and classi-

---

11.   Associated Press. October 23, 2004

12.   Given the lack of data collection, U.S. law enforcement officials admit they do not know to what degree large international organized crime syndicates are engaged in this industry.

13.   Proceedings of "Trafficking of Women & Children: Challenges and Solutions Conference," published by the University of Washington Women's Center, 2001.

fied newspaper ads. There are hundreds of mail-order catalogue agencies operating in the United States. A quick "Google" search produces over three
million hits for "mail-order bride."[14] Brokerage agencies represent the women
as if they are commodities, selling contact information and marketing them as
subservient, submissive and sexually "exotic"—typically drawing on highly
gendered and racialized constructions of Asian and "third world" women.
Marriage brokerage "services" can be differentiated from other dating services
by the inherent socio-economic power imbalances between the men and
women. In mail-order transactions, for example, men from wealthy countries
"purchase" women from poor countries as their brides. The power imbalances
are introduced not only in the commodification of the women, but also in the
unequal access to information regarding the terms of their "migration."

Marriage brokers recruit "brides" from Southeast Asia (primarily the Philippines) and also former Soviet bloc countries, which have been greatly
impacted by civil unrest and/or war, political repression and economic devas-
tation.

Bringing a woman to the United States for the purpose of marriage is not
always considered to be bride trafficking. Some of the men treat their wives
well and are looking for companionship and an equal partnership, not just a
housekeeper who also provides sex. However, where there is not full disclo-
sure and informed consent as to the nature of the relationship or the terms of
her migration, a woman may end up as a trafficking victim in a servile marriage. She may be exploited as a domestic worker and/or sexual slave, confined
to the house, denied the opportunity to learn English, prohibited from driving or communicating with family back home, and kept isolated or even pros-
tituted by her husband.

No national figures exist on the abuse of women trapped in servile marriages. Anecdotal evidence, however, sheds light on the extent of the problem.
While the US Citizenship & Immigration Services (USCIS) (formerly the
Immigration & Naturalization Service or INS) estimates that the 4,000 to
6,000 brides who enter through mail-order or pen-pal arrangements comprise

---

14. A common term for women seeking husbands through international marriage
     brokers is "mail-order bride." This term is generally avoided as many Asian
     women consider it derogatory and because it places a stigma upon women who
     found husbands through these types of arrangements. Other terms, which are
     used to describe trafficking victimization through the use of a "mail-order" ser-
     vice and exclude marriages where abuse and violence has not been an issue are the
     terms "bride trafficking" and "servile marriage."

only three to four percent of all annual immigration involving female spouses, the Asian & Pacific Islander Women & Family Safety Center in Seattle indicates that 35 to 40 % of those who have sought services at their agency because of domestic violence are women who came to the United States in this way. The Asian Women's Shelter in San Francisco and the Asian Task Force Against Domestic Violence in Boston also report that a growing and significant percentage of the populations they serve are women migrants trapped in servile marriages.

In the United States, there have been several high profile cases of Filipinas trapped in servile marriages who were killed by their husbands. In 1994, Jack Reeves of Texas, a serial bride buyer, killed his wife of seven years, Estelita Villar Reeves. Estelita was the third bride Reeves brought over to the United States. The following year, Susana Remerata Blackwell (also 25 and Filipina) and two of her friends were killed by her estranged husband at a Seattle courthouse while waiting for a hearing regarding Susana's divorce petition.

Significant economic, age, and social disparities often exist between men and women in brokered marriages. A survey conducted in 1999 for the former INS revealed that 94 % of the men seeking brides through mail-order catalogues were white, 50 % were college educated, and 6 % held M.D.'s or Ph.D.'s. These men were also more politically and ideologically conservative than average and had higher than average incomes and professional status. Their median age was 47, whereas the median age for brides ranges from 16 to 24 years. Over 90 % of the men surveyed were 20 to 50 years older than their brides and stated that they wanted women that they could "mold" and that were not "too educated." Most of the men surveyed rated "traditional values" as an important attribute of future wives.

While many international marriage brokers may be legitimate businesses, they remain unregulated. They are not required to, and generally do not voluntarily, screen their male clients—some of whom have histories of domestic violence or criminal records. While the companies provide personal details about the women, they do not disclose much about the male customers. The international marriage broker has no legal obligation to inform a woman that the man she will marry has a criminal background or may be a suspected batterer, pimp, or serial bride-buyer.

Fortunately, the 2005 "International Marriage Brokerage Act" (IMBRA) and the 2005 "Violence Against Women Act Reauthorization" (VAWA) were passed to provide protections for these women. IMBRA prohibits brokerage of marriages to women under the age of 18 and requires the broker to:

- provide criminal background checks and marital history of their client to the overseas fiancée;

- conduct a search of federal and state sex offender registries before releasing information about the overseas fiancée to their client;

- obtain written consent from the overseas fiancée prior to release of personal information to the client;

- provide information to the overseas fiancée regarding rights and resources available to her upon coming to the U.S.

In addition, the IRBMA limits the lifetime number of fiancée visas to three per U.S. sponsor (with potential for USCIS waiver).

Amongst other protections for immigrant women, the 2005 VAWA bars deportation of immigrant victims of sexual assault or domestic violence and exempts victims of domestic abuse, sexual assault, or trafficking from sanctions (e.g. for failing to voluntarily depart from the country). It also mandates a review of any history of convictions of domestic violence by the U.S. petitioner and requires petitioners to provide information and resources for immigrant women experiencing domestic violence.

Wealthy Private Households

Ms. Shaefeli Akhta is a Bangladeshi woman who was trafficked into the U.S. for domestic servitude by a Bangladeshi couple in 1995. She worked for five years for this couple, enduring beatings and death threats to herself and her family. She escaped in June 2000 and became a material witness for a federal criminal prosecution trial against the family she had worked for. To prevent her from testifying, Akhta's former employers arranged to have her family's home in Bangladesh burnt down. Akhta refused to be intimidated and the couple was convicted. [15]

Thousands of trafficked women work for wealthy private individuals under conditions of involuntary servitude.[16] These wealthy individuals are primarily

---

15. Interview with Muneer Ahmad, attorney, who represented Ms. Shaefeli Akhtar.
16. Many domestic workers enter the U.S. legally on B-1 visas (temporary work visas). Since USCIS does not keep a record of the number of domestic workers brought in under the B-1 visa category, it is difficult to estimate the number of women who may be in the situation of domestic servitude.

émigrés from countries with great disparities in wealth, such as Indonesia, Bangladesh, Thailand, the Philippines, and Nepal. They often bring their domestic "help" with them to the United States, viewing them as servants rather than as workers with rights.

Violations of domestic migrants' rights have included refusal to pay promised salary, sexual abuse, withholding of health and dental care, and even death threats to the workers' families back home. Domestic workers may work as long as five or more years in a home before escaping.[17] Domestic workers continue working, despite the abuses, in order to support their families back home or to protect their families from threats. In addition, escape may be difficult because of language and cultural barriers, isolation, or close employer-monitoring.

Diplomats and International Officials

> *Shamela Begum, a Bangladeshi woman, was brought to the United States to work as a live-in domestic in New York for an official at the Bahrain Mission to the UN. Upon her arrival in the U.S., her passport was taken away by her employer. Over the 10 months that she worked for him, she worked seven days a week, 12 to 15 hours a day, and was only paid $100 a month, which was sent by her employer to Begum's husband in Bangladesh. When her employers left town, they left Begum no food or money to buy food. She was twice assaulted by her employer's wife and confined to the house. One day Begum overheard a conversation in Bengali among some sidewalk vendors outside her window. When her employers left town later that day, she left the apartment alone for the first time. She reached the vendor and told him her tale. The vendor contacted a Bengali language newspaper, which contacted Andolan, a South Asian workers' rights group. On August 30, 1999, Andolan brought the police to the apartment and Begum was freed.[18]*

Shamela's story draws attention to cases in which diplomats, foreign embassy employees, and even delegates to the United Nations have also been reported as traffickers.

---

17. Women forced into prostitution are usually detected within a year or two because, unlike domestic work, prostitution is a crime for which law enforcement is actively seeking prosecution.
18. Somini Sengupta, An Immigrant's Legal Enterprise: In Suing Her Employer, Maid Fights Diplomatic Immunity, New York Times, Jan, 12, 2000.

Each year, the USCIS issues over 3,000 two-year temporary work visas to diplomats and international bureaucrats based in the U.S. to bring domestic workers to work as nannies, maids, cooks, and gardeners. These visas are issued to diplomats at foreign embassies and consular offices throughout the U.S. and to high-ranking officials of the United Nations, Organization of American States, World Bank and IMF. The diplomat employers of domestic workers come from all over the world, but their domestic helpers are primarily from poorer countries, as well as their own. Of the 3,000 visas issued annually, 49% are issued to women from Asian countries, half of those to Filipinas, and the rest to women from Latin American and African countries. Most diplomatic domestic workers are employed in New York City, the site of United Nations headquarters, and in Washington D.C., the site of many foreign embassies and the main offices of the World Bank and IMF. As diplomats, employers may have full or limited diplomatic immunity from criminal and/or civil prosecution and as a result their domestic employees may not have legal recourse for the abuses and exploitation suffered.

Over a 20-year period, the Spanish Catholic Center in the Washington D.C. area has handled at least 50 cases a year, for a total of 1,000 cases, of women who faced severe exploitation or were held in slave-like conditions by diplomats and international bureaucrats. Advocates believe this is only the tip of the iceberg. These women are confined to homes, forced to work around the clock, seven days a week, with no time off. They are paid between $100 to $400 a month, some working for years without pay. In some cases they are "passed on" to a relative or mistress of the diplomat.

ADVOCACY

I felt that eighty percent of the community was against me. They regarded Supawan [the trafficker] as a 'high soul' ... and couldn't believe how bad Supawan really is ... I felt like I did the right thing. But in Thai culture, I am seen as ungrateful.[19]

---

19. A domestic service worker enslaved in California by the common law wife of Thailand's ambassador to Sweden described in "Hidden Slaves: Forced Labor in the United States" September 2004.

There are a number of promising avenues for advocacy to ensure that survivors of trafficking remain safe and succeed in starting new lives. These include advocacy for culturally competent services, safe and appropriate shelters for them, and financial support for them while their visa applications and/or prosecution of the traffickers are pending, Advocacy is also needed to ensure the implementation of the TVPA. Finally, advocacy work cannot be seen as rescuing the trafficked person. To maintain and develop survivors' sense of agency and self-determination, the advocacy work must be informed by the survivors themselves and their communities.

Advocacy for Safe and Appropriate Shelters for Survivors

The most pressing need of those who escape trafficking is for shelter. The TVPA prohibits the detention of victims in inappropriate facilities and requires that they receive medical care and protection from recapture or harm by the traffickers. However, there is only one shelter in the U.S. exclusively dedicated to survivors of human trafficking.

Homeless shelters are unsafe because many require the resident to leave during the day and return only at night. Some domestic violence shelters accept only victims of intimate partner abuse. In addition, both types of shelters are already overburdened and not trained to handle the extreme forms of exploitation suffered by victims of trafficking.

When survivors of trafficking are placed in a shelter, it is usually a domestic violence shelter. These shelters commonly have increased security measures and can provide food, but are not typically aware of the additional needs of trafficking victims. For example, due to issues of safety and pending prosecution, women are sometimes required to stay within the confines of a shelter, limiting access to culturally relevant interaction and building of emotional support systems. This leaves many women vulnerable to depression and emotional insecurity.

There is a clear need for emergency, transitional, and low-income housing for survivors of trafficking. Appropriate shelters need to be constructed and additional resources given to existing shelters to expand their capacity to accept survivors of trafficking and to train staff to address the legal, case management, and safety needs of survivors of trafficking.

Advocacy for Financial Support for Survivors

After shelters, the second most pressing need of survivors of trafficking is finding ways to support themselves while criminal prosecutions or their visa applications are pending—either of which may last over a year. Survivors are commonly required to go through a lengthy visa application process, without a work permit for 3 to 6 months. Additionally, although they might be given "refugee" status immediately following liberation, many state agencies are not aware of what this new status means, causing many barriers to accessing public benefits.

The TVPA created a new visa category, the T visa, which will allow up to 5,000 victims of trafficking to remain temporarily in the United States per year while their cases are under investigation and/or while prosecution is under way. T visa holders are authorized to work while they remain in the U.S.[20] The TVPA also stipulates that those certified by the government as victims of severe forms of trafficking are eligible, to the same extent as refugees, for public benefits such as food stamps, Temporary Assistance for Needy Families, Medicare, and job training programs. Federal, state, and county welfare agencies need to be educated about these regulations and trained to appropriately handle these cases.

Ensuring Implementation of Federal Laws

Advocacy is needed to ensure that the implementing regulations carry out the intent of the TVPA. Advocates have drafted regulatory language to cover *all* forms of trafficking, whether by organized crime or wealthy individuals and diplomats (without absolute immunity) or by men who "purchase" a bride through a mail order company.

The law requires that victims have access to information about their rights and translation and interpretation services. Victims also need legal representation to protect them from criminal prosecutors who sometimes threaten to prosecute the women as co-conspirators. Legal Services Corporation (LSC) attorneys are authorized under the TVPA to represent undocumented survivors of trafficking. Advocacy is needed to ensure that the women have access to LSC attorneys and that they and other attorneys receive training.

---

20.   If certain conditions are met, a T visa holder may petition to become a permanent legal resident (green card holder) after three years.

Longer-term support services in the U.S. *and* within home countries are needed to prevent re-victimization, given that the period immediately following liberation and/or repatriation is the most vulnerable time for survivors and the risk of re-victimization is high.

Training of Law Enforcement

When trafficked persons escape and turn to law enforcement, they may be victimized a second time by being incarcerated, prosecuted, deported or returned to their abusers. Survivors may be held indefinitely in detention and mixed in with the general prison population while serving as a witness in criminal cases against traffickers. In some cases, traffickers may post bail to have the female victim "released" back into bondage.

Thousands of minors have also been trafficked into the United States, but lack of education among immigration and customs enforcement officers, child protective service agencies, and other law enforcement agencies has prevented effective monitoring or advocacy. Much more needs to be done to protect the rights of and provide appropriate services to trafficked minors.

One step in this direction was taken by the TVPA in requiring specialized training for Department of Justice (DOJ) and Department of State (DOS) personnel in identifying and responding to survivors of trafficking. Other federal, state, and local law enforcement need additional training in identifying survivors of trafficking and referring them to appropriate shelters and the appropriate federal agency, not simply to the Department of Homeland Security (DHS).

Advocacy Informed by Survivors and Their Communities

> *I never thought I will survive(sic). It was a terrible life with them [the traffickers]. But now I have finally come out in the open to fight for justice, not only for myself but also for all the workers of color who have suffered abuses.*[21]

Campaigns which focus on the need to "rescue" trafficked persons do not develop survivors' sense of agency or self-determination. The project of "rescuing" often invokes missionary zeal by "saviors" who may draw on colonial or

---

21.   Elma, a Filipina forced into domestic servitude in New York quoted in The Filipino Express September 2-8, 2002.

criminal constructions of victims. References by human trafficking responders to "our poor dark sisters" and the need to "rehabilitate" them conjure a vision of helpless women or a lack of respect for the human dignity of victims. Anti-human trafficking responses must be careful not to demean survivors' own capacity for self-determination or to reinforce power imbalances between "victims" and "rescuers." A survivor-centered system, guided by the experiences and perspectives of those who have survived and been liberated from trafficking, is essential to successfully protecting victims and preventing re-victimization.

Such a system would also contribute to the potential for prosecution by developing the victim's confidence and trust in the process following liberation. Partnering with survivors from diverse cultures and countries requires introspective analysis on the part of advocates, service providers and other responders who may be part of a society's dominant or mainstream culture. Such an analysis must examine personal biases, ethnocentric belief systems and socio-economic privileges. This introspection can help build trust and the capacity to respond to trafficked persons in culturally relevant ways.

Unfortunately, to date there has been a lack of discourse within the current system of responders regarding the philosophical or ideological viewpoints that guide their work against human trafficking. Rarely is human trafficking seen as resulting from the intersection of class, race, and gender oppressions and/or the imbalance of power and privilege among nations. The "rescue" approach and lack of a human and civil rights perspective to anti-trafficking work explains why responses developed by organizations in the ethnic immigrant communities impacted by human trafficking have hitherto been ignored. It is here, however, where the essential expertise to work with the victims and survivors of trafficking resides.

Survivor-centered approaches have generated new ways of analyzing and responding to the phenomenon of trafficking. Such new perspectives are evidenced by the shift in language from "victim" to "survivor" or "trafficked person" in new and innovative response programs.

The Anti-Trafficking Collaborative—A Promising Practice

The San Francisco Bay Area is a major hub for human trafficking from Asian countries, because of its port, but also because of the diversity of API communities in the region. There is clearly a demand for the labor provided by trafficked people, whether it is for the goods they create in a sweatshop or the services they can perform in the restaurant, home or sex industry. These industries flourish in the Bay Area and prey on the vulnerabilities of many communities.

The Asian Anti-Trafficking Collaborative (AATC) was organized in the Bay Area as a result of an identified need to serve trafficked persons with a culturally relevant and holistic strategy. The AATC partners originally organized to provide co-case management of legal and social services for Asian Pacific Islander (API) immigrant domestic violence survivors. Consequently the well-established coalition, including Asian Pacific Islander Legal Outreach, Asian Women's Shelter, Donaldina Cameron House, and Narika, was poised to address the lack of comprehensive services available to trafficked people.

The AATC model revolves around the teamwork of an attorney and a social service provider, both from immigrant-based community agencies. Since trafficked people experience extreme trauma, possible cultural shame, as well as community retaliation, the coalition focused on creating models of service provision built around culturally relevant strategies designed to build trust rather than building cultural competency into existing models of service provision. AATC staff speak sixteen API languages and house two language banks that include numerous other API languages. The staff represent many cultural communities. At the core of this cultural competence is the shared understanding that there is not one definition of culture and every person AATC serves will identify differently.

The team creates a stream of services and advocacy starting with outreach and technical assistance in the community, among advocates, and with government. From that point, AATC provides seamless services commencing from initial identification and advocacy for benefits to the extensive legal, social and long-term support services. This seamless integration of services at various stages of response, supports trafficked persons in their transition to a safe and independent life. AATC is a partnership of four community-based agencies that, together with trafficked persons, fosters shared cultural understanding of the daily challenges of responding to the needs of trafficked persons.

Life after Human Trafficking: Collaborative and Comprehensive Approaches

While laws, policies, and programs exist to counter the commercial sexual exploitation of children, greater political will, more effective implementation measures, and adequate allocation of resources are needed to give effect to the spirit and letter of these laws, policies, and programs. (World Congress, 1996c; para. 10)

The development of multi-disciplinary public policy, practice models, protocols, and infrastructure informed by survivors and impacted communities (primarily ethnic migrant communities)—partnerships like the AATC—is critical to improving response efforts. Increased private and public funding is needed to fund capacity-building initiatives, which include technology, training, and program evaluation.

Such approaches will involve community-based organizations and advocates, health and human service providers, law enforcement agencies, criminal justice systems, other public service agencies as well as national and international anti-trafficking organizations. Such multi-disciplinary partnerships, striving to achieve seamless multi-level comprehensive services, are the best way to provide adequate and effective response services and foster the development of self-determination for survivors.

REFERENCES

"Police Break Up Sex-Slave Ring That Preyed On Immigrant Girls," Associated Press, Nov. 13, 1998.

Chelala, Cesar, "The Unrelenting Scourge Of Child Prostitution," *San Francisco Chronicle*, Nov. 28, 2000.

"2 Reported In Poverty After Fleeing Employer," *Daily News*, April 3, 1998.

Honey, Martha, "Campaign for Migrant Domestic Workers Rights," Feb. 15, 2000, a presentation at the Congressional Briefing on Trafficking in Domestic Workers.

Hughes, Donna M., *Pimps and Predators on the Internet*, 1999.

Jordon, Ann, "Slave Trade Still Alive In U.S.," *San Francisco Examiner*, Feb. 13, 2000.

Lim, Lin Lean, *The Sex Sector: The Economic And Social Bases Of Prostitution In Southeast Asia*, a study for the International Labor Organization (no date) "House Oks Crackdown On Trafficking In Sex," *Los Angeles Times,* Oct. 7, 2000

"The Dark Side Of The New World Order," *Los Angeles Times,* Jan. 13, 1998.

May, Meredith, "Sex Trafficking: San Francisco Is A Major Center For International Crime Networks That Smuggle And Enslave Women," *San Francisco Chronicle*, Oct. 6, 2006.

McMahon, Katheryn, *Trafficking of Women: A Report from Los Angeles*

Poletunow, Mark, Fr., "Spanish Catholic Center," Feb. 15, 2000, a presentation at the Congressional Briefing on Trafficking in Domestic Workers

Richard, Amy O'Neill, *International Trafficking in Women to the United States: A Contemporary Manifestation of Slavery and Organized Crime*, published by the U.S. Central Intelligence Agency, April 2000.

Scholes, Robert J., *The "Mail-Order Bride" Industry and Its Impact on U.S. Immigration*, A Report to the INS, 1999.

Sengupta, Somini, "An Immigrant's Legal Enterprise: In Suing Employer, Maid Fights Diplomatic Immunity," *New York Times*, Jan.12, 2000.

Sparr, Pamela, *Mortgaging Women's Lives: Feminist Critiques of Structural Adjustment.* Zed Books. London. 1994

U.S. Conference of Catholic Bishops. "Care for Trafficked Children." April 2006.

U.S. Department of Justice Report on Activities to Combat Human Trafficking, Fiscal Years 2001-2005.

Wallace, Bill, "Smuggling, Prostitution Indictments," *San Francisco Chronicle*, Feb. 13, 2001

William, Booth, "13 Charged In Gang Importing Prostitutes," *The Washington Post*, Aug. 21, 1999

Report from the Roundtable on the Meaning of "Trafficking in Persons": A Human Rights Perspective, *Women's Rights Law Reporter*, Rutgers, Vol. 20, No. 1, Fall/Winter 1998.

Picketers at a 1982 demonstration of 20,000 New York Chinese garment workers demanding that contractors renew the union contract.

3

Asian American Garment Workers:
Low Wages, Excessive Hours, and Crippling Injuries

Updated by the author

INTRODUCTION

Man Le Lo worked for 10 years in San Francisco sewing the private label garments of major discount retailers. She worked seven days a week, and except on Sundays, 10 hours a day, some days even longer. After 10 years of setting elastic bands, she sustained repetitive stress injury to her hands, wrists, and arms. In the mornings she could not close her fingers into a fist because of the pain. On piece rates, in the last two years of employment, she averaged $2.00 to $3.00 an hour, half of minimum wage. She was never paid overtime. She reported the violations in her shop to the US Department of Labor (DOL), triggering an investigation of five shops owned by her employer. When she began organizing her co-workers, she was fired. But 200 of her co-workers benefited from her bravery. They recovered $192,000 in unpaid overtime wages as a result of the DOL's investigation.[1]

Ten to twelve hour days, six to seven days a week are the regular hours that garment workers toil in the United States. The majority of garment workers are Asian, Latina, and other immigrant women of color who on piece rates

---

1. The author, who was a staff attorney at the Asian Law Caucus from 1992–2000, represented Man Le Lo in her wrongful termination and wage violation lawsuit and assisted her with her workers' compensation claim.

earn below the federal minimum wage and rarely receive overtime pay. They work under dangerous conditions that include blocked fire exits, unsanitary bathrooms, poor ventilation and suffer from repetitive stress injuries.[2]

The U.S. Government Accountability Office has developed a working definition of a sweatshop as "an employer that violates more than one federal or state labor, industrial homework, occupational safety and health, workers' compensation, or industry registration law."[3] This report focuses on the New York, Los Angeles and San Francisco garment industries and the sweatshops where Asian American women toil.

THE U.S. GARMENT INDUSTRY

At its peak in 1973, the U.S. garment industry provided 1.4 million jobs. The movement of production overseas to Asia beginning in the 1980's and passage of the North American Free Trade Agreement (NAFTA)[4] in 1993 reduced the number of garment jobs to 621,000, a decline of 56%. Only the worldwide system of quotas on apparel goods provided for in the international Multi-Fibre Arrangement of 1974 (MFA) kept the remaining jobs from being moved offshore for another decade. However, on January 1, 2005, the MFA's worldwide quotas for cotton and wool apparel imports were phased out altogether by member countries of the World Trade Organization (WTO). With their complete phase out, the domestic industry has been devastated. The elimination of these quotas gave corporations more incentive to outsource apparel to countries with lower costs and labor standards. China has become the country of choice for garment production. After quotas on brassieres were lifted, China's exports into the U.S. increased by 232%. When quotas on

---

2.   A 2000 survey by the California Department of Industrial Relations' Division of Occupational Safety and Health found that an astounding 98% of the state's inspected factories had "regulatory, general, or serious health and safely violations.

3.   Historically, the word "sweatshop" originated in the 19th century to describe a subcontracting system in which middlemen earned profits from the margin between the amount they received for a contract and the amount they paid to the workers. The margin was said to be "sweated" from the workers who received minimal wages for excessive hours worked under unsanitary conditions.

4.   Under NAFTA, garments assembled in Mexico with North American made yarn and fabrics have no quota limitations or tariffs.

baby clothes were lifted, China's exports to the U.S. increased by 826%. Today, 80% or more of all apparel sold in the U.S. is made overseas.

The U.S. Bureau of Labor Statistics estimates that about roughly 207,800 cut-and-sew[5] garment jobs are left in the U.S.—reflecting a 79% decline in jobs from 1990-2005. In 2006, less than 70,000 garment jobs remain in California and about 40,000 in the New York industries.

Los Angeles

In the 1990s, the Los Angeles garment industry grew to be the country's largest garment center, with 156,000 jobs in 1997, 120,000 of those jobs in the downtown Los Angeles area. LA's garment manufacturers tend to produce locally because its niche market of constantly changing women's casual wear, with brand names like Forever 21, Bugle Boy and Chorus Line requires "Quick Response" production; garments orders are turned around within five to seven weeks or even shorter time periods. A local contractor can process reorders within a week or two. Contractors in Asia require a turnaround time of 10 to 12 weeks or longer. However, with the skills of Mexican garment workers, quality control, and turnaround times improving and with NAFTA having eliminated quotas and tariffs, a greater percentage of California's production has shifted to Mexico. As a consequence, the LA garment industry experienced steep decline post-NAFTA. By the end of 2000, Los Angeles garment worker jobs dropped down to 86,000. After the WTO worldwide phase-out of export quotas, today only 63,500 garment jobs remain, 56,700 in cut-and-sew jobs.

Despite the loss of jobs, the Los Angeles garment industry still produces $13 billion in clothing each year. LA's lucrative garment profits are made off the backs of women of color—96% of whom are immigrant. Based on the 2000 Census, 70% of those workers are Latinas, and about 20% are Asian women. The Asian women are made up mostly of Chinese (44%) and Korean (25%) workers, but there are also Vietnamese (12%) and Filipino (7%) workers. The vast majority are non-English speakers. Work is assigned on the basis of gender. Higher paying cutting and heavy pressing jobs are almost exclusively performed by men while the sewing operations are almost exclusively

---

5.   Cut-and-sew garment jobs are those with contractors primarily engaged in (1) cutting materials owned by others for apparel accessories and/or (2) sewing materials owned by others for apparel and accessories.

performed by women. Over half of Los Angeles' Latino garment workers are undocumented, most arriving within the last 20 years. Immigrant workers are employed by contractors who are also immigrants. Production is concentrated in downtown LA's garment district, but in the last 15 years has spread to the immigrant communities of El Monte, East Los Angeles, Orange County, and San Fernando Valley, as contractors look for cheaper labor and better space.

Given the large numbers of undocumented workers, Los Angeles's workforce is especially vulnerable to exploitation which explains the higher rate of minimum wage and overtime violations than in San Francisco's mostly documented workforce. The DOL estimates that in 2000, nearly 70% of garment factories in Los Angeles failed to pay federal minimum wage and overtime. Passage of the Immigration Reform and Control Act of 1986 (IRCA) only worsened conditions for garment workers. IRCA prohibits the employment of undocumented workers but imposes low sanctions that are rarely enforced, so few employers are deterred. Instead, employers use IRCA as a weapon against workers. Some contractors prefer to hire undocumented workers and then just report them to immigration officials when workers protest conditions. Because of the Illegal Immigrant Reform and Immigrant Responsibility Act of 1996 (IIRIRA), workers who are reported as undocumented are often immediately deported without any due process rights or opportunities to plead their situation. When employers threaten to call "la migra," undocumented workers stay compliant, and a whole sub-class of workers in the Los Angeles garment industry work at sub-minimum wages, driving the wages of the entire Los Angeles industry down with them.

San Francisco

Historically, San Francisco's garment industry was located in Chinatown. For decades, Chinese immigrant women walked to work from the crowded tenements where they lived to small mom and pop sewing shops, employing 10 to 15 employees and operating out of storefronts. In the 1970s and early 1980s, this began to change as entrepreneurial immigrants from Hong Kong began setting up larger, more efficient shops outside of Chinatown in San Francisco's South of Market and Outer Mission districts. The larger, more modern South of Market and Mission district shops survived and grew larger. These more efficient shops of over 100 workers, operating with new machinery and using assembly line methods of production (vs. one worker assembling the whole garment) were able to produce higher quality apparel in greater volumes. They had greater bargaining power to obtain higher contract prices and were able to pay at least minimum wages to 75% or more of their workers. As explained below, these larger shops were able to survive the scrutiny of labor agency inspections and law enforcement while the Chinatown mom and pop shops went into decline and completely disappeared by late 1990s.

At its height in the 1990s, the San Francisco Bay Area garment industry provided over 30,000 jobs. With the implementation of NAFTA, 20,000 garment workers lost their jobs in San Francisco alone, and the industry was reduced by two-thirds. Many of the local manufacturers, such as Esprit, Koret of California, Byers and Eberts, moved production to Southern California or Mexico where wages are lower than in the Bay Area. After the WTO quota phase-out, only 3,610 garment workers remain in San Francisco and about 1,790 workers remain across the bay in Oakland. The California Employment Development Department estimates that by 2012, San Francisco's garment industry will drop to 2,600 jobs and Oakland's will drop to 1,700.

New York

The New York garment industry remains the U.S.'s leading center for high fashion even though production jobs have declined precipitously from a high of over 149,000 in 1980 to a low of between 65,000 and 74,000 in 2000. As in California, movement of apparel production overseas was responsible for the decline in New York garment jobs. But it was the September 11, 2001 attacks on the World Trade Center that devastated the New York garment industry, particularly in Chinatown. Workers and trucks were prohibited from going into lower Manhattan, including Chinatown, for months after the attack. Many factories were forced to close. Today, a little over 43,757 jobs in apparel manufacturing remain.

However, it is anticipated that a local industry will remain because, like Los Angeles and San Francisco, New York manufacturers must also have "Quick Response" strategies for its unpredictable market of women's wear, particularly sportswear. In addition, New York's niche is producing high-end fashion and more formal apparel. This includes dresses, overcoats, blouses, slacks, and tailored women jackets with names like Oscar de la Renta, Donna Karan, and Calvin Klein giving New York fashion its glamour. Many of the higher end fashion houses produce in small batches of hundreds, not thousands, and prefer to stay in New York where their designers can walk across the street to their contract shops to personally oversee the quality of production.

About 54% of sewing shops are concentrated in New York's midtown (in a zoned garment district) and in Chinatown, 26% in Brooklyn (with half in Sunset Park), and the remaining in Queens and the Bronx. As of April 2006, there were 1,058 garment manufacturers and 1,128 contractors registered with New York's Department of Labor, and an additional 1,000 contract shops that are unregistered, bringing the total of contractors to about 3,628 primarily small shops with less than 20 workers each. The small size of a sewing workforce provides manufacturers with a flexible and fragmented workforce that can be laid off easily during seasonal lows. The majority of garment workers are Chinese and Latina immigrant women with a smaller number from other countries.

The majority of the midtown and 80% of Chinatown sewing shops, which consist mostly of Chinese workers, are unionized by UNITE (Union of Needletrades, Industrial and Textile Employees). Korean-owned shops that employ mostly Mexican workers are hardly ever unionized because of the primarily undocumented status of the workers, and the practice of paying in cash. Unfortunately, UNITE has not been effective in enforcing the union contract in these shops and rampant minimum wage and overtime violations continue to exist. In the early 1980s, most garment manufacturers were also under union contract and produced locally. During that period, UNITE members working in the Chinatown shops could earn from $5.00 to $15.00 per hour. Support for the union was strong. In 1982, 20,000 Chinese garment workers went on strike to demand that contractors renew the union contract. However, union manufacturers such as Liz Claiborne, Donna Karan, and Calvin Klein began moving the bulk of their production overseas. With union manufacturers moving their work, union contractors were forced to compete with nonunion contractors for work from nonunion manufacturers. The union contractors were thus forced to accept contract prices too low to pay even minimum wage. Ironically, the unionized Chinese workers earn less than the nonunion Mexican workers who often demand higher wages for particular skill sets. The Mexican workers can leave their employment if the pay is not high enough because they are not loyal to their Korean bosses the same way Chinese workers are often compelled to feel toward their Chinese bosses, especially since Chinese factories operate mostly through a referral system. The New York Department of Labor has little control over the wages of Chinese owned shops because the Chinese workers make few complaints. In response, the labor officials rarely visit those shops, and workers are continually paid low wages.

The 2002 Supreme Court decision, *Hoffman Plastic Compounds, Inc.v. NLRB,* made it even more difficult to get employees to complain. The Court provided undocumented workers who were unlawfully fired for complaining about labor conditions with essentially no remedy. The courts could not force employers to rehire these workers. Moreover, while the undocumented workers could get the wages that they were denied while they worked for the employer—for example, overtime pay—they could not obtain back pay for the time they were unemployed due to the unlawful termination.

Additionally, involuntary servitude is a regular part of the New York industry. Between 1991 and 1994, at least 100,000 people from the city of Fuzhou in the coastal province of Fujian, China, were smuggled into the US, with the majority of them settling in New York. Most of them owe snakeheads (people smugglers) $30,000 or more in fees. A large number were women who ended up in garment sweatshops. These workers were harassed, beaten, and even killed by snakeheads for protesting poor working conditions and not working hard enough to repay their "debt." Desperate to pay off their debts, the Fuzhounese take the lowest paying jobs in the Chinese community and line up outside sewing factories long before the doors open to be the first to begin work. At night, they work until after 10 p.m., sometimes until 4 a.m., sleeping in the factory, and start work again after sunrise. Increasingly, garment manufacturers offer contracts to Chinese subcontractors who hire Fuzhounese, whose willingness to accept low pay and poor working conditions has further dropped standards in the New York Chinatown garment industry.

The combination of jobs going overseas, involuntary servitude, and fear of immigration officials have resulted in wages of New York garment workers dropping to as low as $2 to $6 per hours. Working hours have steadily increased, with legal immigrants and naturalized citizens working six to seven days a week, 10 to 12 hour days. Homework and child labor are becoming more widespread. It is now common in New York shops, including unionized shops, for workers to work several months without receiving a paycheck. It is also not unusual for employers, seeking to reduce their taxes, to pay workers half in cash under the table and half by check, and then take back a percentage of the cash payment.

THE ROOT CAUSES OF SWEATSHOPS

Four key factors contribute to the proliferation of sweatshops in the U.S. and worsening conditions for garment workers.

A Pyramid of Exploitation

The very structure of the garment industry encourages the creation of sweatshops. Retailers sit at the top of the apparel pyramid, placing orders with brand-name manufacturers, who in turn subcontract to sewing contractors to assemble the garments. Contractors receive cut garment parts from manufacturers and recruit, hire, and pay the workers who occupy the bottom level of the pyramid, to assemble finished garments. Most contractors must accept the low price set by the manufacturer, even if the contract price is insufficient to pay minimum wages, as they risk having the work given to another contractor. To stay in business, contractors "sweat" profits out of their workers, cut corners, and operate unsafe workplaces.

Consolidated Power of Retailers

The second factor is the power of retailers. During the past decade the retailing industry has experienced major mergers leading to considerable consolidation of their buying power, especially among discounters. In the U.S., Wal-Mart and Kmart outsell all department stores combined, and the 10 largest retailers account for nearly two-thirds of all apparel sales. With this consolidated buying power, retailers dictate the price of clothing and ultimately what workers earn. Retailers have forced manufacturers to reduce their wholesale prices by as much as 25% or more, with the worker at the sewing machine feeling the biggest pinch.[6] Retailers also control the apparel industry by producing their own private labels instead of buying from brand-name manufacturers. The Federated Department Store's private labels, for example, include INC/International Concepts, Charter Club, and Arnold Palmer. Retailers, acting as manufacturers, design the garment, contract out and oversee produc-

---

6.   The $100 sale price of a garment is typically divided up as follows: $50 to the retailer, $35 to the manufacturer, $10 to the contractor, and $5 to the garment worker. A 25% reduction in price means the workers' earnings drop to $3.75 for assembling the garment.

tion, and set the prices for garments created exclusively for their stores. Over 40% of women's apparel sold in the US is manufactured under retailers' private labels. Retailers' domination of the garment industry means their decisions directly affect whether sweatshop conditions improve or worsen.

Race to the Bottom of the Global Assembly Line

A critical factor leading to the resurgence of sweatshops in the U.S. is the movement of production overseas. Production began moving to Asia in the early 1980s, where hourly wages were as low as 20 cents per hour, and to Mexico after adoption of the NAFTA in 1993. Forced to compete with overseas labor costs, domestic contractors lost their leverage to extract higher prices from manufacturers. Attempts by workers to improve their lot have resulted in manufacturers and retailers "running away." For example, when UNITE targeted Guess factories and contract shops for unionizing in 1995, Guess moved 70% of its jeans production to Mexico, Peru, and Chile. In San Francisco, when Esprit de Corps' Chinatown shop unionized in the mid 1970's, Esprit closed the shop, moved to Hong Kong, and did not return for 10 years. The threat of shop closings has kept workers from organizing even as conditions worsen. Overseas production has led to a race to the bottom in terms of wages, affecting workers in all major garment centers.[7]

Poor Enforcement of Labor Laws

The final factor contributing to the persistence of sweatshops is the chronic under-enforcement of labor laws by state and federal labor agencies, both of which are underfunded and understaffed. In New York, there are currently

---

7.   Heightened media attention on overseas sweatshops has led to consumers looking for the "Made in the USA" label. In response, retailers have shifted some production to US territories in the western Pacific Ocean. On Saipan, part of the Commonwealth of the Northern Marianas Islands, about 15,000 imported Asian women-Chinese, Filipina, Bangladeshi-produce garments for over 25 retailers, including The Gap and Tommy Hilfiger. They work 80 to over 100 hours a week, often "off the clock" without pay or overtime. They earn $2.90 per hour, a little more than half of the US minimum wage. They live seven women to a room in inward-pointing barbed wire enclosed barracks and are subject to lockdowns and curfews. The "Made in the USA" apparel are shipped to the US quota and tariff free.

fifteen state-level DOL inspectors to monitor over 3,000 garment shops as well as workplaces from all other industries in New York. Even if a factory is given a citation for a violation, re-inspection for compliance is rare. In California, in the 1990's, only 25% of all sewing shops were inspected each year by state or federal DOLs. Today, with even less staffing, inspections have dropped to even lower levels. Most contractors violate the law with impunity, assuming they will not be inspected. If inspected, the contractor simply pays the unpaid minimum wages, overtime premiums and fines as part of the "cost of doing business" and returns to business as usual, knowing that the inspectors will not return for many more years. In any case, most contractors do not even remain in business longer than 18 months to three years.

THE FIGHT TO ELIMINATE SWEATSHOPS CONDITIONS

For the past two decades, anti-sweatshop work has been carried out by Asian American organizations. The leaders in this movement are Asian American women, many of whom developed into labor and community leaders through their advocacy on behalf of garment workers. The work of these Asian American women has helped garment workers of every ethnicity and race. Their collaborative approach to organizing and advocacy has also built one of the strongest movements for civil and human rights among people of color.

Given the numerous factors that affect garment workers who labor in sweatshops, advocacy to improve conditions requires a multi-pronged approach. The approach includes making retailers and manufacturers legally accountable for sweatshop practices, improving government enforcement of labor laws, organizing and unionizing of workers, engaging in consumer education and corporate accountability campaigns, as well as initiating impact litigation and legislative advocacy. No one approach is sufficient and each is the necessary complement of the other.

Holding Retailers and Manufacturers Legally Accountable for Sweatshops

State and federal governments' responses to the proliferation of sweatshops has been to go after the sewing shops, often with the media in tow. Harassing contractors has proven to be an ineffective and misdirected strategy. Given that it is the retailers and manufacturers who force contractors to accept contract prices so low that contractors cannot pay minimum wage, it is they who must be responsible for the resulting labor law violations. But because production work is subcontracted out to "independent" contractors, manufacturers are often not considered the employers of the production workers and are shielded from legal liability. Unless manufacturers are held legally responsible for the wage and working hour violations of their contractors, they have no incentive to increase contract prices or avoid using contractors who are chronic violators.

Impact Litigation

Garment worker advocates have used impact litigation successfully to hold retailers and manufacturers jointly liable along with their contractors for minimum wage and overtime violations. The San Francisco-based Asian Law Caucus filed the first such lawsuit in 1983. In a lawsuit in 1993, it obtained the first court judgment in the U.S. holding a manufacturer jointly liable with its contractor. In 1995, the Asian Pacific American Legal Center of Southern California (APALC) filed a lawsuit against major retailers on behalf of 72 Thai garment workers released from involuntary servitude in an El Monte sweatshop, and won a $4 million settlement for the workers. In 1998, New York-based Chinese Staff and Workers Association (CSWA), a worker membership organization, and Asian American Legal Defense and Education Fund (AALDEF), assisted garment workers who sewed DKNY apparel with filing a class action lawsuit against DKNY to end the long work hours, lack of overtime pay, and locked bathrooms in their factory. The lawsuit was settled by the workers before trial. In 2003, in another lawsuit brought by AALDEF, the federal court of appeals in New York established criteria for finding joint-employer status. One criteria was whether the manufacturer was the predominant or only source of work in the factory. Manufacturers responded not by raising their prices to allow the factories to pay the minimum wage and to pay overtime for rush work, but by cutting back on domestic production and dispersing their production over a larger number of factories.

Impact litigation is costly and the outcome uncertain. Plaintiffs face high hurdles in establishing a sufficient degree of control by the manufacturer for it to be held liable. Hence, less than 10 such lawsuits have been filed in the last 20 years. Thus, legislation creating strict manufacturers liability without lengthy litigation is needed.

California's AB 633 Joint Liability Legislation

The most promising piece of anti-sweatshop legislation, Assembly Bill 633 (Steinberg), was passed in California in 1999. AB 633 created a "wage guarantee" requiring manufacturers and retailers acting as manufacturers to guarantee payment of minimum wages and overtime. AB 633 was a joint liability legislation that held retailers, garment manufacturers, and their contractors jointly liable for the unpaid wages of the contractor's employees. When a contractor fails to pay wages, retailers or manufacturers whose garments the workers assembled become the "guarantors" for payment of those wages. In exchange for the guarantee, garment workers must give up the right to enforce the new law in court and agree to bring all wage guarantee cases before the state Department of Labor Standards Enforcement (DLSE) under an expedited administrative process. Unfortunately, this exchange proved to be the weak link that undermined the law's great potential.

Despite significant increases in garment manufacturer and contractor registration fees to pay for enforcement, unfortunately, the DLSE has not been given the resources to fully enforce AB 633. A 2005 study by Sweatshop Watch—the organization that campaigned for its passage—and APALC revealed that though the number of wage claims filed by garment workers had increased four-fold since AB 633 first became law, the number only represented 70% of those workers who had been denied minimum wage and overtime, and the workers still ended up being deprived of two-thirds of their unpaid wages. This paltry rate of wage recovery is due to a number of failures by DLSE. First, the DLSE does not fully investigate all the claims that are filed. For instance, the DLSE identified wage guarantors in approximately half of the cases. Of those identified, it failed to issue subpoenas for business records to over 60% of them and failed to even conduct any investigation of about 13%. Records requested from guarantors are only provided about half of the time, and of the records provided, 90% of them are incomplete. Yet, despite its power to enforce its subpoenas, the DLSE lets guarantors off the hook by not obtaining court orders compelling them to produce the records.

Second, even when a claim goes to hearing and the DLSE issues a wage order, an overwhelming 85% of guarantors ignore the order and pay nothing. As a result, the DLSE only collects 3 out of 12 judgments entered against guarantors. In cases where the parties settled before the DLSE made an order, workers often only received 34% of their wages claimed. The DLSE's failure to pursue post-judgment collection efforts against guarantors result in its dismal rate of wage recovery.

Despite its great promise, AB 633's potential is not being met because of the lack of will and resources of the agency that is charged with protecting California garment workers, and the flagrant disregard by retailers and manufacturers of DLSE's subpoenas and the wage orders since they know there are few repercussions for ignoring the DLSE.

New York's SO7628 Joint Liability Legislation

A strict liability law is needed in New York State. The current version of the joint liability law, SO7628 (Spano), passed in 1998, holds manufacturers liable only if they knew or should have known, with the exercise of reasonable care, of the contractor's failure to comply with labor laws. Meeting the reasonable care standard mires garment workers in time-consuming litigation, which California's AB 633 avoided. In addition, SO7628 fails to hold retailers, the entities most responsible for the continuance of sweatshops, jointly liable for minimum wage and overtime violations of the contractors that produce their garments. Making enforcement even more difficult, in 2005, Governor Pataki proposed to rename the Apparel Industry Task Force, the group currently designated with the responsibility of identifying labor violations in the apparel industry, to the "Fair Wages Task Force" and to broaden its jurisdiction beyond the apparel industry to also cover any industry that may have sweatshops. The task force, with limited resources and investigators, is already overwhelmed with ensuring labor law compliance in garment shops. Pataki's proposal will simply dilute what little impact it currently has with cleaning up the garment industry.

On the federal level, after the 2000, 2002 and 2004 Presidential and Congressional elections, advocates will have to wait until a friendlier political climate in Washington before attempting federal joint liability legislation.

Advocating for Government Enforcement of Labor Laws

Laws do not protect unless vigorously enforced. Advocacy is needed to increase staffing levels at state and federal labor agencies. Advocates must exert pressure on these labor agencies to direct their enforcement efforts against contractors, manufacturers, and retailers. Advocates must oppose the labor agencies' efforts to join with immigration officials in their investigations and their inquiries. Workers will not step forward to complain or cooperate if they fear being apprehended by immigration officials. Vigorous enforcement has brought results. A case in point is the San Francisco Bay Area where minimum wage violations are significantly lower than in Los Angeles and New York. This improvement in wages in the Bay Area is due to the concerted outreach efforts to Chinese garment workers that began in 1990, media coverage on the lack of government efforts, successful lawsuits by the Asian Law Caucus (ALC) against manufacturers and contractors, organizing efforts by UNITE, a national anti-sweatshop campaign launched by the Asian Immigrant Women's Advocates, and pressure by ALC and UNITE on the DOL to use the "hot goods"[8] provision of the Fair Labor Standards Act to confiscate garments made in sweatshops. Using the threat of seizing hot goods, the DOL compelled manufacturers to increase contract prices and monitor their contract shops to bring them into compliance. Monitoring by manufacturers and combined federal and state agency raids on sewing shops led to the demise of San Francisco Chinatown's mom and pop industry, the growth of larger, more efficient and stable garment factories outside of Chinatown, and higher wages for San Francisco garment workers.

Empowering Workers

In the long-run, lasting improvements in the industry can occur only with an empowered and organized workforce. After a lawsuit or government inspection, after wage judgments and fines have been paid, neither government agencies with increased staffing nor lawyers are in a position to monitor factories day to day to ensure compliance with labor laws. After the scrutiny is over, employers revert to violating the law. Only an organized workforce can monitor factory conditions on a routine basis. However, workers face serious challenges to organizing because they are employed in the most globalized industry in the world with shop after shop that has been successfully unionized "running away" to lower wage countries. Undaunted by these challenges, in 2000, Sweatshop Watch launched a worker membership organization, the Garment Workers Center, in Los Angeles' downtown garment district where

---

8.   Goods that are produced in violation of minimum wage and overtime laws are considered "hot goods." The US DOL can seize hot goods and prevent them from being shipped or sold until the wages are paid.

Asian and Latina workers learn about their rights, develop leadership skills through a special curricula for women workers, learn how to use AB 633 to advocate on their own behalf and train other workers to do the same, and organize to win back wages from contractors and manufacturers. However, workers in Southern California do face a formidable challenge to organizing. Over half of the garment workers in the Los Angeles garment industry are undocumented, and the fear of deportation prevents them from becoming an empowered workforce. Garment workers in Southern California need amnesty. For sweatshop conditions to be eliminated, workers need to move from undocumented to legal status. These challenges, while formidable, are not insurmountable and require that new and innovative forms of organizing be developed.

Public Education and Consumer Campaigns

Traditional methods of union organizing, lawsuits, and government enforcement are not enough in today's global economy. As long as garment manufacturers can close shop and run away overseas with impunity, sweatshop conditions will remain and worsen. Garment workers need the support of the public and consumers. The first high profile national campaign was launched in 1992 by the Asian Immigrant Women Advocates (AIWA) against designer Jessica McClintock when one of her contract shops closed, owing its workers weeks of pay. The high point of the campaign, a segment that aired on 60 Minutes in 1994, brought nationwide attention to the plight of garment workers. In August 1995, 72 Thai immigrant women were discovered behind barbed wire fences in an apartment complex in El Monte, California, working under conditions of involuntary servitude: they were sewing the private labels of major retailers such as Mervyn's, Montgomery Ward, and Miller's Outpost. Sustained media attention and intense advocacy by garment worker advocates around the El Monte case, as well as other high profile cases, such as the national media exposure that Kathy Lee Gifford labels were being made in sweatshops, began to turn public opinion. Through these high profile campaigns and lawsuits, the public has been educated and no longer believes manufacturers' claims of ignorance of conditions in their contract shops. Indeed, the support of an educated public contributed to the garment workers' success, after 10 years of effort, in obtaining AB 633 in California.

More recent campaigns, including two in California, have also proved successful. The first was a campaign against Forever 21, Inc., a clothing store well known for its trendy, fashionable clothes sold at especially low prices. In 2001, Los Angeles garment workers with the assistance of APALC filed a lawsuit against Forever 21 to end sweatshop conditions. Sweatshop Watch and the Garment Worker Center waged a public boycott against Forever 21 retail stores. The boycott ended in December 2004 when Forever 21 agreed to implement and maintain lawful labor practices in its garment shops. The second victory, also in December 2004, was against San Francisco-based Ben Davis, a manufacturer of work wear. One hundred Ben Davis workers, all first generation immigrants from China and Mexico, ratified a contract with UNITE-HERE. The contract provided for a significant increase in the average wages, and a decrease in the workers' share of health care premiums. The parties had bargaining difficulties in March 2004, but a widespread campaign and local support from unions, consumers, and community activists put pressure on the employer to offer a fair, solid contract for its workers.

Codes of Conduct and University Logo Products

The plight of garment workers stayed in the public spotlight with the igniting of the student movement against sweatshops in the late 1990s. In 1998, students at Duke University took over their administration building, demanding that the sweatshirts, baseball caps, and other products that they wore with the university's logo be made under sweat-free conditions. The movement to ensure that the garment workers who sewed the products they wore earned living wages spread to other campuses, and more sit-ins followed at Brown, Harvard, the University of Michigan, the University of Wisconsin and the University of California at Berkeley. In July 1998, United Students Against Sweatshops (USAS) was born. In April 2000, USAS helped form the Workers Rights Consortium (WRC) which adopted Codes of Conduct and an independent monitoring system for the production of university products. By February 2006, 152 colleges and universities joined the WRC, including all ten University of California campuses, Georgetown, Harvard, Columbia, and New York University. USAS recently launched its Designated Supplier Program (DSP) to address the problem of companies who comply with labor laws being put at a competitive disadvantage in the sub-sector of the industry that produces collegiate apparel. The DSP calls on universities to phase in a program under which their licensees must contract exclusively with factories which primarily produce collegiate apparel, where workers are represented by independent labor unions and paid a living wage, and that fully comply with their codes of conduct.

University students have also come out in support of worker struggles. For example, when eight garment workers in Los Angeles, who sewed jackets bearing the logo of USC, UCLA, Indiana, Notre Dame, Ohio State and others, filed lawsuit against their employer alleging sweatshop conditions, university students nationwide came out in support of the workers. Students organizing played a key role in helping to settle the case within four months with the garment workers recovering $172,000 in unpaid wages and for their unlawful terminations.

Local Sweat-free Legislation

While advocates grapple with obtaining effective statewide legislation to end sweatshops, they have also turned their attention to cities and counties across the country that purchase uniforms for police, firefighters, hospital workers and other public employees, and ask the question whether these products are made under decent working conditions. Many cities have adopted sweat-free ordinances to ensure that the uniforms they purchase are not made under sweatshop conditions. The first city to adopt such an ordinance was North Olmstead, Ohio in February 1997. Other cities followed suit. In November 2004, the City of Los Angeles passed the Sweat-Free Procurement Ordinance and Amendment to Contractor Responsibility. On September 13, 2005, to ensure that the millions of city dollars spent on purchasing city workers' uniforms are spent on sweat-free apparel, the San Francisco Board of Supervisors unanimously adopted the Sweatfree Contracting ordinance. The law requires all contractors and subcontractors to sign a sweat-free code of conduct. This code requires that garment workers are paid not just minimum wage, but a living wage adjusted for the local labor market. The code also requires safe working conditions, a nondiscriminatory environment, and guarantees workers the right to join independent labor unions. Enforcement of this code is funded by the city and overseen by a nonprofit, independent monitor and a Sweatshop Advisory Group made up of community worker advocates.

Fending Off False Solutions from the Industry

In response to the public education and consumer campaigns, then Secretary of Labor Robert Reich and the fashion industry created The White House

Apparel Industry Partnership, now called the Fair Labor Association (FLA), a coalition of companies such as Liz Claiborne, Nike, Reebok, and human rights organizations. In April 1997, the coalition announced a scheme to eliminate sweatshops worldwide. It rolled out the Workplace Code of Conduct to which industry members of the task force said they would adhere. But major flaws exist in the Code. For example, it institutionalizes indecent wages and inhumane hours for women of color around the world. The Code only requires U.S. firms to pay a country's minimum wage, which, in order to attract apparel firms, governments set so low that it does not cover a family's basic needs. The Code also adopts the 60-hour week as a standard workweek, only requiring overtime pay in countries whose laws mandate overtime premiums. In November 1998, the coalition announced its first "independent monitoring" scheme. The scheme allowed companies to pick the factories that would be inspected by monitors chosen and paid for by the company. Based on inspections of only five percent of factories hand-picked by the company, the FLA could declare the entire company in compliance with the Code. Based on this monitoring scheme, the company was permitted to sew labels onto all of its garments which indicated that the garment was made under fair conditions.

After criticism from garment worker advocates, the FLA now selects and certifies the independent external monitors rather than their being selected and paid for by the companies being audited. These monitors perform unannounced inspection visits of companies' supplier factories. The companies and factories are not given advance notice of the time or location of monitoring visits. When a Code noncompliance is found, the company must work with their supplier to come up with a remediation plan in 60 days, at which time the FLA evaluates the remediation efforts and conducts follow-up inspections as it deems necessary. While the new system may be more successful in identifying Code violations,[9] there remains the question of whether the companies actually maintain their remediation efforts after the FLA has approved the changes. Unless and until they are held legally liable for their plants' labor violations, many of these companies will not have the incentive

---

9. The effectiveness of FLA's monitoring scheme is brought into question when it gives monitoring accreditation to private auditing companies such as Cal Safety who conducts 11,000 factory inspections a year but who failed to discover the El Monte slaveshop that held 72 Thai immigrant workers in involuntary servitude even thought it monitored the slaveshop's front shop.

to end sweatshop conditions and voluntarily join the FLA, or other similar schemes, as essentially a public relations tools for damage control.

A High-Value vs. Low Wage Strategy

For the garment industry that remains in the U.S., it cannot compete through a low-wage strategy since U.S. wages cannot and will not drop as low as wages in developing countries (e.g., about 50 cents per hour in Mexico and the Philippines). Rather, garment advocates believe that the U.S. industry will gain a competitive edge in the global apparel market not by lowering labor costs but by building on the domestic industry's strengths: turnaround time, quality control, and flexibility to do small and medium-sized orders. The future prosperity of the domestic garment industry depends on the ability to devise new niche market strategies and bolster local production capabilities to serve a wide variety of niche markets. Garment advocates believe that the apparel production that can remain in Los Angeles include: a) short cycle, "flash" fashion (which requires quick turnaround times); b) high-end designer fashion with medium to high price points; and c) sweat-free uniforms, collegiate apparel, and other garments produced under government procurement policies.

In California, Sweatshop Watch and APALC have launched the "Made in L.A." campaign for quality garment jobs in Los Angeles—bringing together garment workers, unions, community-based organizations, faith-based groups, industry representatives, and a broad-based coalition of supporters to advocate for government and industry collaboration in modernizing production capacities, creating a pool of efficient factories with model working conditions, and branding L.A. as a city of high-end, sweat-free cool, hip, trendy fashion. By establishing itself within specific niche markets in which local production makes sense and high-wage jobs can be created, garment advocates believe that Los Angeles' garment industry can maintain its competitive edge in the global sourcing market.

A Global Approach to Garment Advocacy

When workers in one country organize to improve wages and working conditions, U.S. retailers and manufacturers move their production to countries where they can pay workers even less. In the 1960s, manufacturers moved production to Hong Kong, South Korea, Japan, and Taiwan. However, over time these economies boomed and wages rose to almost the same levels as in the U.S. In the 1980s, hundreds of thousands of women workers who had worked for 10 to 20 years in the garment industry of these countries (now called the "Asian Tigers") lost their jobs as U.S. manufacturers shifted production to the lower wage countries of Indonesia, Thailand, and the Philippines. In the 1990s, Thailand's garment workers lost their jobs as manufacturers moved production to Vietnam and China where wages were even lower. After the MFA quotas were completely phased out on January 1, 2005, China quickly rose as the dominant producer of textile products.[10] As U.S. apparel companies shift more and more production to China, the jobs of garment workers in countries such as Bangladesh and Cambodia and some African countries are being threatened.

In response to the sudden and large influx of garment imports from China, the U.S. and European Union announced measures to curb imports of certain categories of Chinese textile and clothing products. Anticipating China's potential for immense export growth after the end of the MFA, a condition of China's accession into the WTO was to allow trading partners to impose temporary quotas on China until 2008. In May 2005, the U.S. imposed temporary quotas on seven products, slowing the surge in imports from China. But after 2008 when any type of quota on clothing and textile from China will no longer be allowed, the future is unknown for garments workers around the globe as they await U.S. manufacturers' decision on whether they will continue production in their countries or shift their production to China.

The U.S. garment industry has a global strategy for production, profit making, and exploitation. It has acted with virtual impunity in implementing its strategy. Garment workers in the U.S., who have lost their jobs and those who work in ever worsening conditions, have begun working with workers overseas to build the coalitions and networks needed to challenge the industry's heretofore unfettered exploitation of them.

---

10.   Clothing imports from China to the U.S. alone have gone up between May 2004 and May 2005 from $4.6 billion to $7.6 billion.

REFERENCES

American Textile Manufacturers Institute, *The China Threat to the Textile and Apparel Trade Report* (July 2, 2003)

Bonacich, Edna and Appelbaum, Richard P., *Behind the Label* (University of California Press, 2000)

California Trade and Commerce Agency, Office of Economic Research, "Apparel and Fashion Design" (June 2000)

The Center for Economic and Social Rights, Treated Like Slaves, Donna Karan. Inc. Violates Women Workers' Human Rights, Dec. 1999

Chan, Anita, China's Workers Under Assault: Exploitation and Abuse in a Globa-lizing Economy, Armonk, New York, M.E. Sharpe, 2001

Chin, Margaret M., Sewing Women: Immigrants and the New York City Garment Industry, Columbia University Press, New York, 2005.
Ellis, Kristi, Blame It on NAFTA, Women's Wear Daily, Oct. 1999

Esbenshade, Jill, Monitoring Sweatshops; Workers, Consumers, and the Global Apparel Industry, Temple University Press (June 2004)

Esbenshade, Jill, Monitoring in the Garment Industry: Lessons from Los Angeles, University of California, Chicano/Latino Policy Project's Working Paper Series, July 1999

Fair Labor Association 2005 Annual Report, http://www.fairlabor.org/2005report/mfa/page3.html

Fenton Communications Press Release, First Ever Lawsuits Filed Charging Sweatshop Conspiracy Between Major US Clothing Designers and Retailers, Foreign Textile Producers, Jan. 13, 1998

Fiscal Policy Institute, *NYC's Garment Industry: A New Look?* (August 2003).

Foo, Lora Jo, The Vulnerable and Exploitable Immigrant Workforce and the Need for Strengthening Worker Protective Legislation, 103 Yale L. J. 2179, June 1994

Gary Gereffi, "Global Sourcing in the U.S. Apparel Industry," *Journal of Textile and Apparel, Technology and Management* (Fall 2001).

International Labor Organization Report on the Economy after MFA, retrieved April 7, 2006 at http://www.ilo.org/public/english/dialogue/sector/techmeet/tmtc-pmfa05/tmtc-pmfa-r.pdf.

Kwong, Peter, Forbidden Workers, Illegal Chinese Immigrants and American Labor, 1997

Kwong, Scott, The Triangle Legacy: 90 Years After the Fire, Sweatshops Persist, Women's Wear Daily, March 22, 2001

"Los Angeles-Long Beach-Glendale Metro Div Current Month Industry Employment with Descriptive Narrative (Press Release)" (July 22, 2005).

Munthit, Ker, Garment industry feels threatened in Cambodia, SF Chron, Nov. 15, 2006

Nutter, Steve, The Structure and Growth of the Los Angeles Garment Industry, published in "no sweat" edited by Andrew Ross, 1997

Owens, Jennifer, Apparel Drops 4,000 Jobs, Textiles, 5,000 in July, Women's Wear Daily, Aug. 10, 1998

Ramey, Joanna, Domestic Apparel Employment Continues Downward Trend, Women's Wear Daily, Jan. 8, 2001

Rosen, Ellen, The Globalization of the US Apparel Industry: Free Trade, Neoclassical Economics, and The Origins of Domestic Sweatshops, Aug. 2000

Reavis, Dick J., Sewing discontent, Cut-rate wages in the Dallas apparel underground, The Texas Observer, May 3, 1993

SweatFree Communities, http://www.sweatfree.
org/monitoringconsortium.shtml

Sweatshop Watch and Garment Worker Center, "Crisis or Opportunity? The Future of Los Angeles' Garment Workers, the Apparel Industry and the Local Economy" (November 2004)

Sweatshop Watch Newsletter, New Briefs, April 1997

Sweatshop Watch Newsletter, Fair Labor Association=Starvation Wages, Dec. 1999

Sweatshop Watch Newsletter, Victory for Sweatshop Workers Who Sewed University Gear, Summer 2000

Sweatshop Watch's Response to White House Apparel Industry Partnership Agreement, May 1997, http://www.sweatshopwatch.org/swatch/what/ sw_respon-se .html

Weber, Lauren, Call to Boycott Clothes Maker, Newsday, July 9, 2004

U.S. Department of Labor, News Release "Only One-Third of Southern California Garment Shops in Compliance with Federal Labor Laws (August 25, 2000).

U.S. Department of Labor Codes of Conduct Report, http://www.dol.gov/ ILAB/media/reports/iclp/apparel/3d.htm.

United Students Against Sweatshops,
http://www.studentsagainstsweatshops.org//
index.php?option=com_content&task=view&id=48&Itemid=9

From "Picturing Change," a project of the Service Employees International Union (SEIU), Local 616, that allows homecare workers to portray their struggles and accomplishments.

4

Other Low-Wage Workers: Domestic, Home Care, and Restaurant Workers[1]

Updated by the author

DOMESTIC WORKERS IN THE HIDDEN ECONOMY

About Domestic Workers

There are no reliable statistics on the number of domestic workers employed in the U.S., let alone the number of Asian American domestic workers. Given

---

1.   The section entitled "High-Tech Sweatshops—Asian Immigrant Women in Silicon Valley" that was included in this chapter in the first edition of the book has been deleted from the second edition because of the disappearance of manufacturing jobs in this industry. Five years after publication of the first edition, accordingly to Flora Chu, an occupational safety and health attorney and co-founder of the Santa Clara Center for Occupational Safety and Health (SCCOSH), assembly line jobs have all but disappeared from Silicon Valley. In the late 1990's, there were 800 manufacturing firms in the valley and 50,000 to 70,000 assembly line workers, primarily Asian and Latina immigrant women workers. Most of the manufacturing firms have shut down and today less than 10,000 assembly line jobs remain as IBM, Fairchild, Intel, and others have sent the fabrication work overseas. The Silicon Valley high-tech industry has gone "fab-less," focusing on the design of chips and contracting most all of the fabrication work to shops in China and other points overseas. Along with the disappearance of assembly line jobs where Asian immigrant women worked was the disappearance of organizations such as SCCOSH and others that advocated for these workers. Most of the Asian immigrant women who relied on these jobs have found work in the restaurant, homecare and other service industries.

the small number of organizations that advocate for domestic workers, even anecdotal information is sparse. While it is possible to monitor the number of domestic workers employed by diplomatic personnel by looking at the number of work visas issued each year, the overwhelming majority of domestic workers are employed in the homes of private individuals. In states with large immigrant populations, most domestic workers are immigrant women. More often than not, they receive their wages as cash under the table and as such, are part of a vast underground economy. In the 1970's, Congress estimated that domestic workers comprised approximately half of all female heads of households and that three-quarters earned less than minimum wage. Over the last three decades, while the ethnic make-up may have changed, this remains a low-wage and female dominated workforce

It is estimated that there are 200,000 domestic workers employed in New York City, and about 600,000 in the metropolitan tri-state area of New York, New Jersey and Connecticut.[2] The Committee Against Anti-Asian Violence (CAAAV), an organization that works with domestic workers, estimates that in the tri-state area the vast majority of domestic workers are Caribbean immigrant women, about 25% are Asian immigrants, and a smaller number are Irish women. Among the Asian workers, 80% or about 25,000 are Filipinas, working in the suburbs primarily for white families. Three thousand are Tibetan women. This exact figure is derived from U.S. Citizenship & Immigration Services (CIS, formerly INS) data; Tibetan women enter the U.S. as political asylees and 99% of them work as domestic workers. South Asian domestic workers (from Nepal, Bangladesh, India, Pakistan) and Malaysians make up the rest of the Asian domestic workforce. It is estimated that there are thousands of South Asian domestic workers. Except for the South Asian domestic workers who work for employers of the same ethnicity, e.g., Bangladeshi for Bangladeshi, all other Asian domestics work primarily for white families. Most domestic workers in the tri-state area, except the Tibetans, are undocumented migrant workers who work in the U.S. in order to send money home to their families and many have been here up to a decade or more.

Regardless of ethnicity, the issues domestic workers face are the same across the board: low wages and long hours, isolation, sexual harassment, and lack of health care. Many continue working despite their exploitation because

---

2.   Steven Greenhouse, "Wage Bill Would Protect Housekeepers and Nannies" *New York Times*, 3/25/2002, Sec. B, p. 4.

of their isolation, particularly for suburban live-ins who may become homeless if they were to leave an abusive situation. They are unaware of their rights and fear deportation because of their undocumented status. Employers threaten to turn them over to immigration officials if they complain and many do not leave the house for fear of being picked up by the CIS. Under these circumstances, organizing among undocumented domestic workers is particularly difficult. Among South Asian domestic workers employed by those of the same ethnicity, many work in conditions of involuntary servitude.[3] Their passports are confiscated, they cannot leave the house or use the telephone and may be physically abused, and may work 100 hours a week for wages as low as 50 cents an hour.

Other live-ins isolated in the suburbs, such as Caribbean, Filipino, and Latina immigrants, work long hours for wages that average $2 per hour. Conditions for those who work as live-out domestic workers in Manhattan are better as they have each other for support. They meet in the park, at playgrounds, schools, and play spaces or while walking the dog or shopping at grocery stores. They teach each other how to negotiate with employers and spread the word about job openings. But even these workers work 12 hour days with no overtime pay. Their wages range from $5 to $7 an hour. Another issue is that the average age of domestic workers is in the late 40's and 50's. For many, Social Security taxes have not been paid during their years of work. What will happen to them in retirement?

Gaps in Legal Protection

Exacerbating the abuses spawned by their isolated work situations is the fact that domestic workers are excluded from federal and state labor laws that protect most other workers. Not until 1974 did Congress include domestic workers within the protections of minimum wage and overtime laws of the Fair Labor Standards Act (FLSA). But FLSA's overtime protections do not apply to live-in domestic workers. Nor do they apply to babysitters and companions to the disabled or elderly whose principal duties do not include housekeeping. The National Labor Relations Act, which grants employees the right to organize, does not cover domestic workers. Title VII of the Civil Rights Act of

---

3.   Nahar Alam, an Andolan organizer, estimates that there are 20 cases of indentured servitude of South Asian domestic workers a year in New York. Author's interview of Alam, Dec.14, 2000.

1964 (Title VII), which prohibits discrimination on the basis of race, color, religion, sex, or national origin, only covers employers with 15 or more employees, thereby excluding virtually all private households and domestic workers. As for state laws, a number of states exclude them from their higher minimum wage laws, resulting in domestic workers making the lower federal minimum ($5.15/hour). Over half of states exclude private households and domestic workers from their civil rights and workers compensation laws. And while all states but one offer unemployment benefits to domestic workers, most do not qualify because of requirements such as the need to earn $1,000 per quarter from the same employer; many domestic workers work a few hours a week for several employers.

Organizing Domestic Workers

Advocacy on behalf of immigrant domestic workers is very challenging. They must be located, then educated about their rights and given a place to turn to for help. The ethnic communities from which these domestic workers come do not look at them as workers with rights, but rather as servants. Thus, there are few resources for domestic workers in these communities. The numerous issues they face in addition to low wages and long hours are still hidden. Moreover, to advocate legislatively to address their issues and expand their limited legal rights, hard data is needed to persuade lawmakers. Broad based organizing must be done among domestic workers as a critical part of any advocacy work.

CAAAV's Women Workers Project (WWP), formed in 1998, engages in organizing work. To reach domestic workers, WWP goes into parks, the streets of wealthy neighborhoods, and indoor play areas during rainy days, such as gyms for babies, or on the subways.[4] The WWP provides workshops on basic rights under labor laws, negotiations with employers, and health fairs such as mammogram days. However, the WWP is not a service provider; its emphasis is organizing for broader change. When a domestic worker seeks assistance from the WWP, its Organizing Committee consisting of domestic

---

4. On Monday and Tuesday mornings, between 6 a.m. and 8 a.m., organizers are at the Long Island Railway terminal leafleting live-in domestics workers who are going back to Long Island to work after a day off. Many domestic workers sublet apartments in Queens or Brooklyn where they stay on their days off so that they are not at the beck and call of their employers on their rest days. Their employers are disembarking from the very same trains to go to work.

workers, decides on accepting the case based on whether it will further all workers' rights and whether the woman seeking help agrees to be part of a public campaign. For example, the WWP accepted a case on behalf of a Malaysian woman injured on the job and organized a demonstration in front of her employer's office. The gathering in front of the well-known psychologist's office brought public attention to the occupational hazards faced by domestic workers and the role of employment agencies who send women to employers known to be abusive.

In addition to individual campaigns, WWP has lobbied private banks to adopt codes of conduct for their international staff who hire domestic workers. In a highly publicized case, CAAAV targeted a Crédit Lyonnais executive who was transferred from England to the U.S. and brought a Filipino domestic worker with him. She was paid $2 an hour to work on-call 24 hours a day, seven days a week as a live-in nanny and housekeeper. The nanny sued the executive for unpaid wages. There is no legal precedent to include Crédit Lyonnais as a defendant. In addition, WWP has targeted Citibank and Merrill Lynch but both corporations have refused to respond.

In 2002, CAAAV joined with Andolan Organizing South Asian Workers to form Domestic Workers United (DWU), a city-wide, industry-wide coalition of domestic workers and domestic worker organizations.[5] In June 2003, through its "Dignity for Domestic Workers" campaign, the DWU was successful in getting the New York City Council to adopt Local Law 96-A and Resolution 135 which required that employers and agencies provide domestic workers with a standard contract that guarantees minimum wage laws, health insurance, regular working hours, overtime pay, and enforces other basic labor standards.

Andolan is a New York-based South Asian women worker organization. It is a membership and all-volunteer organization without paid staff or funding. Like CAAAV, Andolan use lawsuits as a way to educate other domestic workers and the public. It also provides services such as pro bono attorneys, self-defense classes, phone advice on how to leave the house and use public transportation, and has helped numerous workers escape involuntary servitude situations. In conjunction with the lawsuits, workers are asked to protest and

---

5.   Lynda Richardson, "PUBLIC LIVES; A Union Maid? Actually a Nanny, Organizing" The New York Times, April 4, 2002, Sec. B p. 2. See also Andolan website at http://andolan.net/campaigns.htm.

demonstrate in front of employers' homes to encourage other domestic workers to step forward and educate the public. Andolan recently launched the "Campaign against Diplomatic Immunity of UN Employers," demanding that diplomatic immunity not be used to shield abusive employers from being held liable for their mistreatment of domestic workers.

ORGANIZING RESTAURANT WORKERS IN SOUTHERN CALIFORNIA'S KOREATOWN[6]

Close to 300 restaurants operate in Los Angeles' Koreatown, employing approximately 2,000 Korean and Latino workers. Of the Korean workers employed, 87.5 percent are women. Until the Korean Immigrant Worker Advocates (KIWA) began organizing them, workers usually labored 10 to 14 hours a day, six days a week, and earned roughly $2.50 an hour. Many waitresses received only $500 a month, or $1.31 an hour with the restaurants assuming that the low wages would be supplemented by tips. This, however, often did not happen. 90% of the workers in Koreatown restaurants did not have any workers' compensation coverage. Most workers had no health insurance, were never paid overtime wages, and had no health or safety protection. Women often experienced sexual harassment, and Latino workers were often discriminated against. Any sign of discontent by a worker would result in severe retaliation, including termination and their blacklisting by Korean business owners. Workers who had no immigration papers were routinely threatened with deportation or being reported to immigration officials.

In 1995, KIWA started the Restaurant Workers Justice Campaign to address these poor working conditions and low wages. It engaged in worker-led confrontational actions to retrieve back wages and fight the practice of blacklisting and unjust terminations. KIWA also turned to litigation to stop the practice of blacklisting of fired workers. It sued the Korean Restaurant Owners Association (KROA) and in 1996 won a settlement that required the KROA to: (1) issue a public apology for its blacklisting practices, (2) establish a Workers Defense Fund of $10,000 to assist workers who become unemployed while resolving workplace disputes, (3) translate basic labor law posters into Korean and distribute them to all member restaurants for posting, (4)

---

6. Information for this section is derived from the Korean Immigrant Worker Advocates' website at www.kiwa.org/e/homefr.htm.

allow KIWA to give labor law seminars at all member restaurant premises, and (5) establish a committee to consider the extent of worker abuses in Koreatown restaurants and to craft responses. Two years later when KROA breached the agreement, a subsequent settlement forced KROA to establish a wage scale for workers based on seniority and business size and to organize a health fair for restaurant workers. A 1999 survey by KIWA found that significant improvements had taken place. In 1997, only 34.3 percent of workers in the restaurant industry reported earnings at or above the minimum wage. By 1999, that figure almost doubled, with 61.7 percent of workers earning at least the minimum wage. Nearly 70 percent of the employers provided workers compensation, up from 20 percent the year before.

HOMECARE WORKERS UNIONIZE-A LABOR SUCCESS STORY

On February 25, 1999, the Service Employees International Union (SEIU) won the right to represent more than 74,000 homecare workers, primarily women of color, in Los Angeles County. This was the biggest organizing victory for the U.S. labor movement since workers at Ford Motor Company's River Rouge plant joined the United Auto Workers in 1941. This stunning achievement was accomplished over 12 years among a low-wage, ethnically diverse, and predominantly female workforce scattered throughout the 4,083 square miles of Los Angeles County. Similar organizing efforts in the Greater San Francisco/San Jose Bay Area have also succeeded with SEIU now representing 60,000 homecare workers, also primarily women of color in Northern California. In the past decade, over 130,000 homecare workers have become union members. Through the union's collective bargaining and backing from elderly and disabled advocates, San Francisco homecare workers now earn $10.65 per hour, with medical and dental benefits. Alameda County workers earn $10.50 per hour with health care benefits, receive free bus passes to get to work, and got funding for a Workers Center. Los Angeles County homecare workers earn $8.45 per hour, and in April 2002, became eligible for health benefits through a Los Angeles County Department of Health Services Community Health Plan (CHP).

A Profile of Homecare Workers

Homecare workers are personal attendants who provide assistance to sick, elderly, and disabled people in their homes. Their duties may include helping their clients bathe, dress, move around the house, eat, and use the toilet. Other routine household tasks might include meal preparation, doing laundry, and managing household money. Homecare workers are also legally permitted to perform medically related tasks such as bowel and bladder care and administration of medications. Their jobs are often difficult and stressful, requiring a variety of skills ranging from heavy lifting to coping with death. In California, homecare workers are paid by the California In-Home Supportive Services (IHSS), which administers funds from Medicaid and other government programs.

In California, currently there are about 270,000 IHSS homecare workers providing care to 330,000 consumers. Overwhelmingly, homecare workers are women of color, many of whom are immigrants. Los Angeles County has some 74,000 homecare workers. 83% are women, 39% are Latinas, 25% are African Americans, 14% are of Armenian or Russian descent, and 7% are Asian/Pacific Islanders. This contrasts with San Francisco and Alameda Counties where approximately 25%–30% of the 15,000 workers are Asian American.

Half of homecare workers are family members of the consumers, e.g., a daughter caring for an elderly mother. Over half of Los Angeles homecare workers are over age 45. Prior to unionization, the wages paid to homecare workers was the state minimum wage, which was below the federal poverty level. Moreover, the workers were not entitled to any medical insurance, pension, or holiday pay.

The Challenges to Organizing and the Union's Strategy

The union was faced with several formidable challenges in organizing the homecare workers. First, the workforce was dispersed throughout the county and difficult to locate. With individuals working in home settings, they had no occasion to come together as a group. They spoke many languages-more than 100 different languages in Los Angeles County alone. Due to the low pay and lack of benefits, and consumer death, their turnover rate was estimated to be a staggering 40%. Second, it was not easy to pinpoint who the employer was. While IHSS performed the administrative functions of issuing paychecks, it did not have the legal authority to enter into negotiations with the union and neither the state nor the county would accept the responsibility of being the workers' employer. Moreover, some traditional functions of employers such as hiring, firing, and directing work, were performed by the consumers, who were unwavering about retaining this right as a means to control their lives. In fact, the consumers themselves were a potential obstacle if they publicly opposed homecare workers unionizing. Some were very concerned that the union would strike and leave them without critical care that no one else could provide, and others were suspicious that the union's intervention would decrease the control they valued over their ability to lead independent lives. Finally, there did not seem to be any leverage that the workers could use to press their concerns. The traditional weapon of a strike was not a viable source of leverage because the workers were often family members of the consumers.

1. The Action Plan

Notwithstanding the formidable challenges, the union committed itself to the following plan of action. As a first step, the union needed to pass statewide legislation to create a public authority in each county, an employer-of-record, with which the union could collectively bargain. Once passed, the next step would be to form public authorities in each county and commence collective bargaining. To achieve these goals, the union utilized a three-pronged strategy in each county: 1) grassroots organizing and political mobilization around day-to-day worker issues, 2) coalition building among workers, consumers, and advocates, and 3) policy changes aimed at restructuring the homecare system to bring higher wages and benefits to workers, while delivering better care to consumers.

2. Grassroots Organizing

Without worker interest, the union could not claim representation rights. Grassroots organizing was critical. In a long-term campaign with a 40% turnover rate, this required constant organizing and reorganizing just to maintain a statewide level of support of 10,000 to 15,000 of homecare workers at any given time. The initial challenge in Los Angeles was to find the 74,000 workers. The union went to senior citizens' centers, doctors' offices, markets, and churches. It established a union office that provided assistance in finding jobs and gave workers a space to come together. It filed a successful lawsuit over late paychecks, organized to raise the minimum wage from $3.75 to $4.25, and fought cuts in funding for homecare workers' services every year from 1989 to 1992. From these early successes, workers realized what could be done collectively. In Alameda County, SEIU set up a community-based Workers Center to conduct outreach. Once workers heard about the union and had a ray of hope that they could earn higher than minimum wages, they readily joined the union. Remarkably, the Los Angeles local was able to sign up 12,000 workers in a three-month period in 1987.

3. Coalition Building

After building a base among homecare workers in each targeted county, the union created partnerships with activists in the elderly and disabled communities. Most consumers came to see that by upgrading the pay and skills of their personal attendants, turnover would decrease and quality of their care would improve. The strength of worker/consumer partnerships formed the basis of a wider community alliance with church and other community-based organizations (CBOs). In the San Francisco Bay Area, Asian American CBOs such as Oakland Chinese Community Council, Korean Community Center, and Self Help for the Elderly supported the homecare workers. Delegations of workers, elderly, disabled persons, and CBOs met with politicians, rallied at government buildings, and chained themselves to the doors of the Capitol, all demanding dignity for homecare workers through a revision of the existing employer system.

4. Policy Making

In 1993, the homecare worker/consumer coalition succeeded in passing state laws providing the statutory authority for counties to establish public authorities. The public authority was designed to bargain with the union, train homecare workers, and provide a registry to match workers with prospective consumers. The union then turned its attention to establishing the public authorities in the counties and funding appropriations for IHSS workers' wage increases. San Francisco was the first to establish one in May 1995 and San Mateo's was the first to become operational in January 1996. In 1997, 10 years after the Los Angeles campaign began, homecare workers celebrated the establishment of their public authority.

After the public authorities were formed, finding common ground between workers and consumers was critical. For instance, while negotiating for the union contract with the public authority, the issue of who should have the right to hire and fire the workers was hotly debated. In the end, the union contract gave consumers the right to hire and fire with or without cause. "I came to understand how intensely personal this job is, and how important it was that the consumers had a choice in who touched their bodies," said a SEIU Executive Vice President. The union contract prohibits striking. A bill passed in 1999 prevents funding wage increases by reducing the hours of care approved for consumers. In return, the union got from consumers their support in pressing for higher state and county appropriations to pay for wage increases.

In 1999, the worker/consumer coalition succeeded in getting a law passed requiring each county to establish an Advisory Board and an "employer-of-record" by 2003. The law also protects against reductions in consumers' hours of care and requires all counties with a caseload of more than 500 individuals to provide the homecare option. Another law passed that year requires counties to provide the union the names, addresses, and phone numbers of all IHSS homecare workers it seeks to represent, solving the problem that the union faced 10 years earlier of locating homecare workers.

5. Establishing a Workers Center

Before the campaign, only one union business agent (paid staff of union) represented some 7,000 workers in Alameda County. To provide more representation to homecare workers, the union decided to create the Homecare Workers Center. Workers are given four months of training on workers' rights, the union contract, and IHSS rules and procedures and can then serve as business agents for fellow workers. Initial funding for the Workers Center came from private foundations. Union dues now pay for operations of the Center, including rent and wages for the five member/organizers who provide assistance in Chinese, Spanish, and English. However, union dues for homecare workers are one-third those of other SEIU members. As a result, there is only enough funding for the Center to provide a few hours of assistance a day and only very limited programs.

6. The Role of Chinese Homecare Workers in the San Francisco Bay Area

In Alameda County, Chinese homecare workers, who made up 13% of the workforce, were the most active union members at every stage of the organizing campaign. They recruited union members, lobbied for the 1993 state law that created the public authorities as employer-of-record, pushed the counties to form public authorities, negotiated the wage increases and health benefits, and represented their fellow workers in solving problems with the county. Non-English-speaking Chinese immigrant women learned to work the phones to enlist their fellow workers and CBOs to turn out at Board of Supervisor and state capitol hearings and testify, rally, or lobby for setting up the public authority or releasing funds for their wage increases. Chinese homecare workers have also run for and won union offices and served on the union's executive board. The thousands of Asian immigrant women who joined the union and played key roles in the organizing campaign have also helped shatter stereotypes that non-English-speaking Asian women are unable to stand up for their rights.

7. Subsequent Victories and Ongoing Organizing

Outside of California and New York, Asian Americans are a much smaller proportion of homecare workers. However, subsequent victories by SEIU nationwide have also benefited them. For example, on March 9, 2006, SEIU Local 880 successfully signed the first union contract for 49,000 homecare workers in Illinois. The contract provides four wage increases over two and a half years, averaging 35% raises overall, with additional 5-20% raises for workers who meet specific training and education guidelines, and funding for health insurance for homecare workers. The landmark contract was secured with the support of homecare consumers, who along with homecare workers themselves flooded the state capitol of Springfield on March 2, 2006, rallying and demanding quality care for homecare workers. In attendance were more than 500 members of SEIU Local 880 and five organizations representing seniors and persons with disabilities.

SEIU now represents over 440,000 homecare workers nationwide. In addition to the victory in Illinois, homecare workers in New York and California continue to make gains with each successive collective bargaining agreement and have secured health care coverage for themselves and their families. Workers in New York have also won paid vacation, sick days, and training and educational opportunities. In addition, homecare workers in Washington State have won worker's compensation when they work more than 20 hours per week.

These impressive organizing successes serve as a model for organizing and empowering other low-wage immigrant workers, including garment, domestic, nail salon, and restaurant workers.

REFERENCES

Domestic Workers

Lee, Chisun, Hard knocks, immigrant housekeeper says psychologist boss should pay for injuries, The Village Voice, Dec. 13, 2000

Lee, Chisun, Home work, immigrant nanny takes executive to court, Village Voice, Feb. 8, 2000

NOW Legal Defense and Education Fund, Out of the Shadows, Strategies for Expanding Labor and Civil Rights Protections for Domestic Workers, 1997

HRW report, retrieved at http://www.hrw.org/reports/2001/usadom/usadom0501.pdf.

Washington Post, June 14, 2001, by Ruben Castaneda, "Some Domestic Left Open to Abuse, Study Says"p. B03.

Homecare Workers

Delp, Linda, Home Care Workers Organizing Strategies, paper written for Professor Jacqueline Leavitt, Department of Urban Planning, University of California, Los Angeles, 2000

Delp, Linda & Quan, Katie, Homecare Worker Organizing in California: An Analysis of a Successful Strategy, Labor Studies Journal, Vol. 27, No.1 (Spring 2002).

Quan, Katie, Social Dialogue in the United States, John F. Henning Center for International Labor Relations, Institute of Industrial Relations, University of Cal-ifornia, Berkeley, Draft, March 2001

Park, Yungsuhn, "The Immigrant Workers Union: Challenges Facing Low-Wage Immigrant Workers in Los Angeles," 12 Asian L. J. 67 (2005).

Pence, Angelica, Home health care workers protest wages, San Mateo contract negotiations falter, San Francisco Chronicle, March 28, 2001

PART II
Health and Well-Being

5

Health Care Needs of Asian American Women

Updated by Courtney Chappell[1]

Susan Matsuko Shinagawa, a Japanese American breast cancer survivor and advocate, had two different breast surgeons tell her that "Asian women don't get breast cancer" and that she had nothing to worry about when she found a lump in her breast. In fact, breast cancer rates for Japanese American women are the highest of all Asian ethnic groups. Susan Shinagawa survived because she had the assertiveness to demand a biopsy.[2]

There are very few studies on the health and well-being of Asian American women in general, and even fewer on specific ethnic subgroups within the population. For example, a search of all published articles on sexual health found that only 2% focus on Asian American women, the lowest percentage for all racial and ethnic groups, and far below the percentage of Asian Americans in the U.S. population.

Where research does exist on Asian American women, the studies are limited because they tend to either include Asians among the minority or "other" category, or as part of large-scale studies where the data collection is not disaggregated by ethnic subpopulation. In these studies, researchers tend too often use the category the "Asian Pacific Islander American" (APIA), which lumps

---

1. Courtney Chappell was formerly the policy and programs director of the National Asian Pacific American Women's Forum where she engages in advocacy at the national and state levels around reproductive justice issues.
2. Asian and Pacific Islander American Health Forum, Women's Health Watch Newsletter (Summer 1997)

all 48 separate, incomparable, and diverse groups of APIA subpopulations into one group. Table 5 details at least 24 distinct Asian subgroups.

Where there is health data on specific API ethnic groups, information has been primarily limited to Chinese, Japanese, and Filipino and, in some cases, Native Hawai'ians and Vietnamese. Not until 1992 did the National Center for Health Statistics separate vital statistics for APIAs into the above groups and further into Indian, Korean, Guamanian/Chamorro, Samoan, and "Remaining API."

The treatment of this diverse population as one single, homogenous unit and the failure to disaggregate by specific Asian subgroups for health research, delivery of services, and policy can have harmful, even fatal consequences.

▶ Table 5.

Asian Population by Detailed Group: 2000

Detailed Group	Asian Alone		Asian in combination with one or more other races		Asian detailed group alone or in any combination
	One Asian group	Two or more Asian groups[1]	One Asian group	Two or more Asian groups	
Total	10,019,405	223,593	1,516,841	138,989	11,898,828
Asian Indian	1,678,765	40,013	165,437	15,384	1,899,599
Bangladeshi	41,280	5,625	9,655	852	57,412
Bhutanese	183	9	17	3	212
Burmese	13,159	1,461	1,837	263	16,720
Cambodian	171,937	11,832	20,830	1,453	206,052
Chinese	2,314,537	130,826	201,688	87,790	2,734,841
Filipino	1,850,314	57,811	385,236	71,454	2,364,815
Hmong	169,428	5,284	11,153	445	186,310
Indo Chinese	113	55	23	8	199
Indonesian	39,757	4,429	17,256	1,631	63,073
Iwo Jiman	15	3	60	-	51
Japanese	796,700	55,537	241,209	55,486	1,148,932
Korean	1,076,872	22,550	114,211	14,794	1,228,427
Laotian	168,707	10,396	17,914	1,186	198,203
Malaysian	10,690	4,339	2,837	700	18,566
Maldivian	27	2	22	-	51
Nepalese	7,858	351	1,128	62	9,399
Okinawan	3,513	2,625	2,816	1,645	10,599
Pakistani	153,533	11,095	37,587	2,094	204,309
Singaporean	1,437	580	307	70	2,394
Sri Lankan	20,145	1,219	2,966	257	24,587
Taiwanese	118,048	14,096	11,394	1,257	144,795
Thai	112,989	7,929	27,170	2,195	150,283
Vietnamese	1,122,528	47,144	48,639	5,425	1,223,736
Other Asian[2]	146,870	19,576	195,449	7,535	396,430

Source: US Census Bureau, Census 2000

[1] Respondents reporting several Asian groups are tallies of Asian responses rather than the number of Asian respondents. Respondents reporting several Asian groups are counted several times. For examples, a respondent reporting "Korean and Filipino" would be included in both the Korean and Filipino numbers.

[2] Includes respondents who checked the "Other Asian" response category on the Census questionnaire or wrote in a generic term such as "Asian" or Asiatic."

DISPARITIES IN HEALTH CARE FOR ASIAN AMERICAN WOMEN

The studies that do exist have found that the health and mental health status of Asian American women are disproportionately worse than the mainstream population. Asian American women suffer from a significant number of health disparities, many of which are preventable, detectable, and treatable if found at the early stages. Yet, Asian American women face particular obstacles that prevent early detection and treatment for these diseases and illnesses. Coronary heart disease, osteoporosis, cancer, sexual and reproductive health are among the most pressing areas for the physical well-being of Asian American women.

Coronary Heart Disease

A report published by National Women's Law Center indicate that although Asian and Pacific Islander women have a lower death rate from coronary heart disease (35.7%) compared to white (43%) and black (41.4%) American women, coronary heart disease is the single largest killer of Asian American women, accounting for more than one-fourth of all deaths. The limited studies that do disaggregate by ethnic subgroups indicate higher rates of death among Asian Indian, Filipino, and Laotian Americans than for the general population.

The risk of hypertension also varies by subgroups. For instance, hypertension is more prevalent among Filipino (25%) than for either Chinese (16%) or Japanese (13%) Americans. In California, while the rate of hypertension for all women in the state is 16%, the rate is only 9% for Vietnamese women and 3% for Korean American women. Further research is needed for all other Asian sub-populations to better understand this disease among the Asian American women's community.

Osteoporosis

Osteoporosis is primarily a women's disease, with women comprising approximately 80% of all cases. Asian American women are at a heightened risk for osteoporosis, most likely because they tend to be lighter in weight, have smaller bones, and have an average calcium intake that is half that of the general U.S. population. According to the National Osteoporosis Risk Assessment Survey, 65% of postmenopausal Asian American women had low bone density, the highest percentage among all racial and ethnic groups, and one of the primary indicators for developing osteoporosis. Twenty percent of Asian American women age 50 and older are estimated to have the disease, increasing their risk for hip, spine, and wrist fractures.

The dangers posed by a hip fracture, for instance, are particularly serious. Within one year after a hip fracture, up to 30% of the victims will die, 24% of the survivors will be confined to long-term care facilities, and 50% will experience long-term loss of mobility. Yet, only 11% of Asian American women between the ages of 40 and 64 in California have had a bone density test for osteoporosis in 1999-2000.

Cancer

Studies have found that Asian American women are at risk for cancer at younger ages and for more aggressive types of cancer than non-Asian women living in the U.S. This is true even though rates for these same cancers may be lower in Asian countries than in Western ones. For example, the rates of breast and cervical cancer increase for Asian women once they immigrate to the United States. The rate of breast cancer for Japanese and Chinese American women is significantly higher than for women in Japan and China.

Not only is the rate of several cancers higher for Asian American women than non-Asian American women, but the cancers Asian American women get often are more aggressive. Japanese American women have the highest rates of invasive breast cancer of all Asian ethnic groups. The risk of death for Asian American women with breast cancer is 1.5 to 1.7 times higher than that of white women. In fact, one study found that breast cancer is the leading cause of death for Asian American women age 45 to 54. Research published in the Oncology Nursing Forum found that Asian American women in California were younger at hospitalization and younger at death from breast cancer than white and Latina women.

The prevalence of cervical cancer is also increasing among certain ethnic Asian subpopulations. For instance, Vietnamese American women have the highest rate of cervical cancer among all racial and ethnic groups, a rate that is 5 times higher than that of white women. Another study found that invasive cervical cancer was much higher among Hmong women than other ethnic groups, and that diagnosis occurred at advanced stages. Japanese, Korean, and

Filipino American women were also found to present later with cervical cancer.

The increasing rate of and the higher risk of death from breast and cervical
cancer in Asian American women stems in part from lack of early screening.
APIA women age 50 years and older have the lowest rate of breast cancer
screening among all racial and ethnic groups. One study found that only 49%
of APIA women over 50 had obtained a mammogram or clinical breast exam
within the previous two years.

The same is true of cervical cancer screening. One study found that 53%
of the surveyed Vietnamese American women had never had a Pap smear,
compared to 6% of women in the general population. Another survey in San
Francisco showed that 21% of the 2,756 Asian and Pacific Islander women
who participated in the research had never received a Pap smear, compared to
5% of white women.

Acculturation rates may also play a role in whether Asian American women
seek preventive care. The San Francisco study mentioned above found that
Vietnamese women who had migrated to the United States more recently
(post-1981) were more likely (76%) to have never had the Pap test than
women who had migrated before 1981 (33%).

In addition, obstacles to early detection of cancer among Asian American
women include a lack of information in their native languages. This lack of
information is a particular problem due to the misinformation that surrounds
cancer in these communities, including the common notion that female
organs cease to function if they are not used for procreation and therefore are
not susceptible to disease and a belief that cancer is inevitably fatal. A San
Francisco survey of Vietnamese women found that 52% believed "there is little one can do to prevent cancer."

Sexual Health

In recent years, APIA women have experienced the highest rate of increase for
certain sexually transmitted diseases (STDs) among women of all racial and
ethnic groups. For instance, although the rate of STDs is decreasing for the
general population, cases of gonorrhea and chlamydia are steadily increasing
for APIA women. In addition, APIA women have four times as many report-
able STDs as APIA men, and the incidence of STDs for APIA women under
age 25 is on the rise. Hepatitis B and HIV/AIDS are areas of particular concern.

Hepatitis B rates for Chinese, Koreans, Filipinos, Southeast Asians, and Pacific Islanders range as high as 15%, compared to 0.2% among the general U.S. population. In particular, Chinese Americans are 6 times at greater risk for Hepatitis B, Korean Americans are 8 times at greater risk, and Vietnamese Americans are 13 times at greater risk than white Americans. Of the 1.25 million Americans living with chronic Hepatitis B, approximately half are Asian American. And among the APIA population, approximately 1 in 10 individuals are infected with Hepatitis B, resulting in the highest rates of liver cancer among all racial and ethnic groups. In 2002, the death rate among Asian Americans with Hepatitis B was 6 times higher than the rate among whites. Perinatal transmission is the most common mode of transmission among Asian women and their children. Every year, approximately 19,000 women infected with the Hepatitis B virus deliver infants in the U.S.; nearly half of these women are Asian.

Less than 1% of all reported HIV-positive cases occur among APIAs, the lowest percentage among all racial and ethnic groups. Between 1999-2003, however, AIDS cases among APIAs increased by 35%, the majority of which are among foreign-born APIAs. APIA women have witnessed the highest rate of increase in new HIV/AIDS infections. APIA women represent 13% of all cumulative AIDS cases within the APIA population. One study found that 49% of adult and adolescent APIA women reported having heterosexual sex with an HIV-positive or high-risk partner, compared to 47% of Latinas, 40% of white women, 39% of African American women, and 37% of Native Americans/Alaska Natives.

Cultural stereotypes about patients at risk for HIV prevent many doctors from offering Asian women HIV tests or from compiling sexual history profiles for Asian patients. Poverty, lack of health insurance, language barriers, and confusing immigration restrictions and eligibility guidelines further discourage many APIA women from accessing services and screening programs. Many Asian American women only learn of their HIV status through tests during pregnancy, job or insurance change, or after their partner becomes ill. Studies have found that white and Asian women tend to be infected for the longest time before discovering their HIV status.

Reproductive Health

Prenatal care is essential to the health of both mothers and children, as it provides early detection for mothers at risk of delivering a premature infant as well as interventions to reduce the risks of low-birth weight infants and other adverse pregnancy conditions and outcomes. Yet, some groups of Asian Pacific Islander American women have lower rates of prenatal care than the general population. For instance, only 52% of Samoan mothers (the lowest percentage among all racial and ethnic groups), 56.1% of Laotian women, 64% of Cambodian American women, and 76% of Native Hawaiian women receive prenatal care during the first trimester, compared to 82% of white women.

One study found that pregnant Hmong women in Wisconsin delayed prenatal visits out of fear that a doctor's touch would result in miscarriage. Another study in Oregon found that of the five major Southeast Asian groups in the state (Khmer, Hmong, Mien, other Lao, and Vietnamese), Hmong American women had the least favorable birth risk profile.

Asian Indians (8.3/1,000) and the group classified as "Other Asians" (8.9/1,000) have the highest infant death rates among Asians and Pacific Islanders. Asian Indians (8.4%), Thai (7.5%), Cambodians (7.1%), and Filipinos (7%) have the highest percentages of low-birth weight infants among all Asians.

After birth, the American Academy of Pediatrics recommends that all mothers breastfeed their children. The benefits to breastfeeding for both mother and child include better health outcomes for the infant, which translate into time, energy, and money saved due to fewer visits to the doctor and fewer missed days from work tending to a sick child. Many Asian American women, however, have lower rates of breastfeeding than the mainstream population. For example, among all women in California, Southeast Asian women have the lowest incidence of breastfeeding. This finding is interesting, given that 93% of Southeast Asian babies born outside of the U.S. are breastfed, compared to only 10% of those born in the U.S. Possible barriers may include lack of information about breastfeeding, limited maternity leave, lack of workplace breastfeeding facilities, and lack of support from peers and family members.

DISPARITIES IN MENTAL HEALTH CARE

Suicide

Asian American women have the highest suicide rates among all women over age 65, and the second highest rate among women ages 15 to 24 in the

United States. Suicide is the eighth leading case of death for Asian American women. A breakdown of Asian female suicide deaths in California found that 56% were Chinese, 22% were Japanese, 11% were Korean, and 8% were Filipina. In addition, the study found that 89% of those who committed suicide were immigrants. The suicide death rate for Chinese women is 20 deaths per 100,000, the highest for all racial and ethnic groups.

Other studies have found slightly higher rates of depression, attempted suicide, and substance abuse for Asian lesbian, bisexuals, transgenders and queers (LBTQs). Although Asian LBTQs are virtually absent in research on women's health, lesbian health, and transgender and queer health, anecdotal evidence suggests that the cultural and social pressures that many Asian LBTQs face are attributed to their higher than average rates of suicide attempts.

Impact of War

For certain Southeast Asian refugees who have suffered persecution, torture, and starvation prior to immigrating to the U.S., psychiatric treatment, psychotherapy, and general health care services are needed.

For instance, while there are no known longitudinal studies, the few that exist show that survivors of the Cambodian holocaust, the Mahantdorai, are experiencing a health crisis that is a direct result of their extraordinary trauma. Those who lived in Cambodia from 1970-80 suffered from major trauma that included starvation, combat conditions, slave labor, imprisonment, witnessing atrocities, physical and psychological torture, death of family members, physical injury, and loss of home, property, and country. A study of Cambodians living in Massachusetts found that by the mid-1980s, those who had lived in Cambodia from 1975-79 were suffering a high incidence of headache, dizziness, fatigue, muscle and bone pain, palpitations, sweating and fever-symptoms associated with starvation.

For those who suffer post-traumatic stress disorder (PTSD), their symptoms increase as they age. A California State Department of Mental Health survey found that 16% of Cambodians met the criteria for PTSD. Other studies have found that 40% to 50% of Khmer teenagers who lived through the Mahantdorai had PTSD. Many years after their trauma experiences, child survivors are having breakdowns and intrusive memories. Women traumatized as children demonstrated an unusual lack of physiologic response to a startle paradigm. Psychosomatic blindness for Cambodian women ages 40 years and older has also been reported.

Researchers are discovering that, like survivors of Nazi concentration camps of World War II, the survivors of the Cambodian holocaust also suffer psychic symptoms such as increased lassitude, failing memory, inability to concentrate, sleeplessness or irritability, and vertigo. The psychic symptoms are the result of starvation-induced organic brain and neurological changes. Studies are beginning to show that a history of torture is associated with hidden or undiagnosed traumatic brain injury that may be interfering with positive responses to psychiatric treatment. This fact raises serious questions as to whether some Manhantdorai survivors will be able to achieve self-sufficiency at a time when the safety net of social protection is being shredded in this country.

BARRIERS TO CARE

There are a number of barriers that prevent Asian American women from accessing the health care system and receiving meaningful and effective care from doctors and health care providers. The following are among some of the major obstacles.

Lack of Disaggregated Health Data and Meaningful Research

As mentioned above, the lack of disaggregated data collection has a negative impact on Asian American women's health care. Studies must collect data by not only ethnic subpopulation, but immigration and refugee status, socioeconomic status, age, acculturation, etc., in order to fully capture the diversity of the Asian American community. Without these statistics, the medical, public health, and health care communities are unaware that certain ethnic subpopulations within the Asian American women's community face a heightened risk for certain health conditions. In addition, health care providers are less likely to train their staff, tailor their outreach programs to educate Asian American patients and communities about the need for early detection and intervention, or provide appropriate care to this population.

Research on women's health, lesbian health, and transgender health virtually ignores the unique concerns and issues faced by the Asian LBTQ community. Because Asian American lesbians face multiple forms of discrimination based on race, gender, and sexual orientation, one can hypothesize that this will have an impact on their overall health. Yet, there are very few studies that analyze how stress affects the particular health and mental health care needs of Asian American lesbians. Studies relating to the health of lesbians generally have shown that lesbians have overall poorer health than the general population, morbidity is greater among lesbians than among heterosexual women, and lesbians use the health care system less often than heterosexual women. In addition, lesbians who do not disclose their sexual orientation may be at increased risk for melanoma or other cancers due to psychogenic suppression of the immune response. There needs to be more effort within the health care community to include Asian LBTQs in studies and data collection.

Uninsured Asian American Women

Another reason for the low utilization of health care services among Asian American women is their lack of health insurance. Approximately 36% of Asian American women under 65 years of age do not have any form of health insurance, a higher rate than the general U.S. population. Asian American women in California ranked second only to Latinas (21% and 32%, respectively) as most likely to be uninsured. And, Korean Americans are the most likely racial or ethnic group to be uninsured. Studies have found that Asian Americans and Pacific Islanders of all ages are less likely than whites to have a regular source of health care. This lack of health insurance is one of the primary barriers to accessing the health care system and obtaining preventative care, routine check-ups, and screenings.

There are a number of reasons attributed to Asian American women's lack of health insurance. First, Asian immigrants are concentrated in low-wage jobs that do not provide health insurance, such as garment shops, restaurants, and private households. Second, many Asian Americans are self-employed. For instance, Korean Americans are disproportionately self-employed, which is one of the factors that explain why they are more likely to be uninsured. For low-income and self-employed Asian American women, purchasing private individual health insurance is cost-prohibitive.

Finally, the 1996 Welfare Reform Act excluded many Asian immigrants living in poverty from federal and/or state-funded Medicaid programs. Those who remain eligible for Medicaid do not apply for fear of adverse immigration consequences. In California, since welfare reform, there has been a 33% decrease in Medicaid coverage among Asian Americans. The Kaiser Commission on Medicaid and the Uninsured found that Medicaid coverage for

Southeast Asians sharply declined between 1994 and 1997, from 41% to 18%. As a result, selected sub-populations of Asian American women are more likely to be without health insurance and more likely to become frequent users of hospital emergency rooms.

Language Barriers to Care

Language barriers impede clear communication between doctor and patient that is vital to ensuring the delivery of quality and meaningful health care. Title VI of the Civil Rights Act of 1964 prohibits any entity that receives federal funds from discriminating against individuals on the basis of race, color, or national origin in their delivery of services. The Supreme Court further interpreted the law to prohibit discrimination on the basis of language. Thus, health care providers, who almost all receive federal funds, are required to provide adequate services to individuals regardless of whether they speak English. Despite these efforts, the lack of linguistically accessible services continues to pose a serious impediment to health care access for Asian American women.

Over 60% of the Asian immigrant population is limited English proficient (LEP). There are far too many anecdotal accounts of immigrant children being asked to interpret for their mothers at the doctor's office. Sometimes interpreters are found at random. One story involved a 52-year-old Korean speaking woman who had a gynecology appointment at a county hospital. A community-based agency called ahead to request a Korean language interpreter for her. When she arrived for her appointment, however, the hospital did not provide an interpreter or bilingual worker. Instead, the hospital staff asked a 16-year-old boy sitting in the waiting room—a complete stranger—to be the interpreter for her gynecology appointment.

One of the most extreme examples of a health care breakdown due to a lack of language accessible services involved a 51-year-old Laotian mother of seven who was imprisoned for 10 months in Fresno, California because she had failed to take all of her tuberculosis medication. She had stopped because of severe side effects, and because, after talking to county health interpreters who did not speak Lao, she thought the medication could kill her. She was arrested by police with guns drawn. At the jail, a translator misunderstood and told officials that she was suicidal. She was held in a cell without light, water, heat, or food for three days. After she became acutely ill due to this mistreatment, she was taken to a hospital where she was chained by her ankles to her bed. After six months, the doctors diagnosed her as being non-contagious, yet she was held another four months before a judge found that she was being illegally detained.

Lack of Culturally Competent Care

Despite the growth and diversity of the Asian American population, the U.S. health care system has yet to fully incorporate culturally competent care and programming in its delivery of services. Culturally competent care requires recognizing, respecting, and responding to the different cultural and spiritual beliefs, values, and practices of individual patients. It includes incorporating traditional and non-Western treatments into clinical practice, diagnosis, treatment, and education.

Studies have shown that Asian Americans tend to be more dissatisfied with the quality of health care they receive than white Americans. One of the primary reasons is that many Asian Americans use traditional or alternative treatments and therapies, yet their physicians or medical staff fail to inquire about, understand, or accept these approaches during the medical visit. When these discussions do take place, Asian American patients report improved satisfaction rates with the health care that they receive.

Culturally competent care is of particular importance for the overall health care status of Asian American women, who are more likely to use traditional health practices and medicines, such as acupuncture and herbal remedies, than Asian men—69% versus 39%. By ethnic group, nearly 96% of Cambodian women, 81% of Laotian women, and 64% of Chinese women use traditional health practices. Their reliance on traditional medicines may explain their high non-compliance rates with Western prescription medications. Instead of viewing the non-compliance as lack of cooperation, however, health care providers could better serve the needs of the Asian American community if they integrate traditional health practices into Western clinical treatments.

For instance, traditional maternal health practices that empower Asian women through the birthing process are often denied to Asian American women because they conflict with Western medical practices. Hmong women, for example, will search far and wide for doctors who do not "cut" during the birthing process and allow them to squat during birth. The custom of saving the placenta after a birth for burial in a special site is not honored in today's hospitals because they consider the placenta a "biohazard." In addition, the common practice of offering ice chips and ice water during labor is antithetical to widespread Asian beliefs about the potential harm that can occur from exposure to coldness. For women who believe in these practices, the lack of support by the medical establishment means their birth experience and reproductive freedom are compromised. Promoting culturally competent care in health and human services will encourage more Asian American women to access the health care system, which will improve their overall health care and well-being.

Barriers to Mental Health Care Services

Despite the alarming statistics on Asian American mental health, Asian Americans generally are only a quarter as likely as whites, and half as likely as African Americans and Hispanic Americans to seek outpatient treatment for mental health. Asian Americans are also less likely than whites to be psychiatric inpatients.

A constellation of barriers deters Asian Americans from seeking treatment, including language and cultural barriers. For instance, approximately 1 out of every 2 Asian Americans who seek mental health care services will encounter language barriers. In addition, many Asian Americans feel ill at ease with the mental health system in the United States. They may find clinicians who do not provide culturally competent care, or who hold biases, misconceptions, and stereotypes of Asian cultures. Another reason for the underutilization of services includes the stigma and "loss of face" over mental health problems found in the Asian American community. These obstacles are even more pronounced for recent Asian immigrants.

Discrimination and Stereotypes

Discrimination against, and stereotypes of, Asian Americans represent additional barriers to accessing and receiving meaningful health and reproductive health care services. The stereotype that Asian Americans are one homogenous group that is healthy, educated, and financially prosperous—the model minority—is one of the primary reasons for the lack of attention and limited resources devoted to serving the needs of the Asian American community. For Asian American women, the myth presumes that they do not encounter sexual or reproductive health care problems, such as high STD rates or cancer or other health disparities. The model minority myth not only oversimplifies the more than 14 million individuals who identify as Asian American, but it is also used to divide people of color and deny the fact that Asian Americans experience discrimination in the health care setting.

With regard to the general lesbian population, it is known that lesbians encounter discrimination by health care providers, such as reluctance or refusal to treat, negative comments during treatment, or rough handling during examinations. As a result, the majority of lesbians, up to 72%, do not disclose their sexual orientation when seeking medical care. Without knowledge about a woman's sexual orientation, however, physicians are unable to provide appropriate, sensitive, and individualized health care. For example, when seeing a gynecologist, she/he may assume that the patient is heterosexual and asks questions that are heterosexist, such as "Do you use birth control?" The doctor will not know to ask questions about family history for breast cancer given that women who do not have children may be at a higher risk for this disease. Gathering accurate information about sexual behavior history is an essential component of good medical care. Yet, if a physician is not aware that a woman is lesbian or is uncomfortable eliciting this information on sexual behavior, she/he cannot advise, for example, on safe sex practices or order tests for particular STDs.

ADVOCACY

Advocacy, education, and outreach are needed at the national, state, and community levels to ensure that Asian American women and girls have access to meaningful health care. Legislation aimed at expanding the health care system for immigrant Asian women and families and changing immigration laws that have a chilling effect on access to health care will create better health outcomes for all Asian American women and girls. A commitment on the part of private health care providers as well as local, state, and national health agencies to devote more money and and resources into hiring and training bilingual health care staff will improve health impacts. Collaboration among community organizations that represent a diverse range of stakeholders will help broaden the health care movement and give increased visibility to these efforts. Finally, more research needs to be conducted so that health care providers, policymakers, and the general public can better understand the unique needs and concerns of Asian American women. More research will also help to dispel stereotypes of the Asian American community.

Successful Campaigns to Expand Health Care Access

Within the past few years, there have been a number of campaigns aimed at supporting the health care needs of Asian American women. For example, national and state Asian American organizations[3] have collaborated with immigrant rights, health care, and other civil rights organizations to advocate for expanded health care coverage for immigrants at both the state and national levels. Many of these groups were the impetus behind the introduction of bipartisan legislation in Congress that would lift the five-year bar to health care benefits under Medicaid and the State Children's Health Improvement Program, which is currently part of the 1996 welfare reform law. Lawfully present immigrant pregnant women and children, two of the most vulnerable groups in society, would no longer be prohibited from receiving these services.

There has also been a grassroots and national movement around HIV/AIDS in the Asian American community.[4] Some of the new organizations that have formed provide culturally and linguistically appropriate services to reach out to Asian American men, women, and youth who are living with HIV/AIDS, while others develop educational programs designed to dispel the myths, stereotypes, and cultural taboos about homosexuality and HIV/AIDS within the Asian American community.

Finally, there are efforts to address the high cervical cancer rate among Asian Americans, particularly Vietnamese American women. Many national and grassroots organizations and government agencies have developed educational materials aimed at increasing awareness about the importance of cervical cancer screening for Asian American women. For instance, the National Cancer Institute recently developed an informational booklet in both English and Vietnamese about cervical cancer, what a Pap smear is, and how to pay for the test if you don't have health insurance.

---

3. Among these organizations are the Asian Americans for Civil Rights and Equality, Asian American Justice Center, Asian and Pacific Islander American Health Forum, Association of Asian Pacific Community Health Organizations, the National Asian Pacific American Women's Forum, and the Southeast Asia Resource Action Center.

4. Some of the organizations that support APIAs living with or at risk for HIV/AIDS include the Asian Pacific AIDS Intervention Team, the Asian and Pacific Islander Wellness Center, the Asian and Pacific Islander American Health Forum, and the Asian and Pacific Islander Coalition on HIV/AIDS.

As part of this work, the reproductive justice movement conducted a successful campaign to promote FDA-approval of the human papilloma virus (HPV) vaccine, since studies have found that two of the HPV strains—16 and 18—cause 70% of cervical cancer cases. The vaccine, approved on June 8, 2006, is nearly 100% effective in protecting women against these two strains. The HPV vaccine would help reduce cervical cancer among Asian American women. Subsequent to the FDA's approval of the drug for the market, additional questions will need to be addressed, such as how expensive the vaccine will be and whether the uninsured or low-income women will have access to the vaccines.

REFERENCES

Ahn, Andrew, Ngo-Metzger, Quyen, Legedza, Anna T.R., Massagli, Michael P., Clarridge, Brian and Phillips, Russell S., "Complementary and Alternative Medical Therapy Use Among Chinese and Vietnamese Americans: Prevalence, Associated Factors, and Effects of Patient-Clinician Communication," 96 *Am. J. Pub. Health* 647 (April 2006)

American Heart Association, Biostatistical Fact Sheets, Leading Causes of Death for Asian/Pacific Islander Females United States: 1998

Asian and Pacific Islander American Health Forum, Making Managed Care Work for Asian and Pacific Islanders, an Action Agenda for Asian Pacific Islander American Communities, Nov. 21, 1997

Asian and Pacific Islander American Health Forum, Health Briefs: *Hmong in the United States* (Aug. 2003)

Association of Asian Pacific Community Health Organizations, Policy Brief. *Hepatitis B* (2006)

Brown, E.R., Ojeda, V.D., Wyn, R., and Levan. R, Racial and Ethnic Disparities in Access to Health Insurance and Health Care. UCLA Center for Health Policy Research and Kaiser Family Foundation, April 2000

California Medical Association Foundation, *Building a Strong Community From the Inside Out*, available at http://www.calmedfoundation.org/projects/pdfs/womenshealth/Osteo%20Complete%20Toolkit.pdf.

Center for Disease Control, National Center for Infectious Diseases (NCID), *Hepatitis B and Asian Americans Fact Sheet*

Gonen, Julianna S., Ph.D, Managed Care and Unintended Pregnancy: Testing the Limits of Prevention, Insights, Jacobs's Institute of Women's Health, July 1997—No. 3

Kaiser Commission on Medicaid and the Uninsured, *Health Insurance Coverage and Access to Care Among Asian Americans and Pacific Islanders* (June 2000)

Kuoch, Theanvy, Khmer Health Advocates, Inc., Health Crisis in the Cambodian-American Community (a working paper), date unknown

Luluquisen, E.M,. Groessl, K.M, and Puttkammer, N.H., The Health and Well-Being of Asian and Pacific Islander Women. Oakland, CA: Asian and Pacific Islanders for Reproductive Health, 1995

National Asian Women's Health Organization, *2, National, Plan of Action on Asian American Women and Breast Cancer* (1999)

National Asian Women's Health Organization, *6, Learning from Communities: A Guide to Addressing the Reproductive Health Needs of Vietnamese American Women* (1998)

National Women's Law Center & Oregon Health and Science University, *Making the Grade on Women's Health: A National and State-by-State Report Card*, 2004

Nowrojee, Sia, and Silliman, Jael, "Asian Women's Health: Organizing a Movement" from Dragon Ladies: Asian American Feminists Breathe Fire, Sonia Shah, Ed. (Boston: South End Press, 1997), p. xii-xxi

Penserga, Luella, "Health Profile of Asian and Pacific Islander Women: Legislative Briefing on Women's Health," Asian and Pacific Islander American Health Forum, March 12, 1997

Polek, C., Klemm, P., Hardie, T., Wheeler, E., Burney, M., and Lynch, K., "Asian/Pacific Islander American Women: Age and Death Rates During Hospitalization for Breast Cancer," *Oncol Nurs Forum* 69 (2004), available at http://www.ons.org/publications/journals/ONF/Volume31/Issue4/pdf/69.pdf.

Srinivasan, Shobha, Asian and Pacific Islander Women's Health: A Review of the Literature, Annotated Bibliography on Asian and Pacific Islander Women's Health, Asian and Pacific Islander American Health Forum, 1998

Suh, Dong, and Penserga, Luella J., Riding the Waves of Change, Improving the Health of Asian and Pacific Islander Women under Medi-Cal Managed Care Expansion, Policy Report of the Asian Pacific Islander American Health Forum, December 1996

U.S. Dep't of Health and Human Services, Office on Women's Health, *The Health of Minority Women*, (July 2003), available at http://www.4woman.gov/OWH/pub/minority/status.htm.

U.S. Dep't of Health and Human Services, *Health Problems in Asian American/Pacific Islander and Native Hawaiian Women*, available at http://www.4woman.gov/minority/asianamerican/suicide.cfm

Spring 2001 participants in Project HOPE's (Health, Opportunities, Problem-Solving & Empowerment) Organizers-in-training program, a project of Asian & Pacific Islanders for Reproductive Health (APIRH.)

6

Sexual and Reproductive Justice for Asian American Women

Updated by Courtney Chappell[1]

INTRODUCTION

For women, sexual and reproductive freedom includes the right to be a sexual being, free from both the patriarchal constraints of controlled pregnancy and the mandate to be heterosexual.[2] Control over sexuality and reproduction are inextricably interrelated.[3] But for too long, society's deep-seated antagonism toward women's sexual freedom has limited the discussion regarding women's reproductive health and rights to a narrow focus centered on control over women's procreative functions. The choice of whether or not to have an abortion is fundamental to women attaining full status as persons. At the same

---

1. Courtney Chappell was formerly the policy and programs director of the National Asian Pacific American Women's Forum where she engages in advocacy at the national and state levels around reproductive justice issues.

2. Same sex relationships also threaten the traditional hegemony of men in the sexual pecking order. The potential for women to have sexual pleasure and to construct relationships and communities without men changes the balance of sexual power in familial relations, precisely the arena most resistant to egalitarian intervention.

3. In the early abortion cases, some advocates pressed this argument and emphasized the differential punishment women suffered as a consequence of sexual activity enjoyed at least as much by men. But antagonism by the courts toward sexual freedom is very deep. Thus, in *Roe v. Wade*, advocates relied primarily on, and the Supreme Court chose, the right of privacy as a constitutional basis to protect a woman's right to abortion, and not the 13th Amendment prohibition against servitude and slavery.

time, reproductive freedom and the notion of "choice" encompasses more than the decision of whether or not to have an abortion. It also includes a broader framework of racial, gender, and economic justice.

For Asian Americans, sexual and reproductive justice includes the struggle for their very existence: their right to establish families when and if they choose; to have control over the number of children they bear; to have access to and to make sexual and reproductive "choices" freely regardless of socioeconomic status, immigration status, or sexual orientation; to obtain culturally relevant sexuality education; and to be assured freedom from environmental exposures that affect women's reproductive health and overall well-being.

SILENCE ABOUT SEX AND SEXUALITY

There are few studies that seek to document how Asian Americans view sexual freedom and other matters related to sexual health and well-being. The few studies that do exist reveal that in certain Asian American communities, sex is a taboo topic—more so than it is in the general American population. One survey of high school students in Los Angeles found that Asian American teens were less likely to talk with their doctors about sexual activity and risk prevention than any other ethnic group.[4] Another study involving HIV and Asian American women revealed that almost all of the respondents agreed that sex is a private subject that is not discussed openly or publicly.[5] Asian American lesbians have also explained that one of the reasons it is so difficult to come out to their parents and communities is that sex is not a topic that is usually or openly discussed within or outside their families. In some Asian cultures, women are not seen as sexual beings; they have sex for the purposes of reproduction or as a marital obligation only, but not for pleasure. To be a lesbian is to choose to be a sexual person and some Asian American parents have a difficult time accepting this. Sexism allows male children greater freedom to express their sexuality and independence than female children.

The dialogue around sexuality is very new. Perhaps the first time that people of color convened nationally to discuss sexuality in their communities was

---

4.   Sumie Okazaki, Influences of Culture on Asian Americans' Sexuality, 39 J. Sex. Research 34, 37 (Feb. 2002).

5.   Dorothy Chin, HIV-Related Sexual Risk Assessment Among Asian/Pacific Islander American Women: An Inductive Model, 49 Social Science and Medicine 241, 245 (1999).

in February 2001 when the Ford Foundation invited experts and activists from around the country to engage in a dialogue. Given that these issues have only recently moved from behind closed doors, there are just a handful of specific studies on Asian American women's sexual rights and well-being. There is a tremendous need for additional resources to examine and investigate how sexuality is defined and the patterns of sexual behavior in different Asian American communities. This is critical for determining how views of sex and sexuality contribute to reproductive health and social problems discussed in this and the following chapter on domestic violence.

OBSTACLES TO REPRODUCTIVE FREEDOM

Teen Pregnancy in the API Community

Studies that break down data collection by ethnic sub-population reveal that teen pregnancy in some Asian American sub-populations is on the rise. One such study by the California Wellness Foundation found that the highest teen birth rates in California are among Laotian teens (18.9%). Similarly, according to the Women's Association of Hmong and Lao in Minnesota, 50% of Hmong girls between the ages 15 and 19 in Twin Cities high schools have children or become pregnant before they graduate.

These numbers do not correspond with national teen pregnancy data. In 2000, the Centers for Disease Control (CDC) reported the lowest teen birth-rates in 60 years for women ages 15 to 19; 4.96 percent for women of all ages and 2.28 percent for Asian women. However, because the data failed to disaggregate by ethnic group, the CDC report gives the public health community the inaccurate impression that teen birth rates are very low among Asian girls. These misleading statistics have made it difficult to finance teen pregnancy prevention programs in Southeast Asian communities where teen pregnancy rates are high.

Mainstream pregnancy prevention programs are based on the premise that teen pregnancy is a pathology. Yet, counselors who work with girls in Southeast Asian communities with high teen birth rates find that, in some cases, it is not financial barriers, ignorance of birth control, lack of access to family planning services, or peer or boyfriend pressure to have sex that cause teen births. Instead, high birth rates among certain Southeast Asian girls, particularly in the Cambodian, Hmong and Mien communities, may be the result of cultural traditions that encourage or pressure girls to marry and have children at a young age. Motherhood is often seen as a rite of passage, and a woman is not given respect and authority within her family and community until she becomes a mother. It is important to note, however, that some teenage girls are fighting against such early marriages that often condemn them to poverty and cut off their dreams to full personhood.[6]

Lingering Traditions of Male Preference

First generation Asian American women often experience reproductive oppression when their husbands and extended families put both overt and subtle pressure on them to bear a male child. It is widely known that unwanted girl babies are abandoned all over Asia every day and that women who bear only girl children are accorded less respect. In many cases, women are pressured into having more children than the family can economically support until a male heir is born.

The devaluation of girls and adult women until they bear male children has led to the practice of aborting female fetuses in certain Asian communities. For instance, in China, because of its one-child policy, women are using ultrasound or amniocentesis to determine the sex of the fetus, with the goal of aborting female fetuses. Similar attitudes and practices can be found in India and other Asian countries. As a result, there is a significant and unbalanced sex ratio problem in some Asian districts. The sex ratio in some communities in India is as low as 766 girls per 1,000 male children. In China in 1996, there were 121 boys ages 1 to 4 for every 100 girls in the same age range. Similar attitudes and practices can be found among some Asians who migrate.

In the U.S., the development and marketing of reproductive genetic technologies for "family balancing" or "gender balance," is making the practice of sex selection increasingly more popular and acceptable. In June 2005, the newest sex selection technology was introduced in the U.S.: the baby gender

---

6.   Teenage mothers face awesome challenges and poor life prospects. Children of teenage mothers are more likely than children of later child-bearers to have health and cognitive disadvantages and to be neglected or abused. Census data from the 1995 special tabulation indicates that 33% of single female heads of households are living in poverty, compared to 11% of single male heads of household and 7% of married households. Particularly with the elimination of welfare as an entitlement for single mothers with children, funding for teen pregnancy prevention programs is needed more than ever.

mentor, which is a home kit that determines the sex of the fetus as early as 5 weeks into pregnancy through a DNA test. A study of prenatal testing conducted at the University of California, San Francisco, found that Asian and white women undergo prenatal diagnosis for chromosomal disorders at a significantly higher rate than Latinas and African Americans. In addition, Chinese women had high utilization rates for prenatal testing, including amniocentesis.

As the reproductive biotechnology industry continues to advance in the U.S., making sex selection more assessable, reproductive rights advocacy must ensure that women have control over their reproductive decisions. Cultural values and traditions that pressure women to abort female fetuses must be challenged while at the same time respect reproductive autonomy. Questions that must be collectively addressed include whether sex selection and the abortion of female fetuses is can be considered "freedom of choice" when women internalize sexist and patriarchal beliefs about the lesser value of girls or when pressure is placed on them to abort their less-valued female fetuses. And, finally, we must begin conversations with mainstream reproductive rights activists and organizations about sex selection issues and broaden the dialogue on abortion rights and "choice" to reflect these unique cultural experiences that Asian American women face when making decisions about their reproductive health.

Abortion and Asian American Women

Abortion remains a critical issue for Asian American women. A 1991 survey by the Asians and Pacific Islanders for Reproductive Health (currently known as Asian Communities for Reproductive Justice) found that 77% identified themselves as "pro-choice" and an overwhelming majority of the over 1,000 respondents were supportive of a woman's right to choose abortion under varying conditions. The survey did not inquire as to the basis for their pro-choice feelings and it remains unclear whether the beliefs expressed are based on a woman's right to sexual freedom or on other grounds.

National data shows that in 2000, 35% of pregnancies ended in abortion for Asian American women, compared to 18% for white women, the second highest percentage for all racial and ethnic groups. In addition, between 1994 and 2000, abortion rates fell for all groups *except* Asian American women.[7]

---

7.   Rachel K. Jones, Jacqueline E. Darroch, and Stanley K. Henshaw, Patterns in the Socioeconomic Characteristics of Women Obtaining Abortions in 2000-2001, 34 Perspectives on Sexual and Reproductive Health 226, 228 (2002).

While some of these abortions are the result of sex selection after planned pregnancies, there are a few studies and anecdotal evidence to help explain why Asian American women experience high unintended pregnancy and abortion rates. One study looked at the birth control practices of Chinese and Filipina American college women and found that Chinese women were four times less likely to use hormonal methods of birth control than white women, and that both Chinese and Filipina American women were more likely to use the withdrawal method, compared to white women, thereby increasing their risk of becoming pregnant and contracting STDs.[8] Another study found that Asian women were more likely to engage in non-direct, non-verbal strategies around condom negotiation with non-Asian partners and with older partners.[9] Finally, Asian American women may experience higher abortion rates due to their lack of knowledge about emergency contraception: what it is, what it is used for, where to access the pills. A California study found that less than half of South and Southeast Asian women knew what emergency contraception was or that it is an option following unprotected sex.[10] All of these things may help to begin a conversation about what health care providers, clinicians, and activists can do to support Asian American's sexual and reproductive health care.

Limited Choice of and Access to Reproductive and Sexual Health Care

Contraceptive Abuse

True sexual and reproductive "choice" means that Asian women are able to utilize family planning, fertility, and abortion services in their own languages,

---

8. Amy G. Lam, Thida C. Tan, Sareen J. Leong, and Amy K. Mak, Unmasking the Reproductive Health Behaviors of Asian American Young Women: A Comparison of Heterosexual Chinese, Filipina, and White American College Students (publication forthcoming).

9. Amy G. Lam and James E. Barnhart, It Takes Two: The Role of Partner Ethnicity and Age Characteristics on Condom Negotiations of Heterosexual Chinese and Filipina American College Women, 18 AIDS Education and Prevention 68 (2006).

10. Center for Reproductive Health Research and Policy, University of California, San Francisco, EC Knowledge Among California Women (2005).

and have their needs met without fear of being denied access to or coerced into using one form of reproductive technology over another.

Studies cited above indicate that college-aged Asian Americans rely too frequently on the withdrawal method. There is anecdotal evidence within the Asian community and Planned Parenthood clinics that one of the most popular methods of contraception among Asian women is Depo-Provera, a contraceptive injection given every three months. Depo-Provera is a form of birth control that has many potential side effects, including loss of bone density. For that reason, most health sources recommend that women use it for no more than two years. It is thus troubling that this form of contraceptive is so popular among Asian American women. More research must be done to explore why Asian women make this choice. Is Depo-Provera popular because of the wide promotion and use of this form of family planning in Southeast Asian refugee camps and in those countries where it first appeared on the market? Or is there a greater need among Asian women for an invisible form of birth control to hide from one's spouse or family? Or is Depo-Provera's popularity due to the fact that it is a convenient, low-maintenance method which requires less time and health education effort from overburdened health providers? These are among some of the questions that need to be answered to ensure that Asian women truly have options when it comes to choosing a form of birth control.

Religious Restrictions and Refusals

Over the past decade, an increasing number of U.S. hospitals and health care providers have restricted access to sexual and reproductive health care services, largely on the basis of religious grounds. For instance, financially-strapped nonprofit and public hospitals that once provided abortion and other reproductive health care services have been bought by Catholic hospitals that—for religious reasons—will not provide abortion, emergency contraception, or tubal ligation.

Sterilization is the most commonly used form of birth control for American women—28% of all women undergo contraceptive tubal ligation. This number leaps to 41% among poor women. Large numbers of low-income Asian American women without health insurance who relied on nonprofit or public hospitals for access to these family planning services are now losing access as these hospitals are bought by Catholic entities.

Restrictions on family planning have also come from anti-choice groups such as the Christian Coalition who actively recruit Asian community churches, especially those with immigrant or refugee memberships, to take on anti-gay and anti-choice political causes. Finally, in recent years there has also been a surge in the number of pharmacists who refuse to fill prescriptions for birth control or emergency contraception because of moral or religious objections, which create significant barriers to accessing critically important, and in some cases time-sensitive, reproductive health care services.

Language and Cultural Access

Language and cultural access to sexual and reproductive health care services, including abortion, remains a significant issue for Asian American women. Planned Parenthood clinics and other public family planning providers are aware of the need to provide bilingual interpreters for women with limited-English proficiency. Such clinics, however, are equipped to handle only early-term/first trimester abortions. Given that women with limited English proficiency often have the least available access to family planning services, it is often these women who end up seeking but having even fewer opportunities to end unwanted late-term pregnancies.

Medicaid Managed Care

The shift by Medicaid to managed care plans has interfered with the ability of low-income women to receive time-sensitive services such as prenatal care, abortion, and contraception. Under managed care, services may be delayed when a primary care provider is required to give prior authorization for visits to obstetricians and gynecologists. Allowing women to choose obstetricians and gynecologists for primary care is one solution, but these doctors often cannot treat a woman for other illnesses. Many states allow self-referrals to obstetric and gynecological services but place limitations on the number or types of visits. The emphasis on care coordination between providers may conflict with the confidentiality concerns of women who go to a family planning provider (FPP) instead of their regular doctors because they may not want other family members to know their sexual or reproductive status. Basic information, such as a patient's right to go to an out-of-plan provider or even which FPPs are part of the patient's plan, is not being distributed to Medicaid patients.

In many cases, some reproductive health care services are not covered by Medicaid managed care (MMC) plans even though the state which the plan serves has authorized these services as a covered benefit. Family planning providers report having difficulty obtaining reimbursement for costly contraceptives such as Depo-Provera, Norplant, and sterilization. In one state, the managed care plans routinely ignore claims for reimbursement for STD diagnosis and treatment. In addition, multilingual translation and interpreter services are not being fully reimbursed.

FPPs, including community-based providers in Asian American communities, are experiencing growing financial difficulties when they treat women enrolled in managed care but are at best only partially reimbursed.

Sexual Health Care

Health must also include sexual well-being, that is, the right to a satisfying and safe sex life, with healthy and pleasurable sex for both men and women. Women must be able to see themselves and be seen as equal sexual partners responsible for their well-being and health. To that end, society must provide information and services that enhance women's capacities to safely negotiate their sexual encounters. People's association of shame, guilt, and secrecy with discussions of sexuality hinders the development of this more healthy view of sexuality. In addition, taboos around sexuality also create barriers to improving reproductive health by preventing discussion about HIV/AIDS, the high rates of unintended pregnancy and abortion, and the full range of contraceptive options available.

Restrictions on Minors' Access to Sexual and Reproductive Health Care

Young Asian American women are impacted by efforts at the federal and state levels to impose additional barriers for minors seeking sexual and reproductive health care services. At the federal level, Congress has introduced several anti-choice bills that supporters have framed as protecting parental rights. For instance, the Child Custody Protection Act or the Child Interstate Abortion Notification Act, introduced in 2005 and in previous congressional sessions, would make it a crime for anyone other than a parent to transport a minor across state lines to circumvent the home state's parental notification statute for an abortion. The House has passed this bill in the past, but the Senate has never voted on the issue. Other national legislation includes the Parent's Right to Know Act, also introduced in 2005, which would require health care clinics that receive federal funds to notify parents of minors seeking contraceptive services such as birth control pills at least five days prior to dispending the contraception. If enacted, these bills would end up harming many Asian

American teens who already face challenges when talking openly about issues related to sexuality, contraception, and abortion with their parents and in their households.

Anti-choice sentiments are also pervasive at the state level. There is a trend among state legislatures to funnel more money into ineffective, unproven, and scientifically inaccurate abstinence-only programming. In addition, 44 states currently restrict young women's access to abortion services through parental notification or consent laws.[11] During the 2005 legislative session, 25 states considered measures that would have imposed additional barriers to young women's access to abortion services by requiring parental consent instead of notification, for instance, or by making existing laws even harsher. These attempts to restrict access to reproductive health care services and information can place many Asian American girls at an increased risk for unplanned pregnancies and STDs and delay them from seeking timely and safer abortion services.

Environmental Toxins' Impact on Reproductive Health Outcomes

Freedom to have healthy births also is linked to living and working in environments free of toxins. For instance, an emerging body of literature supports claims that past exposure to military bombs, Agent Orange (a powerful herbicide), and DDT (a long-banned pesticide in the U.S., but used widely in Southeast Asian and in refugee camps during and after the Vietnam War) has caused poor reproductive health outcomes among Southeast Asian women. Ironically, after escaping the war, many of these same women and their families had to resettle in low-cost housing areas in the U.S. which are in the shadows of the refineries and chemical manufacturing plants that once produced these toxins.

Many Asian American women have found work in the nail salon industry. Nationally, it is estimated that 42% of all licensed nail salon workers are of Asian descent, with Vietnamese comprising 39%. In California, 80% of the industry workers are Vietnamese immigrant women, and more than half are

---

11.   NARAL Pro-Choice America, 25-26 Who Decides? The Status of Women's Reproductive Rights in the United States (Jan. 2006) (noting that 9 of these laws have been found unconstitutional and unenforceable: AK, CA, ID, IL, MT, NV, NH, NJ, NM).

of reproductive age. Many customers of nail salons would be surprised to discover that nail salons produce a toxic environment for their workers. Poor ventilation within nail salon shops has been linked to respiratory health problems, such as asthma. In addition, some studies have found that prolonged exposure to certain chemicals found in nail polish, such as phthalates, has been linked to miscarriages, infertility, and other reproductive harm. At the present time, there is no independent governing agency that reviews cosmetic ingredients for safety before they are placed on the market. Instead, cosmetic manufacturers are responsible for substantiating the safety of their products and are not required to list phthalates in their ingredients label. In response to community outrage and pressure, some U.S. companies have discontinued use of phthalates in their beauty products, but they continue to pose a health threat.

Asian immigrant women are generally attracted to the nail salon profession because it doesn't require a higher level of English proficiency, the large number of Vietnamese-owned shops and instructors appeals to many Vietnamese immigrant women, and the training and certification process are relatively short. Thus, for many Asian immigrant women, particularly Vietnamese immigrant women who come to the U.S. as refugees with limited education, training, and English skills, the nail salon industry represents a very accessible entry point into the workforce. State and federal policies aimed at improving the working conditions of this particular industry will have a unique impact on Asian American women.

Activists for environmental health and for reproductive health have not always worked together. Reproductive health activists fear that entering into discussions about the toxic effects of the environment on a fetus would aid the anti-choice proposal that the fetus be given legal standing. It is easier for mainstream reproductive rights activists to shy away from taking on issues relating to unhealthy workplaces and the links to women's reproductive health than to have to grapple with the difference between the pro-choice position that a woman has the right to protect her health and that of her fetus and the anti-choice position that the fetus has an independent right to health separate from the health of the mother who bears it.

An additional challenge in attaining environmental and reproductive justice for Asian women who live or work in toxic settings is that scientific research is inconclusive as to causation, that is, whether the illnesses that Asian women are having today are directly related to their work environments or are a result of exposures that happened many years ago in their countries of origin. A third fact is the effect of these women's overall lack of health care and the impoverished and often toxic environments in which they may live. More research must be done to disaggregate this data so that researchers can identify the effects of toxic work and homeplace environments in the U.S. on Asian American women's health.

Finally, most primary care providers are not trained in screening for environmental or occupational health diseases, which means that many of the effects of these exposures go undetected and untreated for many years and across generations. More education is required for both health providers and for Asian American women themselves about the sources of environmental and occupational health diseases, and how the conditions that create these diseases can be mitigated.

ADVOCACY

Our judicial system plays a significant role in recognizing and protecting fundamental sexual and reproductive rights. In <u>Roe v. Wade</u>, the U.S. Supreme Court held that a woman's decision to have an abortion is a constitutionally protected right of personal privacy. Decades later, in <u>Lawrence v. Texas</u>, the Court extended that fundamental right to include intimate conduct between two people of the same sex. Despite these precedents, however, conservative social forces continue to attack sexual and reproductive freedom in this country.[12] Opponents are enacting parental notification and consent laws, promoting scientifically inaccurate abstinence-only programs that fail to teach young men and women about birth control, contraception, and safe sexual practices, introducing anti-gay initiatives, and passing anti-abortion legislation. For instance, in 2006, South Dakota passed the most restrictive abortion restriction in this country, prohibiting all abortions unless they are necessary to save the woman's life and making no exception in cases of rape, incest, or the health of the woman. Fortunately, in the 2006 mid-term election, South Dakota residents voted against the ban. Yet, with the addition of John Roberts and Samuel Alito to the Court, nominated by Republican President

---

12. For instance, during the 2006 legislative session, 18 states considered legislation that would ban abortion, and 23 states considered bills that would further restrict young women's access to abortion services. See NARAL Pro-Choice America, www.prochoiceamerica.org.

George W. Bush in 2005, it is likely that the scope and protections of <u>Roe</u> will be diminished in the years to come.

For Asian American women, the stakes have never been higher. Asian American women have high unintended pregnancy, teen pregnancy, and abortion rates, lack knowledge about and access to emergency contraception, and work in toxic settings that may increase their risk for reproductive harm and illnesses. Thus, it is crucial that national, state, and grassroots reproductive rights organizations use this time to mobilize API communities around these issues, form collaborations with a diverse range of stakeholders—including both API and other social justice organizations—to ensure that Asian American women's experiences are visible, and redefine the reproductive rights movement in a way that connects the issues to the broader social justice, human rights, and civil rights movements.

Campaigns to Expand Sexual and Reproductive Justice for API Women

Over the years, a number of campaigns have formed either in response to a particular threat to sexual and reproductive freedom or as a way to be proactive around issues of importance to Asian American women. Examples include the campaigns organized in California in 2005 and 2006 to defeat ballot initiatives which would have amended the California Constitution to require a physician to notify the parent or legal guardian of young women under the age of 18 at least 48 hours prior to providing an abortion. If passed, California would have joined a significant number of other states that have already passed parental notification or consent laws. Months prior to the elections, API organizations joined with mainstream reproductive rights groups to oppose the propositions.[13] They developed outreach strategies to reach different communities, created bilingual materials in various Asian languages, and participated in get-out-the-vote activities. API groups across California that focus on civil rights, education, and reproductive rights also partnered with

---

13. Some of the APA organizations and coalitions that participated in activities around Proposition 73 included Asian Communities for Reproductive Justice, Asian Pacific Americans for an Informed California, Asian Pacific American Legal Center, Asian Pacific Policy and Planning Council, Khmer Girls in Action, Korean Immigrant Worker Advocates, the California chapters of the National Asian Pacific American Women's Forum.

one another to oppose the ballot initiatives. Through phone banking, education forums, and rallies, they stood in solidarity to let the public and policymakers know their opposition to restrictions on abortion services. Because of these efforts, the two propositions ultimately failed.

The campaign to link environmental justice to women's reproductive health care is also gaining momentum and national attention. For instance, in California, a diverse group of stakeholders have formed a coalition—the California Healthy Nail Salon Collaborative[14]—to collectively mobilize communities in the Bay Area, as well as state policymakers, to support meaningful research, policies, and educational programs that would positively impact nail salon and cosmetology workers. In particular, the goals of the Collaborative are to reduce the use of and exposure to toxins in nail salons that may cause cancer, reproductive health harm, and other illnesses, increase the public's knowledge about environmental health in nail salons, and promote increased health and safety of nail salon workers and owners. Their efforts were instrumental in the 2005 passage of a state law that would require manufacturers to disclose to the California Department of Health and Human Services chemicals in cosmetics that are carcinogenic. Similar efforts are taking place in other parts of the country including in the Washington, D.C., metropolitan area, Connecticut, and Seattle.

Organizations are also promoting different models to engage API communities around issues of sexual and reproductive justice. The National Asian Pacific American Women's Forum (NAPAWF) and Choice USA have developed a Young Women's Collaborative with the goal of building a sustainable base of young API women activists on California campuses. The collaborative combines both participatory action research and social justice activism to better understand the particular sexual and reproductive health care needs of API women and girls. Through training and mentorship, these young women will

---

14. Some of the current Collaborative Members include Asian Health Services, Asian Law Caucus, Asian Advocacy Project of Community Action, Asian Communities for Reproductive Justice, Breast Cancer Fund, Breast Cancer Action, Northern California Cancer Center, Orange County Asian Pacific Islander Community Alliance, National Asian Pacific American Women's Forum, Environmental Finance Center, Region 9, National Environmental Trust, California Department of Health Services, Environmental Health Investigations Branch, Physicians for Social Responsibility, Los Angeles, Alameda County Health Care Services Agency, Public Health, United Food and Commercial Workers, and nail salon owners, environmental consultants, and fashion design owners.

gain the skills and knowledge to launch organizing campaigns in their communities and campuses and, at the same time, break down cultural taboos around sexuality, contraception, and reproductive health. Other organizations, such as Asian Communities for Reproductive Justice, also promote participatory action research in their community organizing and leadership development programs.

Finally, several API organizations have developed programs to address the growing teen pregnancy issues among certain sub-populations within the API community. For instance, the San Francisco-based Asian Women's Shelter and the Oakland-based Narika have assisted teenagers who have resisted forced arranged marriages by escaping from their families. Narika has an outreach program on forced arranged marriages, conducting workshops for teens as well as with community members and leaders to raise awareness about the impact of forced arranged marriages on young women. Before it closed its doors, the Women's Association of Hmong and Lao (WAHL) also had a teen pregnancy prevention program, which is described in Chapter Eight, "Hmong Women in the U.S." Through these efforts, Asian American teens will be able to make decisions about marriage, pregnancy, and their sexual and reproductive health without cultural or societal pressures.

REFERENCES

American Academy of Family Physicians, http://familydoctor.org/043.xml

Asians and Pacific Islanders for Choice, 1992, The Asian/Pacific Islander Reproductive Health Survey 1991-1992

Banzhaf, Marian, "Welfare Reform and Reproductive Rights: Talking about Connections" presented to the National Network of Abortion Funds, June 11, 1999

Barron, Sandy, "Sick and dying in Cambodia: Postwar public health system sinks into decay, pestilence," San Francisco Chronicle, Oct. 19, 1998

Copelon, Rhonda, From Privacy to Autonomy: The Conditions for Sexual and Reproductive Freedom, printed in From Abortion to Reproduction Freedom, Transforming a Movement (Marlene Gerber Fried, ed., Boston, MA, South End Press 1990)

The Ford Foundation, Sexuality and Reproductive Health: Strategies for Programming, January 2001

Gay, Jill, Workshop Report for Ford Foundation's Roundtable on Sexuality Issues in Communities of Color, unpublished draft, March 14, 2001

Gonen, Julianna S., Ph. D, Managed Care and Unintended Pregnancy: Testing the Limits of Prevention, Insights, Jacobs's Institute of Women's Health, July 1997—No. 3

Ikemoto, Lisa C., Lessons from the Titanic: Start with the People in Steerage, Women and Children First, in Mother Troubles: Rethinking Contemporary Maternal Dilemmas (Julia E. Hanigsberg & Sara Ruddick eds., Beacon Press 1999)

Jaffe, Robert, Benjamin, Elizabeth and Hickley, Elizabeth, "Reshaping Reproductive Health, A State-by-State Examination of Family Planning Under Medicaid Managed Care," The Institute for Reproductive Health Access, A Program of the NARAL/NY Foundation, 2000

Kuppermann M., Gates E., and Washington, A.E., Racial/ethnic differences in prenatal diagnostic test use and outcomes: Preferences, socioeconomics or patient knowledge? Obstetrics and Gynecology 1996; 87:675-682

Lattin, Don, Vatican pushes birth control edit despite court ruling, San Francisco Chronicle, July 8, 2001

Nails Magazine, 2005 Nail Technician Demographics, available at http://www.nailsmag.com/pdfView.aspx?pdfName=NABB05p024-025.pdf.

National Academy Press and Veterans and Agent Orange: Health Effects of Herbicides Used in Vietnam, Institute of Medicine, National Academy of Sciences, National Academy Press, Washington DC 1994

Peffer, George Anthony, If They Don't Bring Their Women Here: Chinese Female Immigration Before Exclusion, University of Illinois Press 1999

Roberts, Dorothy, "Punishing Drug Addicts Who Have Babies: Women of Color, Equality, and the Right of Privacy," Harvard Law Review, Vol. 104: 1991

Ross, Loretta, "African-American Women and Abortion" in Rickie Solinger (ed.), Abortion Wars: A Half Century of Struggle, 1950-2000. (Berkeley: University of California Press 1998)

San Francisco Chronicle, "The Vietnamese Victims of Agent Orange," January 14, 1996

Veterans and Agent Orange, Update 1996, Committee to Review the Health Effects in Vietnam Veterans of Exposure to Herbicides, Institute of Medicine

San Francisco-based Asian Women's Shelter multi-lingual brochures.
Language barriers often create insurmountable obstacles for Asian
women seeking to escape abusive relationships.

7

Domestic Violence and Asian American Women[1]

PREVALENCE OF DOMESTIC VIOLENCE AGAINST ASIAN AMERICAN WOMEN

Domestic violence, or intimate partner violence, is a pattern of behaviors that includes physical, sexual, verbal, emotional, economic, and/or psychological abuse used by adults or adolescents against intimate partners. For Asian American communities, the paucity of existing data on this phenomenon makes it difficult to estimate the prevalence of domestic violence. This chapter extrapolates from the few specific studies that do exist. These studies suggest that domestic violence is *at least* as prevalent in the Asian American population as the general American population. Furthermore, this chapter compiles new studies that, together, confirm the alarming rates of domestic violence against particular groups of Asian American women. Lastly, this chapter analyzes the barriers to safety for Asian American women and proposes strategies for prevention and intervention.

National studies tend to indicate a lower rate of domestic violence for Asian American women than for the general population. For instance, a telephone survey of 8,000 women and men of all ethnic backgrounds across the nation found that only 12.8% of the Asian and Pacific Islander respondents reported experiencing physical assault by an intimate partner at least once during their lifetime, compared to 21.3% for Whites, 26.3% for African

---

1.   Janel George, Lee Ann Wang and Courtney Chappell, National Asian Pacific American Women's Forum staff, assisted in the updating of this chapter.

Americans, and 21.2% for Hispanics. However, these results may reflect under-reporting among Asian American women.

Certainly, surveys by Asian Pacific American domestic violence organizations contradict the results of the national studies. A 1986 survey of 150 Korean women living in Chicago found that 60% reported physical abuse. A compilation by the Asian & Pacific Islander Institute on Domestic Violence of a decade's worth of community-based studies and surveys points to the high prevalence of domestic violence in Asian communities: 41%–60% of respondents reported experiencing domestic violence (physical and/or sexual) during their lifetime. Even more compelling is a 2006 survey of 178 Asian American women living in the Washington D.C. area by Project AWARE (Asian Women Advocating Respect and Empowerment) that found 81.1% reported experiencing at least one form of intimate partner violence "rarely" to "very frequently," and 31.9% experiencing physical/sexual abuse at least "occasionally" in the past year.

Domestic violence appears to be equally prevalent in queer[2] Asian women's relationships. However, there is little research and data on same-sex relationship violence, and what does exist tends to overlook queer Asian women. There are several reasons for under-reporting violence among queer Asian women. In 1998, in national and local focus groups held by the Family Violence Prevention Fund and the Asian Women's Shelter, queer Asian women divulged that they did not feel safe reporting relationship violence to the police or authorities.[3] They feared that disclosing themselves as lesbian being abused by another lesbian would subject them to further abuse at the hands of the police. Many were hesitant to access service providers due to sexism, racism, homophobia, language and cultural barriers, and fear of disbelief among service providers. Many queer Asian women admitted that they do not feel safe reporting violence to friends. They are also often hesitant to report abusive partners, as they do not wish to further isolate or marginalize partners who have already been subjected to a homophobic, racist legal system.

---

2. The term "queer" is controversial within the lesbian, bisexual, transgendered, and questioning (LBTQ) community. However, many younger LBTQs have reclaimed "queer" as a positive term. This report uses the terms queer, LBTQ, and LGBTQ (when gay men are included) interchangeably (for definition of these terms, see Chapter 10, footnote 2).

3. In these focus groups, survivors expressed discomfort with the label of domestic violence and preferred the term relationship violence to describe violence in queer relationships.

The data that exists on violence against Asian American women, whether straight or queer, shows an alarming trend: Asian women suffer from disproportionately high rates of domestic violence-related fatalities. One study in Santa Clara County, California, found that although Asians comprised 17.5% of the population, Asian women accounted for almost one-third of the 51 domestic violence-related fatalities that occurred between 1994 and 1997, the highest of any ethnic population. A Massachusetts study found that although Asians comprised only 3% of the population, Asian women constituted 18 percent of those killed as a result of domestic violence. The 2002 Washington State Domestic Violence Fatality Review Board concluded that Asian women were 2.3 times more likely to die from domestic violence-related homicide than their white counterparts, the second highest rate of any racial minority (African American women had the highest fatality rate of any ethnic minority at 2.7 times that of white women).

BARRIERS TO SEEKING SAFETY

What accounts for the higher domestic violence-related fatality rates for Asian American women? Why are the safety needs of Asian American women not being met by the systems that exist? To date, there has been little research that answers these questions. We do know that safety is inherently tied to access to services. We also know that Asian American women in abusive relationships face challenges different from women of other ethnicities, for whom most shelter and service programs are designed. These challenges include: language limitations (40% of the Asian American population is Limited English Proficient); cultural differences (which can contribute to discomfort in mainstream domestic violence shelter settings) and immigrant status (undocumented victims often fear deportation if they contact authorities or service providers). Asian American women, therefore, face numerous institutional barriers when seeking safety. The categories of safety-related challenges particular to Asian American women—linguistic barriers; the lack of cultural competence among service providers; anti-immigrant legislation and an inaccessible criminal justice system—are described below.

Lack of Culturally and Linguistically Accessible Services

1. *Lack of Trained Interpreters to Respond to Asian Domestic Violence Victims.*

After her husband lunged at her with a knife, cutting himself on the hand in the process, she ran to a nearby store to call the police. When the police arrived, her husband (who spoke English well) accused her of attacking him. She did not speak English well enough to defend herself and she was arrested.[4]

How do you call 911 when you can't speak English? Although courts have interpreted Title VI of the Civil Rights Act of 1964 to require federally-funded entities to provide linguistically accessible services, few actually do. From 911 services to law enforcement, few if any first responders to violence are equipped to provide for the language needs of those battered women who speak one of the 200 languages and dialects native to Asian Americans. For those Limited English Proficient (LEP) women who do manage to call 911, the police response often fails to provide adequate protection. Since police seldom speak an Asian language and typically do not bring interpreters with them, they often communicate first to the individual who speaks better English, often the batterer. As a result, the woman's story goes unheard. In other instances, children, family and friends have inappropriately been asked to interpret. When those close to the situation have judgmental attitudes and/or fear retaliation by the abuser, they may engage in victim-blaming or they may be unable to accurately or completely convey the battered woman's perspective.

At times language barriers have led to tragic results, such as in the story above where the woman being battered was arrested. Another example occurred in the state of Washington. A battered woman's estranged husband threatened her with a gun, intending to kill her. Due to lack of adequate translation services, the police did not obtain statements from the woman and two witnesses with sufficient detail for the prosecutor to proceed with the case. The abuser was never prosecuted. A year later, the abuser killed his wife.

---

4. Quote: Margaretta Wan Ling Lin & Cheng Imm Tan in *Holding Up More Than Half the Heavens: Domestic Violence in Our Communities, A Call for Justice*, in THE STATE OF ASIAN AMERICA: ACTIVISM AND RESISTANCE IN THE 1990s 323 (Karin Aguilar-San Juan ed., 1994).

Many Asian women in the United States come from countries where police and other institutions do not respond to domestic disputes. In addition, they may view law enforcement in the United States as discriminatory toward immigrants, people of color, and other minorities. These negative perceptions may prevent Asian women from seeking police protection when necessary.

2. Lack of Language Accessible Services for Batterers

Batterers are also affected by lack of language access. In most parts of the United States, linguistically and culturally accessible programs for batterers from Asian American communities do not exist. Court sentences for batterers that require mandatory participation in such programs (which have not been proven to be very effective) are rendered completely meaningless if no such program exists in the batterer's native tongue.[5]

3. Limited and Inadequate Shelter Space

Shelter space in general is limited, but facilities with the capacity to serve Asian women's language and cultural needs are in extremely short supply. In Massachusetts, out of 35 women's shelters, only two have Asians on staff. Some shelters do not accept non-English speaking women at all. When these women cannot access mainstream services, the few Asian service providers who can accommodate the needs of non-English speaking victims are stretched to capacity. For instance, over 4,000 Asian American women and children from across the country use a range of services provided by the Asian Women's Shelter in San Francisco, including its 24-hour Crisis Line. But it is forced to turn away 75% of those who seek its services each year. In 2002, over 1,135 women called the 24-hour hotline of Apna Ghar, a shelter serving South Asian women and children in Chicago. Manavi, a New Jersey service

---

5.   Court sentences that involve serving time and mandatory participation in intervention programs are often insufficient to convey the gravity of the crime to the batterer if he does not share Western cultural values. For these men, there needs to be culturally relevant sentencing. For example, in the Hmong community, when clan elders resolve domestic violence cases through the mediation process, they may order the husband to hire a shaman for a soul-calling ceremony to heal the wife. According to Hmong cultural beliefs, when a wife has been abused, the soul leaves her body because it has been mistreated. When the soul is not well, the body is not well. In a soul-calling ceremony, a shaman calls the soul back to the body.

provider, saw the number of women it serves double in a two-year span. The New York Asian Women's Center provides services to over 3,000 battered women annually. Saheli, in Texas, responded to over 388 calls in 2000 and assisted in 68 cases. All of these agencies report a need for increased funding in order to provide services to the growing number of Asian American domestic violence victims that have nowhere else to turn.

Mainstream women's shelters are clearly not designed to accommodate cultural differences. For example, Hmong women in the St. Paul/Minneapolis area who have larger than average families were not able to make use of most shelters until Asian Women United designed a shelter to accommodate larger families. Nor are most mainstream shelters designed to accommodate the particular needs of many Asian women, including their discomfort with dormitory living and open discussion about intimate matters, their need for privacy, their dietary needs, and their desire to eat and cook their own foods, feed their own children, and keep their children with them most of the time. Many Asian women report feeling very lost when forbidden contact with their mothers—who have traditionally been an important source of social support. Additionally, Asian women often have a difficult time following mainstream shelters' programs and procedures, such as participating in chores selection, because of their inability to communicate with staff and other residents.

The Asian American organizations that *can* provide culturally competent services typically have small staffs, depend on volunteers, and do not receive the large amounts of funding given to mainstream women's organizations. This reality, and the ignorance and indifference of mainstream service providers to the needs of battered Asian women, leave large numbers of battered Asian women without assistance or intervention.

When abused queer Asian women seek help, they find that the vast majority of domestic violence agencies are not able to meet their needs. One factor that contributes to this is the fact that many in the domestic violence movement do not acknowledge same-sex relationship violence. The mainstream domestic violence movement largely understands violence as a patriarchal phenomenon, deriving from sexism, with men using violence to control women. Within the queer women's community, it is not always the more masculine or "butch" woman who is the abuser. Queer women can be both survivors and batterers. The typical response of mainstream domestic violence agencies is to ostracize the batterer. But, banishing the abuser from a small, marginalized queer Asian community is akin to cutting her off from her only family members. Most agencies do not have programs that assist both the batterer and the survivor. The San Francisco-based Asian Women's Shelter is one of the few programs with a Queer Asian Women Services project.

Laws That Trap Asian Women in Violent Domestic Situations

1. Anti-Immigrant Legislation

Anti-immigration legislation poses the most difficult barrier to Asian immigrant women seeking safety. The primary tactic used by abusers of undocumented immigrant women to keep them silent is threat of deportation. Intimidated by this threat, battered undocumented immigrant women often do not tell family members about the violence, access services, or contact law enforcement when abused.

The history of legislation in this area is complex, and constantly changing. Because of changes in immigration laws, even immigrant women who are in the United States lawfully can find themselves trapped in violent domestic situations. Prior to 1986, a U.S. citizen could petition for and obtain lawful permanent residence status (a green card) for his/her immigrant spouse immediately after marriage. However, in 1986 Congress enacted the Immigration Marriage Fraud Amendments (IMFA) that created a new conditional residence status requiring that an immigrant spouse must stay married to a citizen spouse for two years before becoming eligible to apply for permanent status. At the end of two years, the partners must file a joint application to adjust the conditional status to permanent status. As a result of the new two-year waiting period, some immigrant women have been trapped in violent relationships, unable to leave out of fear that their husbands would be unwilling to jointly file the permanent residence application, thereby rendering them undocumented and thus subject to deportation.

After powerful documentation of the physical, emotional, and economic abuses suffered by battered immigrant women was brought to light, Congress passed a series of laws to remedy the unintended consequences of the 1986 law. The 1990 Battered Spouse Waiver Act allowed a battered immigrant woman to leave her U.S. citizen husband and "self-petition" for lawful permanent residence without the cooperation of her husband. In 1994, Congress enacted the Violence Against Women Act (VAWA) to provide broader protections to immigrant women, allowing a woman, documented or undocumented, who is married to a citizen or green card holder to self-petition as a victim of domestic violence. When VAWA was reauthorized by Congress in 2000, other barriers to the self-petition process were removed. These included allowing divorced spouses to self-petition, allowing abused wives living abroad to self-petition (if married to employees of the government or U.S. military), and eliminating the requirement to prove that deportation to the home country would cause extreme hardship to the victims of domestic violence or their children. The 2005 reauthorization of VAWA provided further protections, including the ability to reopen a case upon a final order of deportation and eligibility for work authorization to certain abused spouses of immigrants who hold temporary visas (such as student or work visas).

However, at the end of 2005, anti-immigrant legislation was introduced in the 109th Congress that threatens to jeopardize VAWA's protections. In December 2005, the U.S. House of Representatives passed the Border, Anti-terrorism, and Illegal Immigration Control Act, H.R. 4437, that would make it an aggravated felony for immigrants to be unlawfully present in the United States. It expands the criminal definition of "smuggling" to include those individuals or entities (including social service organizations, churches, and service providers) who knowingly provide assistance to undocumented immigrants to reside or remain in the United States. Individuals convicted of smuggling could face up to 5 years in prison. The "unlawful presence" provision of this bill would have deterred undocumented immigrant women victims from calling the police, seeking protective services, or using VAWA's self-petitioning and other protections.

Fortunately, H.R. 4437 was not passed by the Senate and did not become law. In 2005, the Senate also introduced a series of anti-immigrant bills that would have jeopardized VAWA's protections, but fortunately they also did not become law. However, in early 2007, members of the 110th Congress have indicated that they will be reintroducing bills similar to H.R. 4437.

2. Limitations of the Battered Spouse Waiver and VAWA

The Battered Spouse Waver and VAWA have been on the books for more than a decade. However, because of lack of education and outreach, many monolingual women are unaware of these legal protections. Many immigrant women who are victims of domestic violence are under the impression that their batterers have complete control over their immigration status and therefore continue to live in dangerous and violent domestic situations. Many private immigration attorneys are unaware of relief available to battered women. In addition, there are not enough attorneys trained in immigration law, family law, and domestic violence law to deal with the most complicated VAWA cases, especially those involving undocumented women.

To seek the protections provided by VAWA, a battered woman must report the abuser, typically to law enforcement or other legal authorities. Because the crime of domestic violence is a deportable offense, some Asian immigrant women hesitate to report their batterers to law enforcement. Though they may want to be safe, initiating any process with law enforcement may render them without the financial support of their partner when raising their children and starting a new life. Child support and spousal support orders are rendered meaningless when the spouse has been deported. The children are also destined to a life with no exposure to a deported parent.

In addition, instead of relief under VAWA, in reporting abuse to law enforcement, some immigrant domestic violence survivors find themselves not only wrongly arrested but also deportable when their batterers use the system against them.

In passing the 1986 Immigration Marriage Fraud Amendments, Congress forced women to remain in abusive and violent homes as they await the change from conditional to permanent immigrant status. Congress' passage of VAWA has done little to pull these women out of harm's way.

3. Welfare Reform and Its Impact on Battered Asian Immigrants

The 1996 Welfare Reform Act has resulted in serious financial barriers to Asian immigrant women seeking safety. Recognizing that welfare programs serve as an essential bridge to safety for women fleeing domestic abuse, Congress created exceptions for battered immigrant women. For example, a battered immigrant woman, even if she is undocumented, is eligible for public benefits when she has a pending VAWA or family-sponsored petition. Battered women are exempted from "sponsor deeming" requirements. Congress also created the Family Violence Option (FVO), which allows states to exempt a battered woman from TANF work requirements if meeting these requirements would make it more difficult for the woman to escape an abusive situation. FVO permits the clock on the five-year lifetime cap to stop running until the woman is safe. Under FVO, a state also can waive the paternity establishment and child support requirements.

However, the widespread and erroneous beliefs among both caseworkers and battered women that "immigrants aren't entitled to benefits anymore," have kept battered women from applying and caseworkers from accepting applications. There is anecdotal evidence that caseworkers ignorant of FVO provisions have sanctioned battered women for not complying with job search and work requirements, and reduced or even terminated their benefits. In addition and as described in Chapter 1 of this report, fear of mandatory reporting to U.S. Citizenship & Immigration Services (CIS, formerly INS) and fear of becoming a deportable public charge[6] has also kept eligible Asian immigrants from applying for public benefits.

Without a safety net to keep them from falling into dire circumstances if they leave the batterer, women remain in dangerous and violent situations. One current legislative proposal aims to make access to benefits easier for recent immigrants who are experiencing domestic violence. The Women Immigrants Safe Harbor (WISH) Act, originally introduced in 2001, seeks to eliminate the harm to immigrant victims of domestic violence caused by Welfare Reform. The goal of WISH is to amend the1996 act to provide for the eligibility of certain undocumented immigrants suffering from domestic abuse for SSI, food stamps, TANF, Medicaid, and other public benefit programs. However, the last action taken on the bill was in July of 2001.

CULTURE AND VIOLENCE

Domestic violence ultimately is not a cultural issue. It is about power and control. Violent manifestations of control are found in all cultures.[7] Yet, studies show a higher prevalence of domestic violence in certain Asian ethnic groups and higher rates of fatality. The barriers to seeking safety described

---

6.   INS's May 1999 guidelines state that use of non-cash benefits such as Medicaid and food stamps does not make one a public charge. VAWA 2000 barred the INS from finding a woman a public charge based on her use of non-cash benefits that she is legally qualified to use.

7.   Culture, while never a cause of violence, is often used and manipulated by those who seek an excuse for their violent behavior. In People v. Chen, No 87-7774 (N.Y. Sup. Ct. Dec. 2, 1988), involving a man who murdered his wife because of suspected infidelity, the court accepted the defendant's assertion that in Chinese culture, it was reasonable that a husband who discovered that his wife was having sex with another man would kill her. The Court upheld this "cultural defense" and the man was acquitted of the murder charges. Not only was this an inaccurate portrayal of Chinese cultural beliefs, but the acceptance of culture as legal justification for murder sent a message to all Asian American communities that the American criminal justice system condoned domestic violence against Asian American women.

above in part explain the higher fatality rates. But what are the reasons for the higher prevalence of domestic violence?

Asian American Perceptions of Domestic Violence

A survey conducted by the Boston-based Asian Task Force Against Domestic Violence found that 20 to25% of the respondents from the Cambodian, Chinese, Korean, South Asian, and Vietnamese communities surveyed thought that violence against a woman was justifiable in certain domestic disputes. The report also found that a higher number of Asian men than women condone family violence. Among Korean respondents, 29% (the highest percentage among the five ethnic groups surveyed) felt that a battered woman should not tell anyone. Older Chinese respondents were more tolerant of the use of violence in certain situations, and younger Chinese were less likely to see leaving and divorce as viable options for battered women. Response patterns were similar between the foreign-born and U.S. born respondents. These statistics may reflect a higher level of acceptance of violence against women by Asian American communities than other U.S. ethnic groups.

This higher level of acceptance may be due to the fact that gender roles are tightly prescribed and rigid in many Asian communities. The same Boston Asian Task Force survey also confirmed rigid beliefs about the role of men and women in marriage among many Asians in the United States. Vietnamese respondents, for example, believed that a man has the right to discipline his wife, expect sex whenever he wants it, be the ruler of his home, and beat his wife. South Asian respondents also responded positively to the assertion that a woman in marriage becomes her husband's property and that it is inappropriate for a married woman to ask her family and/or parents to intervene. Cambodian respondents indicated that they did not believe that a woman has the right to divorce, leave a husband who hits her, or that a husband should be arrested for domestic violence.

In addition to these cultural beliefs, the traditional gender roles of male "providers" and female "homemakers" are often disrupted in the context of the U.S. economy where both partners typically need to work outside the home. As described in Chapter 8, while this change in women's gender roles in the United States has been liberating for some Asian women, it has also been viewed as a threat to the social order that privileges men.

How queer Asian American women respond to same-sex relationship violence also is influenced by the Asian communities' perceptions on domestic violence. Violence among queer Asian women is often unreported because of fear of being "outed" to the community. In fact, many queer batterers manipulate their partners' fear of being "outed" and possibly stigmatized by the community in order to maintain control over them. Additionally, many queer Asian women feel that there is community stigma surrounding same sex relationships and do not want to further support negative perceptions of same-sex relationships by admitting that violence is occurring.

Migration and the Breakdown of Family Protective Structures

Migration to the United States also changes other social practices to the detriment of women. In the home countries of many Asian women, extended families often exert collective pressure to prevent the abuse of wives. However, migration to the United States breaks up extended families and the protections they afford to women who often rank lowest in the family structure.

Worse, in some situations, the role of extended families in the United States has been perverted from protector to perpetrator. There are often multiple batterers among in-laws (including mothers, brothers and father-in-laws). Project AWARE's survey found that 28.5% of the survey participants living in the Washington D.C. area knew of a woman who was being abused by her in-laws. NARIKA, a South Asian domestic violence resource center in Berkeley, has reported cases where entire families get involved in abusing a woman, with some members holding her down while others do the hitting.

Cultural Emphasis on Preserving Family

The notion of having to preserve the family in order to "save face" motivates many Asian women to remain in abusive relationships. Women in abusive relationships are frequently blamed for misbehaving and told to tolerate the abuse in order to preserve the family unit. Because some Asian communities are small and close-knit, victim advocates from the communities often face harassment and threats from the abuser and the family for helping women leave the relationship and for upsetting the social order.

Also, this pronounced belief in the sanctity of the family (even in the face of victimization), combined with a cultural antipathy towards divorce, often conflicts with the mainstream cultural perspectives of shelter workers and advocates who may themselves value independence at any cost. The Asian

Task Force Against Domestic Violence notes, "One of the biggest and most important challenges to addressing family violence within Asian communities is reconciling the differences between Western ideals of independence and individualism with Asian ideals of interdependence and group harmony."

ADOVCACY: FROM PROVIDING SAFETY TO ENDING DOMESTIC VIOLENCE

Culture is not static, fixed, and unchangeable. Norms, values, and beliefs are constructed in the interchanges between and among people within cultural groups and are constantly evolving. For Asian immigrants, it can be threatening in light of changes forced by relocating to the United States to think that cultures must also be changed from within. There are aspects of Asian cultures that are worthy of saving and passing on. There are others that must be transformed in order to honor basic human rights—in this case, the right of women to be free from domestic violence. For example, the emphasis on preservation of the family is worthy, but must be transformed so that it is achieved not by pressuring women to stay in violent relationships, but by changing the cultural and social norms that sanction men's use of violence to control women.

Recognizing that all cultures (and particularly migrating cultures) are not static, a number of Asian women's shelters and outreach groups frame their organizing work as "work to perpetuate the core values of each Asian community in the U.S. that are positive and to eliminate those parts that are no longer useful or healthy."

The Shelter and Community Outreach Programs

Asian American women have been organizing for two decades to create shelters that accommodate the needs of Asian victims of domestic violence. Since the first shelter program for Asian American women and children started in Los Angeles in 1981, six other Asian women's shelters have emerged across the country.[8] Most of these shelters began informally, in the homes of community members, friends, and family who wanted to provide shelter for victims of violence. Today, they provide language accessible and culturally-competent services which encompass more than simply providing interpreters. Full language access requires trained interpreters who have an understanding of the dynamics of domestic violence and who accurately translate victims' needs and desires, providing clear explanations of legal processes, available services, and options so that victims feel empowered to determine their own course of action. Interpreters and other service provider staff need to have an understanding of the cultural norms that may influence how a victim responds to violence. Where these shelters exist, though understaffed and under-funded, they provide a life-line to the Asian American women who are shut out by mainstream services, whether through lack of access (language or cultural), provider bias, or lack of outreach to Asian American communities.

The handful of shelters that are available, however, cannot meet the needs of Asian American women, especially limited-English speaking women in communities throughout the United States. To fill the gap, many of the informal networks of service providers within Asian American communities have developed established programs that have outreach, education, and hotline programs for battered Asian American women. These include organizations such as Korean American Women in Need (KAN-WIN) in Chicago, Manavi ("primal woman" in Sanskrit) in New Jersey, Sakhi ("women's friend") for South Asian Women, the Nav Nirmaan Foundation and Pragati ("progress") in New York, Raksha ("protection" in several languages) in Georgia, the Asian/Pacific Islander Women and Family Safety Center and Chaya in Seattle, and Saheli in Texas.

All these groups and shelters conduct some form of community education and outreach as part of their prevention activities to address the root causes of domestic violence. Shelters also conduct local advocacy, such as pressuring police departments to hire interpreters or working with them on protocols to

---

8.   The seven existing shelters are the Asian Women's Home in San Jose, CA; the Asian Women's Shelter in San Francisco, CA; Asian Women United in Minneapolis/St. Paul, MN; the Center for Pacific Asian Families in Los Angeles; the New Moon Shelter in Boston, MA; Apna Ghar in Chicago, IL; and the New York Asian Women's Center in New York, NY. There are also programs within larger shelter programs like the Asian Unit of Interval House in Long Beach, CA. In Atlanta, GA, the International Women's House serves women who do not speak English, including Asian immigrant women.

handle domestic violence calls in Asian communities. Many of these organizations also have worked to raise awareness about community norms that impact experiences of violence:

- The SHIMTUH project, a joint project between the Asian Women's Shelter in San Francisco and the Korean Community Center of the East Bay, reaches out to the social networks and institutions in the Korean community to transform cultural norms. Through cultural events, drumming, singing, working with the Korean press, and outreach to indigenous Korean religious institutions, SHIMTUH engages in public dialogue with religious and other leaders to influence social spheres within the community.

- In the Filipino community, the Family Violence Prevention Fund has reframed of the concept of "hiya" or shame about domestic violence through a poster campaign. It introduced the concept of "nakakahiya"—that a woman should *not* feel ashamed for having bruises and being beaten, and that the community *should* be ashamed if they don't help her.

- The AWS in San Francisco has a ground-breaking program, Queer-to-Queer, to address the needs of queer Asian women and to challenge community homophobia which leads to the under-reporting and minimization of violence by queer women.

Few South Asian women seek help from mainstream domestic violence programs and may not turn to pan-Asian programs. When confronted with violence at home, they turn first to their place of worship and their religious leaders. The Peaceful Families Project of Washington-based Chaya works with Imams and Muslim community leaders, teaching them how to counsel and provide advice to survivors, initiate dialogue on how they can work to end violence and provide models used by leaders in other Muslim communities who are working to effect systemic change. In Peaceful Families Project workshops, quotes from the Q'uran and Sunnah provide an Islamic context, reminding the faithful that God does not tolerate violence. Leaders learn about the many women's rights that are provided within Islam, including the traditional marriage contract that protects women as well as men. Chaya provides a model for one way to integrate faith-based values with domestic violence programs.

National Advocacy and Coalition Work

Meeting Asian American women's safety needs and ensuring that they can escape domestic violence permanently requires national advocacy to reform immigration and public benefits laws. This kind of advocacy cannot always be addressed by local community organizations with limited funds and staff. Coalition building to take on this advocacy work on a national level began in earnest in 1997 when the first large national pan-Asian conference convened in California, bringing together 400 service providers and activists from across the country. Local groups rely on coalitions such as the National Network on Behalf of Battered Immigrant Women to conduct statewide and nationally advocacy campaigns to address the unique challenges Asian American women face.

In 2000 the San Francisco-based Asian Women's Shelter, the Asian & Pacific Islander American Health Forum, the Family Violence Prevention Fund, and the National Resource Center on Domestic Violence, launched the Asian and Pacific Islander Domestic Violence Institute (APIDVI). The Institute serves as a forum for and clearinghouse on information, research, resources, and critical issues concerning violence against women in Asian and Pacific Islander communities. The mission of the APIDVI is to advocate for policy changes, increase ethnically-specific data collection, facilitate the sharing of service models for battered Asian women and children, and promote national discussions on differing Asian American community perceptions of domestic violence and cultural values and community responses to the problem. Since the formation of APIDVI, all the various Asian women's shelters and domestic violence programs have become members. It has conducted several major research projects and produced publications that have added significantly to the body of knowledge that advocates rely on to push for public policy changes.[9]

---

9.   APIDVI publications include: The Lifetime Spiral of Gender Violence (detailing how domestic violence plays out in the life of an APA woman), a 2003 report on Domestic Violence Related Homicides, Innovative Strategies to Address Domestic Violence in Asian and Pacific Islander Communities: Examining Themes, Models, and Interventions (2002), Fact Sheet on Domestic Violence in Asian Communities (updated 2005), TANF Re-authorization and its Effects on Asian and Pacific Islander Families (2002); and Trafficking: Considerations and Recommendations for Domestic Violence Advocates (2004).

Programs for Men

Domestic violence cannot be solved unless programs are created for batterers as well as for survivors. The Tapestri Men's Group, a project of the Refugee Women's Network, Inc. in Atlanta, Georgia, works with men by following a two-fold philosophy. First, it believes that cultural norms are not immutable and can evolve. Second, it views the violence of men not as an individual pathology amenable to counseling or therapeutic intervention in one-on-one sessions, but rather as a social disease, a way of behaving that a man has learned through modeling at home and in a society that accepts the use of violence against women as a way of resolving differences. Thus, Tapestri does not provide anger management because it views men's violence against women not as the actions of an angry man out of control, but as the actions of a man who chooses to be violent to control his partner.

In the men's groups where Asian, Latino, Caribbean, African, and East European men have participated, transformative re-education takes place not by experts imparting information top-down to batterers, but through a process whereby participants critically explore, in an atmosphere of mutual respect and horizontal relationships, the antecedents, dynamics, and effects of their violent behaviors on others. In the process, men's views of themselves and their roles as partners and fathers are transformed, gender identities are de-constructed and re-constructed, and the men become agents of change in their communities. The Tapestri Men's Group and others like it were created when domestic violence survivors, who did not want to leave their marriages, requested intervention programs for their husbands. As the men participate in the 24-week program, women advocates from Tapestri work with their wives to provide support, ensure that they are not in danger, and monitor the progress being made by the men.

Since 2000, the API Women and Family Safety Center has engaged in similar anti-violence work with young men in King County, Washington middle schools, high schools and universities. Currently, its Men's Campaign Organizer leads group discussions in two high schools, where students are pulled out of classes once a week (during different periods so they do not miss the same classes). Using an anti-oppression framework, the focus of the pull-out groups is prevention and empowerment. The pull-out groups—one for Asian American girls, one for Pacific Islander girls and one for API boys—are safe spaces created for them to talk about date violence and other problems and pressures they face in the home, in school, etc. When they graduate from high school and enter university, many of the young men who participate in Safety Center's pull-out groups bring the anti-violence work to the fraternities that they join. Over the past six years, these participants have held "Dialogue," a young adult and youth led conference against dating violence and sexual assault. Dialogue One was organized by a Filipino fraternity who also brought a sorority into the conference.

Asian American women face a higher rate of fatality from domestic violence than women in any other ethnic group. For these women to leave violent homes and start new lives, barriers to Asian American women seeking safety must be removed. This includes changing immigration laws that keep women trapped in violent marital relationships; advocating for language accessible services, including trained interpreters among first responders such as law enforcement; increased funding for the numerous under-resourced Asian American service providers that can and do can provide culturally-competent services; and increased training for mainstream service providers to provide language accessible and culturally-competent services. To address the higher prevalence of domestic violence in certain Asian ethnic groups, anti-violence organizations within the Asian American communities must expand their programs to outreach and education to change the communities' perception that the use of violence to control women is acceptable.

REFERENCES

Asian Pacific/Islander Domestic Violence Resource Project (API DVRP), AWARE (Asian Women Advocating Respect and Empowerment) Survey, *available at* www.dvrp.org/brochures/aware.pdf

Asian and Pacific Islander Institute on Domestic Violence, *Fact Sheet: Domestic Violence in Asian Communities, available at* www.apiahf.org/apidvinstitute, last revised July 2005

Asian Task Force Against Domestic Violence, Asian Family Violence Report, *available at* www.atask.org

Asian Women's Shelter, San Francisco, CA: http://www.sfaws.org/home.html

Chan, Sue, M.D., "Domestic Violence in Asian and Pacific Islander (API) Communities," compilation of studies, statistics, and data on domestic violence and API's, Asian Health Services

Chappell, Courtney, *Reclaiming Choice, Broadening the Movement: Sexual and Reproductive Justice and Asian Pacific American Women, A National Agenda for Action*, National Asian Pacific American Women's Forum, 2 (2005)

Chaya, Seattle, WA: http://www.chayaseattle.org/

Chung, Christine and Lee, Summer (Leni Marin, ed.), *Raising Our Voices: Queer Asian Women's Response to Relationship Violence, available at* www.endabuse.org

Family Violence Prevention Fund, January 1999, "Caught at the Public Policy Crossroads: The Impact of Welfare Reform on Battered Immigrant Women"

Korean Community Center of the East Bay, Oakland, CA: http://www.kcceb.org/english/

Korean American Women In Need, Kan-Win, Chicago, IL: http://www.angelfire.com/il/kanwin/

Legal Momentum, *Federal Law Permits FVO Adoption at States' Option*, at www.legalmomentum.org

Manavi, New Brunswick, NJ: http://www.manavi.org/

Nav Nirman Foundation: http://www.navnirmanfoundation.org/

New York Asian Women's Center History, at www.nyawc.org/index.cfm?fuseaction=Page.viewPage&pageID=504

Perilla, Julia L., "Domestic Violence as a Human Rights Issue: The Case of Immigrant Latinos," reprinted from Hispanic Journal of Behavioral Sciences, Vol. 21, No. 2, May 1999, pp. 107-133

Pragati: RGTIINC@aol.com.

Preda, Moira Fisher, Cecilia Olavarria, and Leslye Orloff. "Alternative Forms of Relief for Battered Immigrants and Immigrant Victims of Crime: U Visas and Gender-based Asylum." Legal Momentum. Washington DC. May, 2005.

Raksha, Atlanta, GA: http://www.raksha.org/

Saheli, Austin, TX: http://www.saheli-austin.org/

Sakhi for South Asian Women, New York: http://www.sakhi.com/

Santa Clara County Death Review Sub-Committee for the Domestic Violence Council, Final Report, 1997

Shimtuh, Korean Domestic Violence Program, *Korean American Community of the Bay Area Domestic Violence Needs Assessment Report*, Oakland, CA: October 21, 2000.

Song-Kim YI, Battered Korean Women in Urban United States, in Furuto SM, Renuka B, Chung DK, Murase K, Ross-Sheriff F, eds. Social Work Practice With Asian Americans: Sage Sourcebooks for the Human Services Series, Vol. 20, Newbury Park, CA, 1992

Tripp, Aili Mari, et al., *Domestic Violence in a Cultural Context*, 27 FAM. ADVOC. 32 (Fall 2004)

Warrier, Sujatha, Ph.D, et al., The Family Violence Prevention Fund, *(Un)heard Voices: Domestic Violence in the Asian American Community*, available at www.fvpf.org

Warrier, Sujata, Ph.D, "(Un)heard Voices: Domestic Violence in the Asian American Community," Family Violence Prevention Fund, produced with a grant from the Violence Against Women Office, Office of Justice Programs, US Department of Justice

Washington State Domestic Violence Fatality Review, *Tell the World What Happened to Me* (December 2002), *available at* www.wscadv.org/projects/FR/index.htm

Yoshioka, Marianne, Ph.D., M.S.W., "Asian Family Violence Report: A Study of the Cambodian, Chinese, Korean, South Asian and Vietnamese Communities in Massachusetts," Nov. 2000, Boston, MA

PART III
Special Focus

8

Hmong Women in the United States

Updated by Mai Moua[1]

INTRODUCTION

The story of Hmong women in America is a story about women with an inde-
fatigable will to survive, to acculturate and to overcome new economic and
social challenges. At the same time, however, it is a story about women who have
not survived, crushed by experiences of violence or carrying burdens that were
too much to bear. Hmong women continue to marry and have children at
young ages, often limiting their educational opportunities in the U.S. They
work full-time jobs—often two jobs—and cope with raising large families.
Sometimes these women are the sole breadwinners for their family. While many
Hmong American women have learned how to navigate around changing traditional cultural norms and have survived by gaining new strategies and skills,
almost all have had to cope with scarce economic and social resources. The load
for Hmong women in the U.S. is formidable.

In the U.S., many Hmong women have realized freedoms that didn't exist
for them back in Laos. Nancy Donnelly, one of the first researchers to write
about the changing roles of Hmong women in the U.S., noted that upon arriving in America, "[Hmong] women were expected to learn to work away from
home, to spend money, to drive a car, to speak English with non-Hmong, to
have ideas of their own. Many felt free to choose their own marriage partners,

---

1. Mai Moua is President of Leadership Paradigms, Inc. and has 10 years of management and leadership experience with several non-profit organizations in Minnesota and Washington. She is a consultant in the fields of organizational
development, leadership, and evaluation.

free to pursue jobs or an education, and free to get out of a bad or loveless marriage." Previously denied educational opportunities in Laos, many Hmong women of all socioeconomic classes have seized educational opportunities and have entered education and professional fields at numbers never before seen in Hmong history. For example, the first Hmong Ph.D. in anthropology in the U.S. was a woman, and the majority of Hmong lawyers in Minnesota are women. Collectively they started the first and only Hmong Bar Association in the country. Hmong women have also found a place for themselves in mainstream politics. Currently there is a Hmong woman in the Minnesota State Senate and a Hmong woman on the Saint Paul Board of Education. Today, Hmong women work as public officials, serve as school principals throughout the U.S., and are forging paths as executive directors, business owners, and professionals of all kinds. One Hmong woman noted this difference in the following way, "For my grandmother, she always had to find and open doors. But for me, the door is open and I get to choose."

Within three decades of U.S. resettlement as refugees, Hmong women have achieved increased visibility and power within both Hmong and American cultures. Social and economic changes have forced them to embrace, and at times, struggle against a combination of westernized ideals and traditional Hmong values. Although Hmong women's roles have been affected, the changes are not specific to just them. As Minnesota State Representative Cy Thao noted about the changing roles of Hmong women in the U.S., "When Hmong women's roles changed, so did everyone else's."

At the same time, such success stories have been accompanied by horror stories, widely publicized in the American press. The changing gendered social and economic roles of Hmong men and women in the U.S. have been accompanied by an increase in domestic violence-related fatalities. Some women have found themselves in what can only be described as dead-end situations because they could no longer bear their burdens. In June 1998, a 13-year-old Hmong girl, Lee Vang of Wisconsin, killed the infant she had just given birth to. This infant was the product of rape by her even younger male cousin. In September 1998, 24-year-old Khoua Her of Minnesota killed her six children and attempted suicide. Khoua Her was raped, at age 12, by the man whom she was forced to marry, had her first child at age 13 in Laos, and had six children by the time she was 19. In Khoua Her's case, police had been called 16 times to her apartment over a one-year period in response to reports of domestic disturbances. The same month, Bao Lor, age 28 and mother of seven children, disappeared the day before her abusive, estranged husband shot and killed himself. Her bones were found two years later.

Voices within the community that attempted to speak out about the violence against Hmong women were discredited as being too "radically feminist." But more murders followed. At the end of 2000, four more Hmong women in Minnesota were killed by their husbands. Two of these men committed suicide after killing their wives. On July 17, 2001, 26-year-old Mee Xiong, was arrested for killing two of her six children, following a suspected suicide attempt. In St. Paul in February 2006, Kou Khang fatally stabbed his wife, Joane, 25, and himself. Other parts of the country have also faced these devastating domestic situations. For example, in Oshkosh, Wisconsin, on April 5, 2006, Yang Pao Lo fatally shot his wife, Zia Yang, who wanted a divorce. The couple had seven children, ages 4 to 17.

Hmong women activists have had to grapple with their desire to remain loyal to their culture and traditions and with their anger and dismay at the deaths and killings of women and children. Hmong in the U.S. believe that in Laos, the country where the U.S. Hmong immigrated from, domestic violence and suicide/homicides were not as prevalent. Why, they ask, in America, are some Hmong so hopeless that mothers believe that death is the only escape and fathers decide to kill their wives, families and themselves?

To begin to understand the complexity of the Hmong experience in America and to search for answers, this report provides a history of the Hmong, explores their migration to the U.S., and probes into traditions and cultural norms that many Hmong women feel have kept them stuck in traditional gender roles that at times turn violent. This report also looks at the changing economic status of Hmong women and how the community is responding to these changes. Finally, the report describes the efforts of Hmong women, men, and their organizations to address gender issues, including the recent disappearance of Hmong women's organizations.

The information in this chapter does not reflect upon "one true Hmong culture." It is widely recognized in the community that Hmong societies and its culture are diverse, depending on region, sub-clan, religion, and so on. The information presented in this chapter is illustrative of what is shared as a whole within the culture, with the recognition that some of these practices may differ depending on inter-cultural systems.

In the first edition of this book, the author's research and analysis yielded information that pointed directly to a connection between patriarchy and the community's responses to sexual assault, domestic violence, rape, and other violent treatment of Hmong women. This information caused uproar, especially among Hmong men who felt the chapter was biased towards women, not an accurate portrayal of their relationships with Hmong women, and portrayed Hmong men to non-Hmong societies as uncivilized. There was a cry that *Hmong men's voices,* which they felt have been lost in the midst of a women's movement, be heard also. Some even criticized the fact that a non-Hmong person wrote the chapter and that she could not possibly understand the intricacies of the Hmong culture. In updating this chapter, careful consideration has been given to the community's responses, and a special effort has been made to include the perspectives of Hmong men.[2]

HISTORY OF HMONG

Scholars of the Hmong are uncertain as to this culture's original roots. Some believe the Hmong originated in Siberia; others that they came from Mesopotamia. In either case, most agree that the Hmong migrated to China around 2000 years ago. Although the origins of the Hmong are debatable, most scholars agree that the Hmong culture is an ancient culture—spanning more than 4,000 years and remaining remarkably intact given their long history of oppression and migration. Hmong scholar Dr. Yang Dao notes that the Hmong's "clan-based social organization, which more than anything, helped the Hmong maintain their historical solidarity as a people" is pivotal to understanding how Hmong collective identity produces strong social and cultural ties to their ancestral heritage. This collective identity based on a strong clan structure impacts the communities of Hmong in the United States today.

---

2.   Mai Moua, who updated this chapter and is a Hmong woman, explains: "I know that there are biases inherent in my own history, my own stories, and that those biases can color my analysis of men's and women's roles. I am careful to maintain what anthropologists call an "etic" perspective; that is, treating the information as an "outsider" even though I, as a Hmong person and a Hmong woman, am an "insider," privy to information that non-Hmong persons are unable to obtain. In that aspect, my role is further complicated by this duality of "insider/outsider. The intent of this research is to bring about an understanding of the interplays of gender, race, ethnicity, religion, age, and other socio-cultural constructs. I have aimed to evaluate the gendered experiences of men and women in their totality and to consider their cultural and social histories to create a holistic understanding of Hmong women's roles in the U.S."

The Hmong in the United States came primarily from the highlands of Laos, to which they had migrated during a rebellion against the Chinese government in the 19th century. They lived in closely-knit patriarchal tribal communities which consisted of extended families called clans to which members owed allegiance. The Hmong clan system is centuries old. There are 18 major Hmong clans (with 18 surnames) and members are related by blood.

The clan system emphasizes and reinforces the collective identity of the Hmong, thereby determining male and female access to resources, activities, and constraints. Clan decisions are made based on the benefit to the clan or household unit, not the individual. Likewise, there is great concern about individual actions and how these actions may affect the reputations of the family and the clan. This is true for men and for women. Both sexes experience a culture clash around issues of gender, as they try to navigate between the requirements of collective identity and an American culture that emphasizes individuality and individual rights.

CHANGING GENDER ROLES AND SOCIAL CUSTOMS

Nine fireplaces are not as bright as the sun.
Nine daughters are not worth as much as one son.
—Hmong proverb

Gender Roles

Although the Hmong community itself operates collectively, the structures of the culture dictate specific gendered roles. As the above proverb reveals, Hmong women were and are considered far less valuable than men. As one scholar, Patricia Symonds, notes "Hmong lineage, spiritual rituals and public life are male. Hmong women as well as men say that "maleness is Hmong" and believe that even if every Hmong woman died or ran away, the patriline would continue because Hmong men would be able to marry women from other groups, and those women would then become Hmong."

Cultural notions of gender roles proscribe what being a "good" Hmong woman means: having a good temper, strong work skills, and being obedient to husband and parents are the characteristics most valued in young women. For a Hmong man, what is most valued is physical strength, the ability to provide for his family, knowing the "Hmong way" and having the ability to teach it to his sons, and making decisions that can be carried forward from generation to generation. These gendered roles are reinforced through the traditions and rituals that mark the "Hmong way."[3] Roles related to family and marriage in particular are taught and reinforced through stories, myths, and folklore told to Hmong children at a young age. Male children also are expected to mirror their father's actions, attitudes, and belief systems; this was critical because sons were expected to pass on the family lineage.

Hmong sons are traditionally given access to resources, freely and often without question. In Laos where education was a scarce resource, boys were sent to school for an education whereas girls remained in the homes to help their families, further polarizing sex roles. As a Hmong woman noted, "The Hmong man wants his daughter to be successful, but if he has $1 he would invest in his son because it benefits the immediate family. The value in people comes from very limited resources." A daughter's value is further diminished for the family by the knowledge that any investment in a girl means an investment in the clan she marries, and not in her own family and clan.

Not all Hmong men see an advantage to traditional male roles, nor do they want to be burdened with responsibilities that sometimes trap them in prescribed relationships. Particularly in the U.S. where certain Hmong and U.S. cultural values and norms are so vastly different, Hmong men may be indecisive about what values to uphold; in doing so, they may be seen as threatening a manhood that has been cultivated for thousands of years. A Hmong American man remarked about his gendered identity in this way, "What would other Hmong people think if I did not put my foot down as a man and just let my wife go out whenever she liked? Or would I be seen as a modern husband if I allowed her all the freedom she wanted?" This comment illustrates how in the U.S. the community still views it as men's role to continue to hold responsibility over women in all aspects of Hmong society.

---

3.   In Hmong culture, behaviors follow a socialized pattern known as *kev cai*, "ways of the custom." *Kev cai* determines the role gender has in Hmong society, one's behaviors towards elders, ritual and ceremony preparations, and interactions between and among Hmong clans. This principle of *kev cai* would come under attack and undergo some changes during the Hmong migration and resettlement in western societies.

Marriage

Adulthood in traditional Hmong society is only achieved when a young Hmong marries and produces offspring. The concept of parenting for both men and women is important to fulfilling Hmong cultural traditions. In Laos, girls could be married starting as young as 13.

The traditional Hmong marriage process involves very complex negotiations to bind not just the woman and man together, but also the extended families. An intermediary is asked to broker the marriage. Marriage negotiations can bring up animosities that go back generations. Debts from generations back must be paid to make amends for all past wrongdoings before the couple can wed. As part of these negotiations, the groom's family pays a bride price to the bride's family.

Once the marriage has been made, from a community standpoint the bride's body and soul belong to the husband's extended family. By tradition, whomever a woman's body and soul "belong" to is responsible for taking care of her at the point of her death or her child's birth. She is no longer part of her birth family. As one father explained to his daughter on her wedding day:

Your mother is not your real mother. You've found your real mother now. You only borrowed this mother's womb. When you go places, you will have to call us "them."[4]

The Bride Price

Most Hmong now believe love should be present in a marriage and young adults should choose their marriage partners. But ritual kidnapping and even real kidnapping of an unwilling bride have been acceptable parts of Hmong traditions. Here is the story of one refugee woman in Sacramento:

In 1980, when she was 13-years-old and a sixth-grader living in Utah, a 22-year-old friend of her stepbrother's kidnapped her and declared that he was going to marry her. Her mother could do nothing because, while the man did not touch her, she was kept in his home for three days. According to Hmong tradition, after passage of three days spent with a man in his home, a woman must marry him as long as he could

---

4.   See Paj Ntaub Voice, The Bride Price Community Forum: Part 1, Dating, Sex, & Marriage, Summer 2000, Vol. 7, No. 1.

pay the bride price. She was bought for $1,500. They had six children in rapid suc-cession.[5]

While kidnapping a bride has all but ended in the U.S., arranged marriages are still prevalent and women often feel forced to marry the man her elders choose.

In keeping with tradition, most husbands are still expected to pay a bride price, which can range from $3,000 to $4,000 in Minnesota and from $6,000 to as high as $10,000 in California. Some in the community view the bride price as mostly symbolic and a relic they brought with them to America. Some view the bride price as measuring the high regard that families place on a daughter or future daughter-in-law and as a protection against abuse and divorce. But the symbolism of a "bride price" becomes murky in the context of an American cul-ture; although it is supposed to represent a "reciprocity so that the two families remain equal," many Hmong females often speak about their distaste for such a symbol. The woman kidnapped in Utah says, "Why did you want to sell your daughter like an animal? Every time you have a fight with your husband or your in-laws ... they remind you how much they paid for you."

Polygamy

Polygamy has also been a part of recent Hmong cultural tradition. Less preva-lent before the twentieth century, it became more common as men died in war. In Laos, widows of soldiers who died fighting were expected to marry their hus-bands' brothers. Polygamy also increased as there were fewer men (many having died in war) and as some men who were left were able to increase their income (often from payments for service to the CIA).

In other cases, some divorced and widowed women became second wives in order to protect themselves from male in-laws who pressured them for sex. Divorcees and widows are no longer virgins and some Hmong men consider them fair game for sexual pursuit. Economic realities, such as women's lack of income and inability to raise orphaned children, also contributed to the rise in polygamy. Finally, polygamy sometimes occurred if women were unable to have children; for the family, having children is not only an important part of a

---

5.   See Stephen Magagnini, Building Bridges, Hmong women helping others adjust to modern America, Sacramento Bee, September 11, 2000.

woman's role in Hmong customs, but is seen as vital to sustaining Hmong culture.

Although there has been some fight against maintaining this polygamous tradition in U.S. communities, the tradition continues. Some Hmong men return to the refugee camps in Thailand and bring home second wives. As recently as the spring of 2006, a prominent Hmong woman living in Minnesota committed suicide after hearing that her husband wanted to seek a second wife.

Family Planning

In traditional Hmong families, men control decisions affecting the lives of all family members. If a man wants 10 children, his wife has little say, and would rarely question her husband. That said, it should be pointed out that traditional Hmong decision-making does not mean that males do not consult their wives or their mothers; it means that the final decision is in male hands.

In the past, the number of children a couple was able to raise afforded them higher status in their villages. Subsistence farmers, in the face of high infant mortality rates, required large families to provide labor in the fields. In the U.S., many Hmong continue the tradition of large families. The average Hmong American family has five children compared to the average of two children per Caucasian families. One reason large Hmong families persist is that couples continue having children until they have a boy, since having a boy guarantees a family lineage. Hmong activists believe these traditions are changing, and that the third generation of Hmong women will have only one or two kids. The challenge for the community will be whether or not baby girls can be seen as transmitters of family heritage.

Divorce

The Hmong tradition does not have a place for divorce. The community disapproves, and both extended families are shamed for not being able to intercede and prevent it. The Hmong prefer clan counseling to salvage the relationship, that is, by persuading the wife to reconcile herself to her situation and persuading the husband not to be irresponsible. Even in times of domestic abuse or violence, husband and wife are urged to remain together. Reasons for this can be attributed to clan or collective identity—individuals must do what is best for the clan and not the individual. Divorce is a problem because the clan—and

"Hmongness" is defined largely through the Hmong family unit (*father, mother,* sons, and daughters).

Hmong women are increasingly questioning the strictures against divorce, especially in cases of domestic violence. An editorial in a national Hmong newspaper, written by a Hmong woman asked, "Why should a Hmong woman suffer through a marriage fraught with abuse and disrespect only to keep her family respectable?"

When divorces are nonetheless inevitable, a court-ordered divorce is insufficient to dissolve that connection. The couple must be properly divorced through the traditional method of mediation by the two extended families and an agreement by both that the divorce should happen. Divorce is the marriage process in reverse, undoing the family ties, including repaying the bride price.

Views on Sexual Assault

In the case of rape, a Hmong woman or girl still may be forced into marriage. When a rape occurs in the Hmong community, it is considered not just a violation of the woman but also a shaming of the family; it is taken seriously. However the response to rape may not be what the girl or woman expects or needs.

To re-establish peace and balance between the two families, the assailant is expected to make a public apology. His family must pay restitution to the woman's family in addition to the bride price if a marriage is negotiated. Sometimes, the victim's family insists that the assailant marry the daughter because her family and community view her as tainted and no other Hmong man would want to marry her. By marrying her off to the assailant, the assailant's clan must take responsibility for the now even more devalued daughter. While the victim's parents may love her and feel the injustice of the situation, often reinstating the family's reputation is more important than the girl's feelings in such a situation.

Hmong culture does not approve of sexual assault. Yet the community's response seldom results in actions that put the victim first. The Hmong approach to preventing sexual assault is often to tell girls to keep themselves safe by staying home (therefore not going to the library, participating in extracurricular activities, or going on fieldtrips, and certainly not dating or going to dances or living alone). As a result, when a girl is raped, she is typically blamed, with the community typically thinking "How else could the man have access to her unless she let him?"

Within the Hmong community, there is widespread denial of the existence of sexual abuse and a lack of punishment for perpetrators. Learned behavior of domestic violence is a continuing problem as children watch similar behaviors continue in male family members and friends. Victims are re-victimized: blamed for the rape, forced to marry the perpetrator, shunned by the community, stigmatized instead of provided with counseling, and held responsible for the ruined reputations of themselves and their families. Until the Women's Association of Hmong and Lao (WAHL) started its Sexual Assault Program in 1998, with a 24-hour hotline, there were very few resources for the victims. Many did not seek help for fear of being disowned by their families if they told their stories. In such a close-knit community, a woman may decide not go to a clinic to get examined for fear that there is no confidentiality and someone she knows will find out.

There is evidence that attitudes are changing. Some parents saw WAHL's program as a way for their daughters to be taken care of, receive counseling and get help. Older women in their 30's and 40's also went to WAHL for assistance. Unfortunately, WAHL's program has ended; its doors closed in 2004.

MIGRATION AND RESETTLEMENT IN THE UNITED STATES

Hmong women's roles have been in flux throughout the past century, as changes in the political and economic environment followed paths of migration. In the mid 1970s after the U.S. military pulled out of Southeast Asia, the Hmong were forced to vacate their villages. Thousands fled persecution by the communist Pathet Lao and escaped into the jungles or to neighboring countries to find refuge in government-operated refugee camps. Others remained with resistance groups. Within the refugee camp structures, Hmong families tried to function as normally as possible. Many aspects of the culture such as shamanism rituals, celebrations of births, and funerals remained vital components to maintaining their cultural heritage. As residency in the camps increased, the Hmong learned how to work with other ethnic cultures, especially the Thai people and Western relief workers. Camps such as Ban Vinai, located in northern Thailand, became the epicenter for Hmong life, containing thousands of refugees by the end of 1978.

Camp life changed the Hmong's ancestral traditions. In particular, Hmong women's roles changed within camp life. Traditionally, Hmong women participated in household agricultural production and often were laborers for their husbands or for male household heads. Young girls mirrored their mothers' behaviors and were taught roles such as cooking, housekeeping, and sewing. In the camps, however, Western relief workers noticed the artistic and monetary value of the *paj ntaub* (a tapestry sewn by Hmong women) to the non-Hmong community, and began encouraging Hmong women to market these tapestries. "Sewing became an important economic function; sewing was no longer 'women's work' and Hmong men began to sew for income or they assumed cooking and childcare responsibilities so women [could] sew full time."[6] Relief workers unknowingly had shifted the Hmong woman from the domestic sphere to the public sphere, thus changing the ways women and men behaved.

These economic changes, however, did not necessarily drive changes in other gender roles. Rather, Hmong women continued to believe that "men's words were more important than women's, that men's decisions carried more weight than women's, and that a woman took on the social standing of her husband, never the other way around."[7]

From the mid 1970s to early 1980s, Hmong refugees received sponsorships for residency in various international countries and many families were relocated to the U.S. The 2000 U.S. Census Bureau places the U.S. Hmong population at approximately 186,000, with the majority living in the Sacramento and Fresno areas of California (65,000), the Twin Cities area of Minnesota (41,800), and in Wisconsin (33,791). Community leaders believe these figures are significantly lower than the actual population, which is estimated at 95,000 for California, 70,000 for Minnesota, and 50,000 for Wisconsin. Hmong migration and resettlement in the U.S. follows a systematic pattern of organizing around enclaves. Traditionally, Hmong enclaves were forms of support and cultural preservation; in a sense, they were supporting units of the Hmong collective identity. Enclaves were and continue to be solid components of transmitting gender and social roles and norms.

Whereas in past migrations, the Hmong could start a new life, free, independent and isolated from the mainstream, this was not possible in the U.S. refugee resettlement process and the Hmong found adjusting particularly difficult. Few were educated when they arrived and came with only minimal possessions to start their lives in America.

During the resettlement process, the community underwent tremendous psychological, physical, and emotional strain due to cultural and language barriers. Stories in newspapers across the country reflected the hardship Hmong families faced in their new society, especially Hmong males. Hmong men were quick to understand that in America Hmong women would have more equality; however, many men were slow to accept the changes. Unlike their male counterparts, many Hmong women quickly accepted and welcomed their newfound rights, not so much to embrace feminist and Western ideals, but to seize the resources available to help their family survive in a new culture. They understood the change in their roles as a way to help maintain family structure, something they were socialized to do.

Changing Economic Roles

The Hmong men's traditional occupations as farmers and soldiers and the women's traditional reproductive and productive work in the home and in the fields did not easily translate into jobs in the U.S. In America, the Hmong were not retrained in these areas, and they had to seek new skills; thus, the 2000 Census reports a mere 1% of the Hmong population in the U.S. are employed in the farming, fishing, and forestry jobs that would have been traditional to the Hmong in Southeast Asia.

In Minnesota, many Hmong families still remain isolated in urban ghettoes and dependent on public welfare, although some have been able to follow the white exodus to wealthier suburbs. In California, the Hmong live in the more rural areas of the Central Valley where jobs are few. Overall, the Hmong live in more dire circumstances than most Asian Americans. While the poverty rate for all Asian Americans is 12.6%, it is 37.6% for the Hmong. To maintain a job, especially one that pays well in the U.S., means that one has to have a good education and speak English well. The 2000 Census reveals that while 4.1% of the total U.S. population and 24.7% of Asian Americans live in linguistically isolated households, for the Hmong the rate is 35.1%[8]. Nor do the Hmong have high rates of formal schooling. The 2000 U.S. Census Bureau reports that while only 1.4% of the overall U.S. population and 4.2% of Asian Americans had no formal schooling, 45% of Hmong have no formal schooling. While 24.4% of the total U.S. population has attained a Bachelor's Degree or higher, only 7.4% of Hmong persons have achieved a higher degree. Disaggregating the numbers further reveals that only 4.7% of Hmong women have achieved a Bachelor's

---

8.   A linguistically isolated household is one in which all adults (high school age and older) have some limitation in communicating in English. A household is classified as "linguistically isolated" if no household members age 14 years or over speak only English, and no household members age 14 years or over who speak a language other than English speaks English "Very well".

Degree or higher, and 10.1% of Hmong men have done the same. Of the estimated 186,000 Hmong persons reported living in the U.S. in 2000, 258 Hmong women reported obtaining a master's degree or higher and only 3 Hmong women reported having obtained their doctoral degree. These figures will likely change given the increase of Hmong females pursuing a higher education. However, language barriers and the lack of education continue to prohibit the full participation of the Hmong in American society, thereby contributing to continued poverty and socio-economic insecurity and limiting mobility.

Impact of Welfare Reform on the Hmong

In recent years, the unraveling of the traditional Hmong culture has been accelerated by the Welfare Reform Act of 1996 which created Temporary Assistance for Needy Families (TANF).

The bureaucratic procedures instituted by programs like TANF often have unexpected cultural consequences. For example, in Sacramento, California, welfare departments require that a TANF case file be established in the mother's name. Not knowing that they can instruct the welfare office otherwise, Hmong families receive funds issued in the wife's name. Some Hmong men resent this because of the appearance that they are not the breadwinners, and because their wives now control the finances. This was power women did not have in Laos.

Many Hmong women have used TANF as a means to move toward self-sufficiency. Welfare reform forced both wife and husband into job training, ESL classes, and jobs outside their ethnic enclave. Some men refuse to attend classes with women as they find it demeaning and a loss of face to be learning alongside women. On the other hand, women tend to be eager to learn and are willing to take jobs men won't take. Consequently, many more Hmong women than men, from age 25 to 50, are graduating with ESL diplomas, and are the ones getting jobs, sometimes with health insurance and sometimes earning higher wages than their husbands.[9]

---

9.   Unlike Asian immigrant women in the rest of the country, because of the availability of factory jobs in the Twin Cities area, Hmong women were able to secure higher than minimum wage jobs in meat packing, vegetable canneries, and light assembly in such companies as Pillsbury, 3M and General Mills. Hmong women prefer working in manufacturing jobs where they carpool to the suburbs instead of working in the service sector such as domestic and janitorial. In these jobs, they can earn from $7 to $12 an hour, though if they have large families of eight to 12, their earnings remain below the poverty line.

Changing Leadership and Political Roles

By the close of the 20th century, Hmong women were vying for leadership positions in mainstream society and were successful at obtaining them. As Cy Thao notes, "Kazoua Kong Thao [St. Paul School Board Member] and Senator Mee Moua were elected by the broader community, meaning support were from both the men and women in the community. Solutions and decisions are now made by women like Senator Mee Moua."

But no matter how visible the success of Hmong women on a cross-cultural level, many continue to face challenges to leading effectively, including the Hmong community's reluctance to accept women as leaders and at such young ages. Most women leaders are in their 20s or 30s, and leadership has always been recognized as a right given to men and elders. Hmong women in recognizable leadership positions like Ilean Her, Executive Director of the Council on Asian-Pacific Minnesotans, and Senator Mee Moua have been criticized for their stance on the recent Hmong marriage bill[10] in Minnesota as well as other issues, and often times are pitted against each other.

Other female-centered organizations and women activists are often labeled "radicals," "fundamentalists," "men haters," or "not Hmong enough." At other times, Hmong women's choices are recognized by the mainstream community but barely acknowledged within the Hmong community. On the other hand, there are factors that support and nurture their leadership; these include the participation and support of family members, particularly their husbands, fathers, and brothers, and the mentorship and network of other Hmong women in similar positions.

---

10. The Hmong Marriage Bill proposal in Minnesota would give a *mej koob*, the negotiator in Hmong marriages, the authority to legally solemnize Hmong marriages. If passed, a mej koob would be responsible for reporting underage marriages, which some members of the Hmong community have argued is still commonly practiced. Thus, this bill serves a dual purpose as a child protection bill while recognizing Hmong marriages. Those who oppose this bill note that traditionally a mej koob serves only as a negotiator, not a legal solemnizer of the marriage; therefore, this is going outside of the scope of his duties. Furthermore, they argue that underage marriages are not a huge problem as it once was and that the responsibility should be placed on the parents and adults rather than the mej koob.

Changes in public and private life

As Hmong women learn English, become wage earners, and attain higher levels of economic independence, the power dynamics within families change, albeit incrementally at first. For example, in Minnesota in the early phases of Hmong arrival in America through the mid 1980's, Hmong women were not seen in public with their husbands. They were pressured to stay home and not attend outings, such as weddings or Hmong New Year celebrations. The women activists at the Association for the Advancement of Hmong Women in Minnesota (AAHWM) tackled these problems by insisting their own husbands take them to these events. Slowly, other women began attending. In 1989, the AAHWM estimate that 20% of the men brought their wives to events. In 1990, half brought their wives and by 1998, it was socially acceptable for a woman to accompany her husband to public events. Though seeing couples together has become socially acceptable, most Hmong women can attest that they are still not part of traditional clan leadership structures.

CHALLENGES REMAINING FOR HMONG WOMEN

Despite the resistance of the clan elders, the Hmong community is changing its attitudes towards family, gender roles, and work. As Hmong men and women learned to adapt to their U.S. environment, several issues emerged as critical to threatening Hmong cultural identity and social systems. Generational conflicts between Hmong children and their parents escalated to dangerous levels; issues foreign to Hmong families previously, such as truancy, youth gangs, and substance abuse, emerged as grave issues. Many first-generation or American-born Hmong children have diverged from their parents' traditional ways of thinking, which was inconceivable within traditional Hmong society. But it is the issue of changing gender roles that seems to draw the most attention from the Hmong communities and remains hotly contested.

Despite their accomplishments, Hmong women still continue to face tremendous challenges in their roles as women, daughters, mothers, aunts, grandmothers, and sisters. Interviews with women who participated in creating the first Hmong female organizations in the late 1980s and early 1990s demonstrated that their concerns about the treatment of Hmong women remain the same. Several women from the Hmong Women's Action Team have noted that the painful stories they told in their late teens and early twenties about polygamy, early marriages, sexism, sexual assault and rape are still being told today by adolescent females. Not only are the issues the same, but within the community the same advice is still being given; that is, *Go back to your husbands and work things out* or *If you were a good Hmong girl you wouldn't have gotten into that situation.* But what has changed for many of these activists is an increasing concern for Hmong boys; they now believe that if sexism, patriarchy, or male dominance is not addressed, it is not just Hmong females that will suffer the consequences.

But whenever questions are raised about gender roles, what inevitably follow are questions about Hmong identity and cultural and social norms. *Who are the Hmong? How is Hmongness defined and by whom—men or women?* At times, the debate becomes heated and a large chasm between the sexes is created. Some young men maintain that patriarchal traditions and stories of polygamy and domestic abuse are old history, and resent Hmong women for shining a spotlight on them. Other men ask: *Why just focus on women and girls? Hmong males are falling behind too. Why not focus on them? Why are men portrayed as perpetrators of violence? Not all Hmong males treat Hmong women poorly.*

Not all Hmong males in the U.S. today still believe the "nine fireplaces/nine daughters" proverb. Clearly, there are Hmong males that treat Hmong women with respect and are proud of the accomplishments of Hmong women. One young man shared his deep respect for his mother,

> *My mother gave me hopes and dreams of a better life until the day that she died of cancer in 1994. It was because of her that I graduated from St. Thomas in 1997 and am living out the dreams that she painted. She is my hero.... It is an honor to be her son.*

Another man commented that, "We Hmong men need to change our thinking and our parents need to do what is right for their young daughters in a bad marriage, not what everyone thinks they should do."

Thus, while there are some Hmong men that continue the patriarchal traditions of the old country in the U.S., there are other progressive Hmong American men who understand the important role of women in Hmong culture and advocate for women's issues.

HMONG AMERICAN FEMINIST APPROACH

Hmong women in different parts of the U.S., who come from different life experiences, are exploring multiple ways to address gender issues, including the continuing violence against women in their communities and how they can work to improve the lives of Hmong women and girls.

One group of Hmong women in California, for example, has developed their own Hmong style of feminism that includes working closely with clan elders. They view the transformation of their culture as a combination of "what is positive from the old culture with what is good in this country." Their approach includes adhering to the close-knit clan structure and its moral authority; for example, the Hmong Women's Heritage Association (HWHA) they founded has, as part of its governing structure, a Clan Advisory Council made up of all men. Some have criticized the exclusion of women in the Council, but traditionally, women did not serve on clan councils. HWHA believes that because it has male clan elders integrated into its organizational structure, the community has been more accepting of its work. When the executive director received death threats and criticism after making statements to *The Sacramento Bee*, the Council stood behind her and smoothed tensions in the community. HWHA has honored clan leaders at dinners, and at the same time criticized the old Hmong guard for living in the past. When issues arise and the clan leaders want to respond in the traditional way, HWHA points out the conflict between Hmong traditions and U.S. law and works to negotiate a middle ground. The Council meets regularly to mediate sensitive cases, such as domestic disputes and divorces. The HWHA believes that only when clan leaders and men are empowered through inclusion in conversations that push them to think in new terms can they be moved to accept change.

In Minnesota, younger women's experiences with their clan leadership give them less confidence in the traditional ways and the traditionally male-dominated systems of community decision-making and leadership. They have criticized the traditional all-male elders' councils. They have created a new tradition of honoring Hmong women leaders and women of courage. For example, in the past, the Hmong Women's Action Team held an annual leadership and courage award banquet to bestow honor on Hmong women leaders and to recognize the contributions Hmong men have to improving the lives of women in their communities. Hmong women in Minnesota are also struggling to change their personal lives—in their roles as wives, in their husbands' roles, and most importantly in the need for the men in their lives (husbands, brothers, fathers, uncles, elders, etc.) to openly support them and other women.

As successful as Hmong women have been at strategizing and creating systemic change, the community has recently seen a disappearance of Hmong female-centered organizations and groups within the U.S. Organizations that in the past addressed systemic issues of gender discrimination are slowing disappearing, or in some cases, have disappeared completely. In 2004, a major Hmong women's organization, the Women's Association of Hmong and Lao (WAHL) stopped providing services to its constituents. Throughout its operations, particularly in the early 1980s, WAHL had provided much needed services to women around domestic abuse and sexual violence even though staff members were threatened, harassed, and their properties vandalized simply because of their advocacy work. This "backlash" continued to frame the way WAHL presented women's issues to the community, and in some ways, hindered it from truly addressing women's issues. For example, violence against women had to be framed under gang violence or truancy, issues that were "safe", in order to even garner support for eliminating violence against women. But it wasn't only the lack of community support that finally ended WAHL's run; it was a combination of several factors. Former WAHL staff members noted that lack of leadership from all levels of the organization, gaps in funding resources, funders' lack of understanding the community's needs, and the lack of commitment and support from community members, regardless of gender, to Hmong women's issues finally closed WAHL's doors.

Currently there are just two formal organizations for Hmong women, the Hmong Women's Heritage Association in Sacramento, CA and the Association for the Advancement of Hmong Women in Minnesota in Minneapolis, MN. These organizations center on direct services to women, which have been tremendously helpful; however, some of the direct services tend to bypass the systemic issues that relate to women and men's access to resources and sources of power. Other Hmong organizations have programs that address the needs of women and children but are often criticized for backing away when controversial issues, such as domestic violence, sexual assault, polygamy, or rape, are brought up. This leads to the question: *How is gender equity achieved within the Hmong community if organizations either are not in existence to address gender issues or if organizations and its members tip toe around them?*

Some argue that if women-based organizations are to survive there is a need for stronger leadership from Hmong women. Others say it is more about defining organizational vision and focus for Hmong women's issues than it is about lack of community support, while others maintain that female-centered organizations will continue to suffer because there is no recognition or support for Hmong women's issues within and outside the Hmong community. Still others noted the lack of cultural sensitivity and understanding from funders in granting money to organizations focused on Hmong women's issues.

As diverse as the opinions given, there is a common thread throughout the conversations—activists have been unable to rally the voices and visions of a diverse population to the cause of women's issues. In particular, *how does one gather the assortment of voices existing among Hmong women to support the cause of gender equity?* GaoLy Yang has remarked that the disappearance of female-centered organizations is not entirely caused by a lack of support for women's causes but also a lack of consensus building among Hmong women. She said, "At first it was resistance from men but now we don't know how to work together or lead. They [men] don't support but that doesn't mean they cause the stoppage. If you don't have strong leadership to keep people focused, no strong leadership to focus on the vision of the organization, then all the energy is dispersed." Similarly, another Hmong woman noted, "We have failed at teamwork in helping and supporting each other.... we haven't created "buy-in" amongst ourselves and within the community for this need."

Even though Hmong women's organizations are disappearing, there is still a pressing need, perhaps now more than ever, to have their presence in the community. Since the first version of this report came out, Hmong women have gathered together to organize informal groups to better serve the needs and issues of Hmong women. Groups like the Professional Hmong Women's Association, a network of professional Hmong women; the Hmong Women's Giving Circle, a philanthropic group that grants money to organizations for systemic change; the Hmong Women's Circle, which helps build leadership capacity among young Hmong girls; the Hmong Women's Action Team; and even the first Hmong Women's Conference in Minneapolis in 2005 have sprung into being. All are attempts to continue the cause that early Hmong women activists began. In some ways, these informal groups are representing a new way of organizing for advocacy work. Some literature on female organizations within minority cultures suggests that informal groups sometimes serve a better purpose and are able to frame issues more directly than formal organization. For example, a member of HWAT commented that if HWAT was a formal organization, then all the bureaucracy and politics of the Hmong community would hinder its systemic work on sexism and violence. But, because it is informal, it has used its informal structures as a *strength* to address issues that Hmong organizations are afraid to touch.

Ultimately, a concerted effort on the part of all segments of the community is needed to begin the dialogue to find solutions. It is clear that women and men, adults and youth are calling out for a consensus to addressing issues of gender equity; that without support and commitment the Hmong community will continue to struggle with issues of gender. Changing cultural norms is vital, whether through men's groups, public education programs, or other means. Equally important is the understanding that the Hmong has survived thousands of years of migrations because aspects of gender roles have changed to preserve the essence of Hmong culture, whatever that may be given the socio-cultural environment of its people. More so now than ever before, Hmong women are voicing the importance of male support for the elimination of sexism and the creation of a Hmong society that honors the roles of women while maintaining the richness of the culture.

REFERENCES

Associated Press, "BRF-Restroom Baby," June 6, 1998

Associated Press, "Hmong leaders trying to curb domestic violence," Dec. 11, 2000

Bentley, Rosalind, and Her, Lucy Y., "2 children dead; mother in critical condition," *Star Tribune*, July 18, 2001

Dao, Y.. "Hmong refugees from Laos: The challenge of social change." In N. Tapp, J. Michaud, C. Culas, & G.Y. Lee (Eds.), *Hmong/Miao in Asia* (pp. 477-485). Chiang Mai, Thailand: Silkworm, 2004

Donnelly, N. D.. *Changing lives of refugee Hmong women*. Seattle, WA: University of WA, 1997

Chan, S. (Ed.). *Hmong means free: Life in Laos and America*. Philadelphia: Temple University, 1994

Fact Finding Commission. *Fact finding commission: The U. S. "Secret War" Veterans*. Retrieved November 15, 2004, from http://www.factfindingcommission.org

Faderman, L. . *I begin my life all over: The Hmong and the American Immigrant*
experience. Boston: Beacon, 1998

Goldstein, Beth L., "Resolving Sexual Assault: Hmong and the American Legal System," published in *The Hmong in Transition*, Glenn L. Hendricks, et al., editors

Hang, May Kao Y., "Lost and Found: Marie Heu and Bao Lor," *Hnub Tsiab*, Newsletter of Hmong Women's Action Team, October 2000

Her, Lucy, "Urging education, 100 protest violence against Hmong women," *Star Tribune*, 1998

Hmong in the '90s: Stepping Towards the Future, a report of the Hmong American Partnership, Dec. 1993

Hmong Women's Peace, Sexual Assault in the Hmong Community, Focus Group Results, April 1999

Huynh, Deborah, "Abused Hmong Women Learn to Overcome Cultural Dilemma," *AAJA Voices*, Aug. 14, 1996

Ireson, C., *Field, Forest, And Family: Women's Work And Power In Rural Laos.* Boulder, CO: Westview, 1996

Kaiser, T. L. . "Caught Between Cultures: Hmong Parents In America's Sibling
Society." *Hmong Studies Journal*, 5, 1-14, 2004

Kasindorf, Martin, "L.A. Confronts Asian Family Abuse," *USA TODAY*, May 17, 2006,
http://www.usatoday.com/news/nation/2006-05-17-koreatown_x.htm

Lavilla, Stacy, "Why Her? Hmong Activists Address The Despair That Turned Deadly For One Minnesota Family," *Asian Week*, Sept. 17-23, 1998

Lee, G. Y. . "Transnational Adaptation: An Overview Of The Hmong Of Laos." In N. Tapp, J. Michaud, C. Culas, & G.Y. Lee (Eds.), *Hmong/Miao in Asia* (pp. 441-455). Chiang Mai, Thailand: Silkworm, 2004

Lee, M. N. (1998). "The Thousand Year Myth: Construction And Characterization Of Hmong." *Hmong Studies Journal*. 2(1). Retrieved November 10, 2004, from
http://members.aol.com/hmongstudiesjrnl/HSJv2n1_Lee.html

Lyfoung, Pacyinz, Editorial Opinion, "Denial: The Core Problem, Hmong Advocate Calls For End To Silence," *Asian Week*, Sept. 17–23, 1998

Magagnini, Stephen, "Building Bridges, Hmong Women Helping Others Adjust To Modern America," *Sacramento Bee*, September 11, 2000

McCall, A. . "More Than A Pretty Cloth: Teaching Hmong History And Culture Through Textile Art." *Theory and Research in Social Education*, 25(2), 137-167, 1997

Meredith, William H., and Rowe, George P., "Changes in Hmong Refugee Marital Attitudes in America," published in *The Hmong in Transition*, Glenn L. Hendricks, et al., eds

Nelson, Todd, "Mom Arrested In Slaying Of 2 Kids In St. Paul," *Pioneer Planet/Pioneer Press*, July 18, 2001

Pfeiffer, M.E., & Lee, S. (n.d.). "Hmong Population, Demographic, Socio-economic, And Educational Trends In The 2000 Census." *Hmong 2000 Census Publication: Data and analysis.* (pp. 3-11). Washington, D.C: Hmong National Development

Quincy, K. . *Hmong: History of a people* (2nd ed.). Cheney, WA: Eastern Washington University, 1995

Rybak, Deborah Caulfield, "Generation X-cellent," *Star Tribune*, (date unknown)

Shur, Jim, "Rape Allegations Shake Hmong Refugees," Associated Press, Oct. 13, 1999

Southeast Asian American Mutual Assistance Association Directory 2000, published by the Southeast East Asia Resource Action Center

Symonds, P. V. . *Calling in the soul: Gender and the cycle of life in a Hmong village.* Seattle, WA: University of WA, 2004

Taus, Margaret, "Minnesota Woman In Custody In Deaths Of Her Six Children," Associated Press, Sept. 4, 1998

Thao, Chong Yang, Editorial Opinion, *St. Paul Pioneer Press*; reprinted in *Hnub Tshiab, A Hmong Women's Publication*, Jan. 2001

"The Bride Price Community Forum: Part 1, Dating, Sex, & Marriage," Summer 2000, Vol. 7, No. 1, Paj Ntaub Voice

Vang, Chia Youyee, *Childbearing Patterns: A Case Study of Hmong Refugees in Minnesota*, Nov. 25, 1996

Vang, H. "Hmong American Women's Educational Attainment: Implications For Hmong American Women And Men." *Hmong 2000 Census Publication: Data and analysis.* (pp. 22-25). Washington, D.C: Hmong National Development, (n.d.)

Xiong, Z. B.., & Tuicompee, A. . "Hmong Families In America In 2000: Continuity And Change." *Hmong 2000 Census Publication: Data and analysis.* (pp. 12-22). Washington, D.C: Hmong National Development, (n.d.)

Yang, K. (1997). "Hmong Men's Adaptation To Life In The United States." *Hmong Studies Journal*, *1*(2), 1-22.

Yang, K. (2003). "Hmong Americans: A Review Of Felt Needs, Problems, And Community development." *Hmong Studies Journal*, *4*, 1-23

Yang, May Kao, "Growing Up Hmong American: Truancy Policy and Girls," Master's Degree Paper, Hubert H. Humphrey Institute of Public Affairs, April 24, 1996

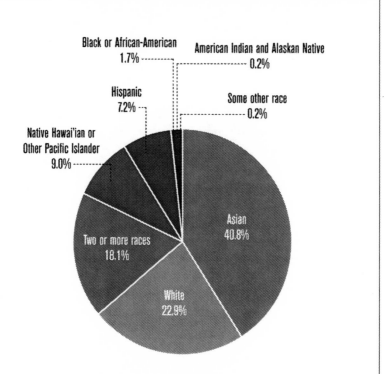

Note: Two or more races: Of persons reporting two or more races, not including Hispanics, 157,880 reported being at least part Asian, Native Hawai'ian and Other Pacific Islander, Some other race or some combination of all three groups.

Source: U.S. Census Bureau. Population by Race and Hispanic or Latino Origin, for All Ages and for 18 years and Over, for Hawai'i: 2000

Hawaii's Ethnic Pie

9

Hawai'i¹—A Different Paradigm

INTRODUCTION

Hawai'i is home to the third largest population of Asian Americans in the U.S. In contrast to the U.S. mainland where Asian Americans are 4% of the U.S. population, close to 70% of Hawai'i's population is Asian or part Asian. However, unlike the general U.S. Asian American population, which is 63% immigrant, in Hawai'i, 84% are U.S. born. The author of this report looked into the following questions: Do Asian Americans, who make up the vast majority of the state and control its political apparatus, suffer human and civil rights violations? The answer was "yes" though with variations not seen on the mainland. With regard to the question: "Is there an Asian American identity or sense of solidarity on the islands?," the answer was "no."²

On the mainland, the white dominant culture's perception of all Asians as being the same and the resulting oppression that does not discriminate among Chinese, Japanese, Filipinas, and Southeast Asians contributes to the creation of Asian American identity and solidarity. With Hawai'i's population being majority Asian, however, there is no white/Asian dichotomy. Rather, each Asian ethnicity occupies a different place in the social hierarchy, and Native Hawai'ians surely do not place themselves within the "Asian Pacific Islander" identity construct that is sometimes seen on the mainland. Indeed, in

---

1. State residents prefer this punctuation.
2. Instead, persons of Asian descent self-identify by ethnicity, such as Japanese, Chinese, or Oriental (used by those without the political consciousness to use the term Asian), or they will say, "I'm local," meaning not haole or Japanese tourist. The darker one is, the more one will self-identify as local or others will identify one as local.

Hawai'i, it is the Japanese ethnic group that wields political power and, along with whites who hold economic power, are among the sources of the human and civil rights violations inflicted on other Asian Americans (Filipinos and newer immigrants) and Native Hawai'ians who occupy the bottom of the socioeconomic ladder.[3]

In order to understand the socioeconomic and political positions of the different ethnic communities in present day Hawai'i, this chapter first gives a brief history of the settlement of Hawai'i by haoles[4] from the mainland, the immigration of laborers from Asia, and the creation of the Japanese American middle and professional classes. The report will then examine the issues facing the ethnic groups at the bottom of socioeconomic ladder and possible steps for future action and advocacy.

BRIEF HISTORY OF SETTLEMENT AND IMMIGRATION TO HAWAI'I

1. Overview

Native Hawai'ians' first came into contact with the U.S. in the late 1700's. The first missionaries began arriving in Hawai'i in 1830. The immediate off-spring of four missionary families began accumulating immense wealth, beginning with sugar and pineapple plantations. Intermarriage among the four families, intrafamily holdings, and interlocking directors created the Big Five companies which came to control the economy of the islands, expanding beyond sugar and pineapple to encompass the steamship, railway, utilities, cattle, and hotel industries.[5] In the 1860's, the lands of Native Hawai'ians were stolen by the descendants of these haole missionaries and turned into sugar cane fields for the world market. Labor was needed to work the fields, but outside diseases such as small pox and diphtheria decimated the Native Hawai'ian population.

---

3.   While the former governor and lieutenant governor are Filipino and the current lieutenant governor has Native Hawaiian roots, however, Japanese Americans hold the majority of political offices.
4.   Residents of Hawai'i refer to Caucasians as "haole."
5.   The Big Five includes American Factors, C. Brewer, Alexander and Baldwin, Castle & Cook, and Theo H. Davies.

From 1778 to 1893, the Native Hawai'ian population dropped from an estimated one million to 40,000. Sugar plantations owners turned to Asian labor. In 1852, the first Chinese immigrants arrived, with 46,000 arriving before anti-Chinese sentiments resulted in Chinese Exclusion laws in 1883. Chinese laborers were replaced by Japanese immigrants, who were arriving in large number by 1885 and then by Koreans in 1903. From the 1850's to 1950's, close to 400,000 people, primarily from Asia, were brought to Hawai'i to work in the sugarcane fields. Asians are a numerical majority in Hawai'i today because of the massive depopulation of Hawai'i's indigenous people and importation of Asian immigrant labor for the sugar industry. The Kingdom of Hawai'i was overthrown in 1893 by the U.S. military and annexed as a territory in 1898. The Big Five controlled every aspect of island life, economic, social, and political and had absolute control over plantation workers. Hawai'i became the 50th state of the U.S. in 1959.

2. Japanese Immigration

Japanese immigration to Hawai'i began in 1868 and occurred in five waves, with men outnumbering women 20 to 1 in the early period and later the ratio dropped to five to one. The first generation of women, the Issei, went to work in the sugar cane fields. By 1890, Japanese women made up nearly two-thirds of wage-earning women in Hawai'i's economy and nearly all of them were laborers. In 1900, the territorial government abolished contract servitude and Japanese plantation workers went on strike to join unions and organized for wage increases and better conditions. One of the strike demands was for two months paid maternity leave, a reflection of the large number of women field-workers.

A treaty with Japan in 1908 allowed larger numbers of Japanese women to immigrate to join their husbands to reconstitute or create new families. Between 1908 and 1924, the Japanese population grew rapidly in Hawai'i. Anti-immigrant backlash from whites in Hawai'i resulted in passage of a 1924 immigration law that virtually ended immigration from Asia until the 1965 repeal of the various bans on immigration of Asians into the U.S. Nonetheless, because both Japanese men and women were allowed to enter Hawai'i, Japanese families, communities, and infrastructure developed early, with their Nisei (second generation) born in the 1920's and 1930's, Sansei (third generation) born in the 1950's and 1960's, Yonsei (fourth generation) born in the 1970's and 1980's, and now Gonsei (fifth generation) born in the 1990's. As described below, the Sansei and later generations were able to rise to the middle and professional classes.

3. Post World War II

Hawai'i's workforce underwent drastic changes when Japan attacked Pearl Harbor in December 1941. Martial law was imposed. It was only the fact that 37% of the islands' workforce was now Japanese, that prevented relocation to mainland internment camps. During World War II, like their mainland counterparts, women in Hawai'i moved into heavy industry. When the war ended, the Rosie the Riveters of Hawai'i and the mainland lost good-paying manufacturing jobs and were pushed into female dominated clerical work in expanding offices. Younger Hawai'i born women of Japanese and Chinese descent made up this new white-collar work force that personifies the movement of women from the fields into offices.

In 1945, Hawai'i passed the Hawai'i Employee Relations Act, which gave agricultural workers the right to organize. The International Longshore Workers Union (ILWU) successfully organized the first multi-racial union, integrating all Asian ethnicities, in the sugar industry. The 1946 strike of 26,000 sugar workers, known as the Great Hawai'i Sugar Strike, shut down the sugar industry island wide, winning them the first industry contract. Their victory broke the oligopoly and stranglehold of The Big Five over the economic and social life of the islands and changed the balance of power between workers and the plantations. Strikes in other industries followed. The multi-ethnic communities forged in these strikes laid the foundation for ending the Big Five and Republican control of Hawai'i eight years later.

4. The Democratic Revolution of 1954

When the Japanese American veterans returned to Hawai'i after World War II, they returned to a segregated society, not dissimilar to that of the US south. Up until the 1960's, Hawai'i had segregated schools, with haole children attending private English Standard Schools and Asian and Native Hawai'ian students attending the county public schools, taught in pidgin or Hawai'ian Creole. Segregation also existed in housing (through racial covenants in deeds that prohibited the sale of real property to non-whites) and employment. The veterans came home and went to college using the GI Bill but were locked out of corporate firms. Immigrants could not vote because they could not become US citizens. In civil and criminal trials, they did not have a right to a jury of their peers but were at the mercy of all-white jurors, usually white plantation managers. The Japanese American veterans who grew up on plantations began seeking change by running for political office. In what is called the Democratic Revolution of 1954, these veterans took over control of the state territorial legislature, breaking the stranglehold Republicans and The Big Five had on state government since annexation. Their base of support was the plantation workers unionized by the ILWU and other union workers who made up nearly one-third of the workforce. Once elected, they started passing social and civil rights legislation, including ending segregation by creating a statewide school system taught in standard English that replaced the poorly funded county school districts. Hawai'i was the first state to adopt a civil rights law that predates the federal Civil Rights Act of 1964, ratify the Equal Rights Amendment, and recognize the right to abortion and same-sex marriage. These policies were pushed by a strong and progressive labor movement, which provided the Democratic Party with its platform and base of support.

While Japanese Americans are the political elite, economic power still lies with haoles, including the corporations descended from The Big Five and the U.S. mainland owned resorts and hotel chains. Dole Pineapple owns the island of Lanai and the Robinson family owns the island of Ni'ihau. In Hawai'i, like the rest of the U.S., those who hold economic power also have great sway over politics. A glass ceiling for Asian Americans, even for Japanese Americans, exist in upper levels of corporate management. For example, the CEOs of the large hotels are white while the middle management is Japanese American. Television newscasters are white and 70% of the tenured professors at the University of Hawai'i are white, mostly from the mainland.[6] The lecturers are predominately women of color. The white faculty resent having to answer to a state legislature that is predominately people of color.

5. Post War Changes for Japanese Women in Hawai'i

In the 1950's, Hawai'i began moving from an agriculture-dominated economy to a service economy, relying on tourism and support services for military families. World War II, the labor movement, the political ascension of the Democratic Party, and statehood opened up many more opportunities for

---

6.   The colonial mentality of the locals accounts for much of this. Anything from the mainland is thought to be of better quality. Locals will send their children to any mainland college rather than to the University of Hawai'i. There is a lot of deference by Asians to white authority.

the Nisei women. They moved into jobs in hotels, offices, and retail where they continue to predominate today. Younger Nisei women whose families could pay for their higher education entered the feminine gendered professions and became teachers, librarians, nurses, and social workers. The public sector tended to be less discriminatory toward racial and ethnic minorities and many women gravitated to government jobs. Sansei women also went to college, entered into the female-gendered professions like their Nisei mothers, but also chose careers in law, journalism, academia, medicine, and politics. Their Yonsei daughters obtain even more prestigious and exclusive secondary, baccalaureate, and post-graduate education. But Native Hawai'ian women were discriminated against and kept out of the white collar positions and relegated to food service and housekeeping.

DISCRIMINATION AGAINST THE NEWER ASIAN IMMIGRANTS

1. Chinese and Filipino Immigration and Racial Discrimination

Unlike the Japanese immigrants, Chinese and Filipino laborers were prohibited from bringing their wives and families to Hawai'i. Filipinos were forced to live in bachelor societies and it was not until after 1965 that they could bring their families to Hawai'i. Chinese men married Hawai'ian women, but their children faced discrimination and their descendants did not move up the socioeconomic ladder in the same way as the Japanese. The particular history of immigration to Hawai'i has influenced the socioeconomic stratification of Hawai'i, which consists of a Chinese merchant and business class that largely stays out of politics, a middle and professional class of Japanese that dominates politics, and a working poor or impoverished class made up of Filipinos, Southeast Asian refugees, mixed ethnicities, and Native Hawai'ans.[7]

Much of the discrimination and violation of civil and human rights suffered by Filipinos and Native Hawai'ians is inflicted by Japanese American politicians or white, Japanese and Chinese employers, managers and those in positions of power and authority. An example of an employment decision by

---

7.   There are of course poor and struggling Japanese American families and well-to-do professional Filipino families. But statistically, most Japanese Americans are in the middle or higher classes and a larger proportion of Filipino Americans are among the working poor.

a Japanese American involving a Filipino American that was allegedly discriminatory occurred in the 1989 Fragante v. City and County of Honolulu case that went up to the Ninth Circuit Court of Appeals. Fragante, a Filipino, had applied for an entry-level clerk position dealing with the public with the Hawai'i Department of Motor Vehicles. His interviewers, one of whom was a Japanese American, declined to hire him because they found his Filipino accent difficult to understand. Fragante sued for accent discrimination, a form of national origin discrimination. He ultimately lost the case. When power resides in Japanese Americans who have made discriminatory employment and other decisions regarding Filipino Americans, there can be no Asian American identity or solidarity in Hawai'i.

The animosity Filipinos feel for Japanese Americans' long-standing discrimination against them came to a head in 1998. Filipino Americans protested and reversed the decision of the Association of Asian American Studies to present a Japanese American writer, Hawai'ian-born Lois Yamanaka, with its Fiction Award for her book, *Blu's Hanging*, which depicted a Filipino man as a sexual pervert who rapes a Japanese American boy. The opening poem of Yamanaka's earlier book, *Saturday Night at the Pahala Theatre*, also portrayed a Filipino man as a sexual predator of young Japanese girls. The racist stereotypes of Filipino men as sexual threats originated 90 years earlier in the days when Filipino men lived in bachelor camps on the plantations. Filipinos had protested the racist portrayals in *Saturday Night* and were appalled to learn that Yamanaka was receiving an award for a second book that again perpetuated the stereotype. This conflict pitted Japanese Americans who defended Yamanaka against Filipinos who were criticized for censorship and over-sensitivity for protesting yet another manifestation of the racism against them.

2. Poverty and Inequities

In Hawai'i, the most serious civil and human rights violations are, as on the U.S. mainland, inflicted on the working poor and impoverished women, in this case, Filipinas and Native Hawai'ian women. Since the 1940s, the lower wages paid first by an agricultural economy, then a service economy, along with a high cost of living in Hawai'i, (about 35% to 40% higher than the national average), have meant that full-time employment for two or more adults in a family is common. This has resulted in Hawai'i's women leading the nation in female labor force participation. A large part of the family income goes to childcare. Hawai'i's housing market is limited and very expensive because most land is owned by a few private estates, corporations, and the government and locals also must compete with tourists for rentals or end up moving further away from their jobs and children's schools, increasing the cost of transportation.

In the last 10 years, the loss of jobs from sugar and pineapple plantations and downturn in tourism because of Japan's weak economy has caused high unemployment. In Molokai, one-third of the population lost their jobs with the recent closing of one resort. There are no jobs on the island of Lanai and much of Molokai. Twenty-eight percent of the Temporary Assistance for Needy Families (TANF) recipients are part Hawai'ian; 92% being women. Eight percent are Filipinas and 38% are local (mixed ethnicity, other than Hawai'ian). With the five-year lifetime limit on TANF benefits expiring in a year, Native Hawai'ians, Filipinas, and persons of mixed ethnicities will find themselves in dire circumstances. Most of the issues that they face are directly related to their poverty:

Incarceration Rates

Hawai'i has the largest proportion of females in the prison population in the country. Girls are arrested and incarcerated at a higher rate in Hawai'i than anywhere else in America. The women and girl prisoners are primarily Native Hawai'ian. In 1970, there was one women incarcerated in the state; that number increased to 500 in 2001, 99% for nonviolent crimes such as drug possession. As high as 95% of incarcerated women need substance abuse treatment and are not getting it. Far more incarcerated girls (45%) than boys (7%) have attempted suicide and 38% of girls and 14% of boys reported being sexually abused in prison.

Health Disparities

Hawai'ians/Part Hawai'ians (23%) and Filipinas (20%) have the highest number of AIDS cases among all women in Hawai'i. Hawai'ians/Part Hawai'ians suffer the highest cancer rates. Working poor Hawai'ians and Asians, who mostly live in the rural parts of Oahu or the other islands, do not have transportation to access health services such as AIDS testing, prenatal care, pelvic exams, etc. Mobile mammography vans are often the only way that rural women can obtain mammograms, but such vans are not available on the neighbor islands. There is also a higher prevalence of domestic violence among Filipinos and Hawai'ians, at 18.2% and 16.1%, respectively.

Gaps in Education

Hawai'i is returning to a two-tiered segregated school system with Hawai'ians/Part Hawai'ians at the bottom. The children of middle class and more affluent Japanese and Chinese Americans attend private schools and the public schools are populated by Filipinos, Native Hawai'ians, and new Southeast Asian immigrants. The public schools are 19% Filipino and 25% Hawai'ian/Part Hawai'ian. However, respectively, these groups make up only 1.4% and 8.9% of the University of Hawai'i, Manoa campus.

Unequal Access to Employment

In the hotels, higher paid bell captains, front desk clerks, and maître d's have traditionally been Japanese Americans. Filipinos and Native Hawai'ians worked in the back of the house. Only now are second and third generation Filipinas moving into front desk positions. In the service sector, 80% of home care workers are Filipinas.

Homelessness

Of all Asian groups, Filipinos have the highest numbers of single female and family units who are homeless (5.77% single, 4.23% families). The largest Asian/Pacific Islander group with homeless single women and families are Hawai'ians/Part Hawai'ians (25.24% single women, 40.78% families) and Mixed/Cosmopolitan[8] (7.89% single, 12.69% families).

Welfare Reform

After the passage of welfare reform in 1996, Hawai'i did not create state substitute programs for food stamps or SSI for immigrants, pre- or post-enactment. Not until four years later, in 2000, did Hawai'i provide Medicaid for post-enactment children. Language access to these services is poor.

---

8.   A category sometimes used to capture any combination of two or more ethnic/racial backgrounds.

THE NATIVE HAWAI'IAN SOVEREIGNTY MOVEMENT

Native Hawai'ians have a markedly different view of Asian immigration and political ascendancy. The most outspoken in the sovereignty movement have been Native Hawai'ian women:

Modern Hawai'i, like its colonial parent the United States, is a settler society; that is, Hawai'i is a society in which the indigenous culture and people have been murdered, suppressed, or marginalized for the benefit of settlers who dominate our islands. In settler societies, the issue of civil rights is primarily an issue about how to protect settlers against each other and against the state. Injustices done against Native people, such as genocide, land dispossession, language banning, family disintegration, and cultural exploitation, are not part of this intrasettler discussion and therefore not within the parameters of civil rights.[9]

The Hawai'ian sovereignty movement asserts that Hawai'i has been overrun by non-Natives, including Asians. Haunani Trask explains: "Calling themselves 'local,' the children of Asian settlers greatly outnumber us. They claim Hawai'i as their own, denying indigenous history, their long collaboration with our continued dispossession, and the benefits therefrom." The sovereignty movement sees the triumphant story of the Japanese Americans over white racism and rise from plantation life to the middle class and political dominance as part of the history of Native Hawai'ian colonization. It sees that local Asians' efforts to differentiate themselves from haoles in Hawai'i only masks Native struggles against Asian settler colonialism. To the sovereignty movement there are no immigrants, only settlers and their children, and Asian Americans are seen as no different than white South Afrikaners and Israeli settlers on occupied territory. Many Native Hawai'ian women do not see their oppression and exploitation stemming only from class, race, and gender discrimination, but rather as violations of their human and sovereign rights as a people.

---

9.   Haunani-Kay Trask, "Settlers of Color and "Immigrant" Hegemony: "Locals" in Hawai'i," Amerasia Journal, Whose Vision? Asian Settler Colonialism in Hawai'i, UCLA Asian American Studies Center, Vol. 26, No.2, 2000.

Needless to say, Asian Americans in Hawai'i are threatened by losing the only home they have ever known. Former Senator Daniel Inoye had refused to introduce legislation designating Native Hawai'ians as an indigenous people in the same way Native Americans on the mainland have been designated and given ownership and jurisdiction over their own lands. Even the most progressive Asian Americans have an ambivalent relationship with the sovereignty movement.[10]

THE ORGANIZATIONS

There are very few organizations that advocate on behalf of Filipinos and Native Hawai'ians. Na Loio No Na Kanaka, a nonprofit legal service located in Honolulu, serves primarily low-income, limited-English speaking immigrants, with Filipinos being their largest client base since over half, or 56%, of annual immigration to Hawai'i is from the Philippines. Na Loio provides legal services in the areas of immigration, naturalization, political asylum, and domestic violence. Na Loio also engages in advocacy on behalf of immigrants before the state legislature.

The National Hawai'ian Legal Corporation is a nonprofit, public interest law firm representing Native Hawai'ians in their assertions of rights to land and natural resources and other entitlements. The Corporation has handled cases involving quiet titles (claims to disputed lands), Hawai'ian home lands program, ceded lands issues, tenants, water, access, fishing and religious rights, and historic preservation.

The Hawai'i Commission on the Status of Women is a state administrative agency which each year lobbies and tracks legislation pertaining to women. It conducts research and seeks and coordinates testimony to garner support or opposition for a bill. It provides support to the bipartisan Women's Legislative Caucus, that works to introduce bills concerning women. Its Violence Prevention Program monitored court cases and found that judges were issuing lenient sentences to sexual assault offenders. Its advocacy led to commitments from the prosecutor's office and the courts to seek and order sentences that reflected the seriousness of the crime. It has two staff members and its funding

---

10.   Ironically, while the descendents of Asians on Hawai'i do not self-identify as Asian American, Native Hawai'ians perceive Chinese, Japanese, Korean, Filipino, and Southeast Asians as the same and any differences between them are merely differences among intrasettlers

is threatened every year in the state budget process. It is incorporating as a 501(c)(3) so that it can raise funds to expand its work.

There is no other grassroots organizing among Filipinas to address their issues. The grassroots organizing in which Native Hawai'ian women are involved concern their fight for sovereignty, not civil rights. Most of the issues facing Filipina and Native Hawai'ian women are not being addressed.

REFERENCES

Bill, Teresa, Into the Marketplace: Working Class Women in 20th Century Hawai'i Labor's Heritage, Quarterly of the George Meany Memorial Archives, Vol. 9, No. 1, Summer 1997

Chinen, Joyce N., Ph.D., Japanese American Women in Hawai'i, Japanese American National Museum Quarterly, Vol.12, No.3, Winter 1997-98

Chinen, Joyce N., Ph.D., Sewing Resistance into the Grain: Hawai'i's Garment Workers at Work and at Home, Race, Gender & Class: Vo.4, No.3, 1997

Fujikane, Candace, Asian Settler Colonialism in Hawai'i, published in Amerasia Journal, Whose Vision? UCLA Asian American Studies Center, Vol. 26, No.2, 2000

Fujikane, Candace, Sweeping Racism under the Rug of "Censorship": The Controversy over Lois-Ann Yamanaka's Blu's Hanging, published in Amerasia Journal, Whose Vision? Asian Settler Colonialism in Hawai'i, UCLA Asian American Studies Center, Vol. 26, No. 2, 2000

Hawai'i State Data Book, 1999

Institute for Women's Policy Research, The Status of Women in Hawai'i: Politics, Economics, Health, Demographics, Washington DC, 2000

Rodrigues, Darlene, Imagining Ourselves: Reflections on the Controversy over Lois-Ann Yamanaka's Blu's Hanging, published in Amerasia Journal, Whose Vision? Asian Settler Colonialism in Hawai'i, UCLA Asian American Studies Center, Vol. 26, No. 2, 2000

Trask, Haunani-Kay, Settlers of Color and "Immigrant" Hegemony: "Locals" in Hawai'i, published in Amerasia Journal, Whose Vision? Asian Settler Colonialism in Hawai'i, UCLA Asian American Studies Center, Vol. 26, No.2, 2000

Women's Legislative Caucus, Package 2001, The Power of Leadership

Michelle "Monst*r" Esguerra and Boo Torres de Esguerra, plaintiffs in
a lawsuit, *Anderson v. King County, Washington*, seeking equal marriage rights for same sex partners and honorees at NAPAWF's 10th
Anniversary Fierce Sister Awards Dinner, 2006.

10

Asian American Lesbian, Bisexual, Transgender, and Queer Women—Moving from Isolation to Visibility

Updated by Rebecca Sawyer[1]

INTRODUCTION

The lives of Asian American lesbian, bisexual, transgender, and queer (LBTQ) women are impacted and complicated by their multiple and interconnected identities as racial, sexual and gender minorities.[2] They face all of the issues

---

1. Rebecca Sawyer, a queer hapa feminist, is chair for lesbian, bisexual, transgender, queer and questioning issues for the Washington, DC chapter of the National Asian Pacific American Women's Forum.

2. The abbreviation 'LBTQ' will be used throughout this chapter to refer to the lesbian, bisexual, transgender and queer communities. The term *gay* is not included in this discussion of the Asian American women's communities as it is largely understood to describe male homosexuality. When referring to lesbian, gay, bisexual, transgender and queer communities, the abbreviation 'LGBTQ' will be used. While the terms *lesbian* and *bisexual* are understood by most, a quick definition of *queer* and *transgender* is warranted for this discussion. *Queer* is a term that was once considered derogatory, but has since been reclaimed by a younger generation. Those individuals who view sexual orientation and gender identity and expression as inherently fluid embrace the term *queer*. Individuals of transgender experience are those individuals whose gender identity and expression do not match that of their biological gender. LBTQ should also be understood to include those individuals who are questioning their sexual orientation or gender identity.

that heterosexual Asian American women are affected by—from oppression based on immigration status to lack of adequate health care, as described in the previous chapters of this report. Asian American LBTQs are also impacted by the oppression and discrimination that all LBTQ women face in employment, housing, the military, family law, and other socioeconomic areas.

All lesbian, bisexual, transgender and queer women, including Asian American LBTQs, are denied many of the rights that heterosexual people take for granted. Most prominent among the rights denied LBTQs is the right to marry, encompassing over 1,000 federal rights associated with legal marriage. Same-sex couples are excluded from protections afforded by community property and intestate laws, and denied many rights that protect heterosexual partners and families, including the right to hospital visitation, the right to make health care decisions, and the right to health care coverage. Immigrations rights associated with marriage are especially important for bi-national couples. Without marriage rights, bi-national same-sex couples are denied the right to seek permanent residency and citizenship for the non-citizen partner. Moreover, many states do not allow same-sex couples to adopt children. Unlike married heterosexual couples, joint custody by the parent who is not the biological mother of a child is not automatic.

The fight for LBTQ equality goes far beyond marriage and adoption rights. In many states, LBTQs can be fired from their jobs simply for being who they are. Under the military's "Don't Ask, Don't Tell" law, LBTQs cannot serve in the armed forces openly. The health care needs of LBTQs are still not being met, as described in chapter 5. Like all LBTQs, Asian American LBTQ women are often the victims of hate crimes and suffer from domestic violence at the hands of their intimate partners.

The intricate multiplicity of Asian American LBTQ identities makes the exploration of how different forms of discrimination intersect and manifest for the Asian American LBTQ communities a key question for this chapter. This exploration begins with an outline of some of the coming out issues faced by Asian American LBTQs and the subsequent cultural isolation felt by many from both the heterosexual Asian American communities and the non-Asian LGBTQ communities. It should be noted that, given the scores of Asian subgroups, it is difficult to generalize about issues facing all Asian American LBTQs.

Additionally, only a handful of research studies and articles address the particular concerns of Asian American LBTQs. Asian American LGBTQ issues are marginalized in many areas of research, including health care research, as exemplified in the 1998 Institute of Medicine study on health care needs of lesbians and gays that excluded Asian American LBTQs.

This chapter attempts to describe the issues faced by Asian American LBTQs based on interviews of activists, an October 2000 survey by the Asian Pacific Islander Lesbian, Bisexual, Queer & Transgender Task Force (APL-BQT),[3] testimonies given to the Presidential Commission on Asian Americans and Pacific Islanders on November 13, 2000, and existing literature. The information gathered from these sources reveals the ways in which pan-Asian LBTQ women's issues are unique and different from the issues of other non-Asian LBTQ women and from straight Asian American women, and as such, requires advocacy specific to Asian American LBTQs.

COMING OUT AND OTHER ISSUES FACING ASIAN AMERICAN LBTQS

1. "There Are No Asian Lesbians!"

To the American public, the face of a lesbian is all too often the face of a white middle-class woman. Asian American LBTQs have very little presence in the mainstream or alternative media. Very rarely do they appear in commercial ads or brochures for the national outreach and educational campaigns of the white LGBTQ communities. Because Asian American LBTQs are invisible to the general public, many people believe that they simply do not exist. Although an increasing number of Asian American LBTQs are coming out and becoming more vocal in some areas of the country, there are still few visible role models for many young Asian American LBTQs and their families.

---

3.   This was a small pilot survey to assess the needs and attitudes of the Asian LGBT communities. It was conducted in English only over a two-and-a-half week period in October 2000 with 153 women of 11 Asian ethnicities from 19 states of the US participating. The results were presented to the Presidential Commission. Of the respondents, 42% were between the ages of 20 and 29 and 34% between 30 and 39; 67% were either born in the US or immigrated at a young age; and 46% were college educated.

For Asian Americans of transgender experience[4], the lack of visibility—and, where there is visibility, the lack of positive representation—is also problematic. Transgender individuals are not only discriminated against by the heterosexual population, but the lesbian, gay, bisexual and queer communities have not readily accepted them either. Because the term *transgender* reflects a gender identity or expression, some lesbian, gay, bisexual, and queer individuals do not see the struggles of the transgender communities as a part of their struggles.[5] This renders the lives of transgender individuals invisible not only to the heterosexual communities, but also to the lesbian, gay, bisexual and queer communities.

This overall lack of representation for LBTQs makes coming out to one's family very difficult. One Asian mother said to her daughter when she came out, "You can't be gay; Koreans aren't gay." Certain Asian American communities consider homosexuality a "Western" or "white" disease and think that their children would not be gay if they were still living in their home country. Certain Asian immigrant communities are isolated from or lack access to the public discourse on sexual orientation taking place in the United States that increasingly recognizes LGBTQ rights. This distance prevents these communities from understanding that LGBTQ individuals are a part of all cultures and hinders them from becoming more tolerant and accepting of a person's sexual orientation.

Some progress has been made in increasing the visibility of the Asian American LBTQ communities, especially in the arena of pop culture with films such as *Saving Face*, the 2004 film chronicling the lives of two Asian American lesbians. While representation of Asian American LBTQ women in the mainstream and alternative media has gradually increased, much more

---

4.   It should be noted that the term *transgender* is preferred over *transvestite* or *transsexual* as the former is considered derogatory and the latter limiting as it encompasses only those who've begun hormone treatment or undergone gender reassignment surgery. Additionally, the definition of transgender should be expanded to include gender expression, as the usage of the term in such phrases as "people of transgender experience" reflects recognition of gender fluidity.

5.   The limited rights that the lesbian, gay, bisexual and queer communities have gained do not necessarily provide similar protections to the transgender communities. For example, a hate crimes statute that protects a person because of his or her sexual orientation may not apply to an assault of a transgender person if the crime was based on the person's gender identity. However, transgender individuals would be protected if the statute included "gender identity and expression" as a protected class.

work is needed to ensure accurate and positive representation of the diversity of the Asian American LBTQ communities. Positive representation of Asian Americans of transgender experience is sorely needed. With increased visibility, not only will Asian American LBTQs gain a sense of empowerment, but also others—from the straight Asian American to the non-Asian LGBTQ communities—will gain a greater understanding of the issues that Asian American LBTQ communities face. Difficulties with family acceptance, personal safety, and other issues of concern for Asian American LBTQs could very well be mitigated.

2. Family Acceptance

Given the cultural barriers and the lack of representation of Asian American LBTQs, the coming out process for many Asian American LBTQs and their parents can be particularly traumatic. In the APLBQT survey, 40% of respondents ranked family acceptance as their most important need and 76% ranked it as a need overall. There are a number of difficulties unique to Asian American LBTQ women in coming out to their families. First, as explained in Chapter Six, in some Asian cultures, women are not seen as sexual beings. To declare one's lesbianism is to proclaim that one is a sexual being. Some Asian parents are shocked and have a difficult time accepting that their daughter is sexual, let alone that she is sexual in the context of a non-heterosexual relationship.

Additionally, first generation Asian family ties are very strong. Some Asian American daughters continue living with their parents as adults until they marry. When an Asian American lesbian continues to live at home, it is that much more difficult for her to come out because she is vulnerable to her parents, emotionally and financially.

In numerous testimonies before the Presidential Commission, Asian American LBTQs revealed how, in coming out to their parents, they were yelled at, physically abused, disowned, or kicked out of the house with all financial support severed. Some parents have responded violently, threatening to kill their daughters. If a woman is financially dependent on her parents, coming out is often not an option.

Being disowned is particularly traumatic for many Asian American LBTQs. As one Asian LBTQ activist explains, "Coming out to my parents was by far the most difficult aspect of being a lesbian—despite having been 'out' at work and to everyone else for many years, it was only recently, after having been active in both the Asian and lesbian and gay communities for over 20 years, that I overcame the fear of losing my parents and I finally came out to them." Regarding strong family ties, one Korean lesbian stated that Asian American daughters want to take care of their parents in their old age, and they face the difficult situation of having to choose between their personal happiness and their family's happiness.

Particularly in immigrant families, Asian American LBTQs do not want to bring shame onto their parents. As a Filipina testifies, "When Asian lesbians 'come out,' our families, especially our parents, go deep into the closet." Fearing that they will bring shame to the extended family, Asian parents remain silent, suffering in pain and isolation, not knowing who to tell or turn to. Very few resources exist for Asian parents to understand the coming out process. To date, only one organization, the San Francisco-based API Family Pride Council, strives to help Asian American families understand LGBTQ identities.

As more Asian American LBTQs come out at younger and younger ages, many may be forced to leave home. Not surprisingly, the increasing numbers of homeless Asian American LBTQs has become a critical problem. There are few shelters and resources devoted to their special needs, especially if they face language barriers or are undocumented. With no means of financial support, many end up on the streets trying to survive by prostituting themselves. Because of the great pressure to keep silent about their sexual orientation or the lack of places to turn for help, queer Asian American women, particularly Asian American LBTQ youth, may suffer higher than average rates of suicide attempts. As described in Chapter Five of this report, suicide rates among Asian American women ages 15 to 24 are the second highest in the nation. Suicide rates among lesbian, gay, bisexual and queer youth are also among the highest in the nation, with estimates that lesbian, gay, bisexual and queer youth attempt suicide at a rate 2-3 times higher than their straight peers; for transgender youth, the rate of suicide attempts is estimated at higher than 50%.[6] More studies need to be done to determine whether Asian American LBTQ youth are particularly at risk.

3. Personal Safety

In the APLBQT survey, respondents ranked personal safety as their second most important need. Eighty-seven percent of survey respondents reported

---

6. Source: University of New Hampshire's Counseling Center (http://www.unhcc.unh.edu/resources/glbt/glbtsuicide.html).

being yelled at or insulted because they were or were thought to be LBTQ. More than half of the respondents reported threats of physical violence, and 15% reported physical injury. These attacks may be because of their gender identity, race, or sexual orientation—or a combination of all of these identities. An Asian American lesbian who presents herself masculinely might be called a 'fag' when the attacker mistakes her for an effeminate gay Asian American man. Because the image of a masculine Asian American woman is so far from the attacker's stereotyped conception of what an Asian American woman should be, the attacker assumes her to be a man. The percentage of hate crimes were slightly higher among youth ages 18 to 23 and police protection emerged as one of the five top needs for this age group.

Transgender women are often the target of hate crimes, especially by police. In many areas of the U.S., it is a crime to cross dress. Transgender women tend to evoke particularly violent reactions from straight men. For example, a transgender woman from Thailand, married to an American citizen, was at a final INS interview for her green card. When the INS officer saw her Thai documents reflected her gender as "male," he harassed her aggressively and threatened to kill her, saying that he had a gun.

Job opportunities are minimal at best for Asian American transgender women, and many are forced to work as prostitutes, increasing their risk of contracting HIV/AIDS and other sexually transmitted infections.

FACING CULTURAL ISOLATION: RACISM, SEXISM, AND HOMOPHOBIA

As noted above, Asian American LBTQs face the same needs and issues as all other lesbians and Asian American women, yet none of the communities they are a part of, including the LGBTQ and mainstream straight Asian American communities, explicitly, let alone adequately, address their needs. Asian American LBTQ women are marginalized as they face combinations of cultural isolation, racism, sexism, homophobia, and xenophobia from one or more of their communities.

1. Isolation from the Non-Asian Lesbian Communities

Some Asian American LBTQs may not feel much kinship with white or non-Asian lesbians. The white lesbian communities often promote the concept of being "loud and proud" and many Asian LBTQs are not comfortable with this communication style. Just as stereotypes of Asian American women pervade the larger American society, white lesbians may also hold certain racial stereotypes about Asian women. For instance, when Jenny Shimizu first started appearing in the Calvin Klein ads, Asian women considered her butch and masculine. Many white women, however, insisted she could not be butch, and was simply androgynous. The racist stereotypes work in reverse when these same white women see African American lesbians; they assume African American lesbians are masculine and butch.

Furthermore, the services provided to white lesbians may not be applicable Asian American lesbians. For example, some advise LBTQs to come out to their parents when they are old enough to leave home but, as noted above, this strategy may not work for an Asian American LBTQ since she may not want to jeopardize losing her family by coming out. Cultural and language differences makes some Asian American LBTQ women uncomfortable in social settings or support groups with non-Asian lesbians. There is also lack of targeted outreach by LBTQ women's services organizations to Asian Americans LBTQs. Many lesbian health awareness programs or coming out brochures are not inclusive of Asian American LBTQs, and do no depict Asian American LBTQS. Furthermore, much of the information is in English only, rendering it problematic for non-English speaking Asian LBTQs. As a result, many Asian American LBTQs express a strong need to create a "safe space" for their communities and needs.

2. Racism and Sexism in the Larger Gay Communities

Racism within the white gay male community is perhaps more challenging for Asian American LBTQs. Often, the only thing an Asian American lesbian has in common with a gay white man is that neither are heterosexual. Some gay white men may have a difficult time understanding or relating to the issues of Asian American lesbians or any LGBT person of color because they enjoy, and do not recognize, the privileges of being white and male in a racist, patriarchal society. Racism on the part of gay men is disappointing since it means that the discriminatory experiences they have had as gay men have not sensitized them to the discrimination of other oppressed groups. A 2004 study from the National Gay and Lesbian Task Force found that 82% of surveyed

Asian American LGBTQs experience racism within the white LGBTQ communities.[7]

At a Gay Pride parade in New York one year, a Nazi gay man marched with a swastika. When an Asian American lesbian confronted him, the parade marshals stopped her. The parade marshals stated that any gay person has a right to march, even if he spews racism and hate toward people of color. In 1992, the Lambda Legal Defense and Education Fund, a national civil rights and law organization that champions gay and lesbian rights, used the racist and sexist Broadway play "Miss Saigon" as a benefit fund-raiser, ignoring objections by Asian American LGBTQs. Asian American activists initially protested the yellow-face casting of a white actor in the Asian male lead role. Asian American LBTQs were the first to point out the racist and sexist nature of the play itself. The Asian American queer communities, along with other queer communities of color, often finds itself in the position of pointing out racial discrimination and stereotyping in the broader LGBTQ communities.

The larger gay communities, in struggles to influence legislation, have further marginalized Asian American LBTQs. The state of Hawai'i's ballot initiative on same sex marriage was dominated by mainland-based white organizations, in particular, the Human Rights Campaign (HRC). HRC excluded Native Hawai'ians and Asian Americans LGBTQs from framing the issues and appearing in public to support the initiative. Instead, HRC mounted an abstract campaign with an obtuse message that the initiative was not about lesbian and gay rights, but rather, it was about defending constitutional rights. The Republicans and the religious right defeated the initiative as most voters, not hearing the voices of their Asian American and Native Hawai'ian sisters and brothers, mothers and fathers, did not see this as their issue.

Sexism also plays a role in the marginalization of Asian American LBTQS by the gay communities. The gay communities often only recognize the Asian American gay, bisexual and queer men's communities (often hypersexualizing or exoticizing these men), and neglect to recognize the existence of Asian American LBTQ women. This further renders invisible the lives of Asian American LBTQ women. Like non-Asian queer women, Asian American

---

7.   The *Asian Pacific American Lesbian, Gay, Bisexual and Transgender People: A Community Portrait* from the National Gay and Lesbian Task Force surveyed over 100 participants at the Queer Asian Pacific Legacy Conference in New York City in 2004. The survey participants included men, women and individuals of transgender experience.

LBTQ women also contend with the often patriarchal and sexist gay white men's communities.

3. Male-Dominated Asian American Gay Organizations

The issue of sexism is not one that is limited to the gay white men's communities. Asian American LBTQ women also face sexism from the Asian American gay men's communities. Some gay Asian American men's organizations have made efforts to address Asian American LBTQ's issues. However, sexism or insensitivity to women's issues contributes to their inability to provide long-term support for women's programs.

An example can be seen in co-gender HIV/STD prevention programs. In San Francisco at the API Wellness Center, AQUA (Asian and Pacific Islander, Queer & Questioning, 25 and Under, Altogether) operated for over three years organizing among young gay men before QUACK (Queer Asian Chicks) was formed to provide support and a safe space for Asian American LBTQs. When QUACK ran out of funding, the Wellness Center planned to end the program. The efforts of Asian American lesbians outside the organization ensured QUACK's survival.

4. Straight Asian Ethnic Organizations

Unless the issue involves HIV/AIDS, most Asian Pacific Islander community-based organizations do not consider Asian LBTQs to be their constituents. Most do not have anti-discrimination policies that include protections based on gender identity or sexual orientation. Staff are not trained on these issues or given sensitivity training in assisting LBTQ clients. In the National Gay and Lesbian Task Force study, over 73% of respondents stated that mainstream national Asian American organizations did not adequately address LGBT rights.

When the Korean Americans for Civil Rights in Los Angeles requested various API community-based organizations to lend their names to opposing an anti-gay state initiative sponsored by Korean Republicans, some readily agreed but the staff in others could not decide and punted the issue to their Board of Directors.

Another example of the discrimination LBTQ can experience from the API community is the experience of the South Asian Lesbian and Gay Association (SALGA) when it sought permission to participate in the annual India Day Parade in New York City. For seven years, the Federation of Indian Associations (FIA) refused to permit SALGA to march in the parade, citing various and inconsistently applied bureaucratic reasons. The FIA pointed out that SALGA was not an FIA member, even though it allowed other non-FIA members to participate. With the support of local politicians, communities organizations, South Asian activist groups and gay and lesbian organizations, SALGA was finally granted permission to participate in 2000.

However, not all mainstream Asian American organizations neglect to include Asian American LBTQs in their agenda. Progress continues to be made as organizations like the Asian American Justice Center (formerly National Asian Pacific American Legal Consortium, or NAPALC) and the National Asian Pacific American Women's Forum (NAPAWF) embrace and advocate for LGBTQ issues.

5. Barriers to Social Services

Given the cultural isolation, homophobia, racism, and sexism that exist for Asian American LBTQ women, it is not surprising that their needs are not being met. For example, a Korean-speaking lesbian recently arrived in the U.S. might be extremely reluctant to approach a Korean social service agency for fear of exposure as a lesbian. She might not be aware of the existence of LGBTQ social service providers and even if she found one, she probably would not find Korean-speaking staff and culturally appropriate services. Mental health professionals and other service providers are generally ill-equipped to address the multiple oppression queer Asian women face.

Families of Asian lesbians also have few resources to deal with the coming out process. Parents, Families & Friends of Lesbians and Gays (PFLAG), with over 350 chapters around the country, supports families through the coming out process, but participants in their support groups are 95% Caucasian and sessions are conducted in English only. A monolingual immigrant parent of an Asian lesbian would not be able to participate. Even English-speaking Asian American parents find it difficult to participate because, as previously noted, many Asians believe that they must solve their problems within the family, and are reluctant to seek outside support and share private family issues with outsiders. Unfortunately, despite repeated requests to do so, PFLAG has not adequately addressed the needs of Asian families with LBTQ daughters. As mentioned above, the API Family Pride Council remains one of few resources for families of Asian American LBTQs.

ADVOCACY

1. Strengthened Coalitional Identity

With few resources available specifically for Asian American LBTQ women, much work is needed to strengthen how mainstream Asian American and LGBTQ organizations address the particular needs and issues of Asian American LBTQs. An understanding of the identities of Asian American LBTQ women as a coalitional one is the first step in addressing the needs of Asian American LBTQ women.

Progressive-minded, predominantly straight Asian American organizations have led the charge by embracing LGBTQ equality as a basic issue of civil rights. Organizations such as the Japanese American Citizens League, NAPAWF, and the Asian American Justice Center have all publicly voiced support for marriage equality for LGBTQ people. Predominantly non-Asian LGBTQ organizations need to include Asian Americans in their agenda by not only including representations of Asian American LBTQs in their work, but by also including the issues of all communities of color. LGBTQ organizations need to begin to defend immigrants' rights and need to organize and provide social services in languages other than English.

Recent examples of organizing around marriage equality exemplify the type of coalitional work deeply needed. In 2004, the national coalition Asian Equality (formerly Asian Pacific American Coalition for Equality), brought together not only Asian American LGBTQ community leaders, but also members of the Asian American and LGBTQ communities across the country in their work to educate others on marriage equality and its impact on Asian American LGBTQ communities. In late 2005, a Washington, D.C. area coalition of Asian Equality, the DC Chapter of the NAPAWF, local Asian American LGBTQ organizations, and student organizations from the University of Maryland at College Park worked together to put on an educational town hall on marriage equality and the Asian American LGBTQ communities. The coalition brought in Gita Deane, a South Asian lesbian who is a plaintiff in a Maryland marriage equality lawsuit, to speak firsthand about the effects of a lack of marriage rights on her family. Such events not only do much toward understanding the intersectionality of racial, sexual and gender identities, but they also strengthen a greater sense of community across racial, sexual and gender lines.

2. Moving Forward: from Social to Political Organizing

Within the Asian American LGBTQ communities specifically, in order to begin to tackle coalition work with other organizations, a paradigm shift from social organizing to political organizing needs to occur.

Asian American LBTQs have been organizing since the mid 1970's when they first discovered each other within the "feminist" or "women's" movement and people of color communities during the time of Third World Liberation politics. Initially, Asian women and lesbians came together for support. By the mid 1980's, local Asian lesbian groups throughout the U.S. began to form in San Francisco, New York, Los Angeles, Chicago, Minneapolis, Madison, Boston, and other major metropolitan areas. The first and only national grassroots organization, the Asian Pacific Lesbian, Bisexual Women's and Transgender Network (APLBTN), was founded in 1987, networking nearly 31 queer Asian women's organizations across the country. APLBTN, pronounced "Apple Button," was the central force behind the Presidential Commission's November 13, 2000 hearing, organizing the APLBTN Task Force, which prepared several hundred pages of a report and testimonies that were presented to the Commission. APLBTN also has organized many events, including national and regional retreats and conferences, and an Activist Institute to provide leadership training and skills-building for young Asian LBTQs. It has mobilized contingents to participate in national marches in Washington DC and New York and educated its constituency on political issues such as pushing for support of same-sex marriage within the Japanese American Citizens League, Hawai'i, California, and Vermont. APLBTN does all this, yet operates without an office, staff, or budget. As an all-volunteer organization, APLBTN is very fragile as an institution. Without funding, it cannot follow up on its many initiatives, and so must function mostly as a network or clearinghouse.

Despite the political work of APLBTN and other similar national grassroots networks, many of the existing organizations specifically for Asian American LBTQs exist solely to organize social events for their members. While this is itself an important function, in order to achieve visibility and understanding around the multiplicity of Asian American LBTQ identity much needs to be done in the political arena. The support for such a paradigm shift can—and should—come from within those organizations. It should also, however, come from national mainstream Asian American and LGBTQ organizations, as well as funders. Local Asian American LBTQ organizations have few, if any, resources—both in terms of financial resources and membership capacity—to do the type of organizing needed to improve the lives of their members. If mainstream organizations were to say to Asian American LBTQ community members that they wanted to tackle the particular issues of Asian American LBTQs in their agenda, it would not only positively assert the visibility of Asian American LBTQ issues, but would also motivate and mobilize those from within the Asian American LBTQ communities to further action.

This further action should not only address the full gamut of issues faced by Asian American LBTQs, but it should also include the creation of a support structure for mentorship of young leaders. The nurturing and creation of Asian American LBTQ leaders is a needed next step towards raising the visibility of the Asian American LBTQ communities. Creating a mentorship program, where youth are provided with positive role models, will help educate and empower young Asian American LBTQs. By taking this first step toward a viable, sustainable leadership and a further politicizing of the Asian American LBTQ communities, acceptance and understanding will be at reached.

REFERENCES

Alcantara, Margarita et al., Yellowdykecore: "Queer, Punk 'n' Asian, A Rountable Discussion," published in *Dragon Ladies, Asian American Feminists Breathe Fire*, Sonia Shah, ed., South End Press, 1997

Asian Pacific Islander Lesbian, Bisexual, Queer & Transgender Task Force, *Report to the Presidential Commission on Asian Americans and Pacific Islanders*, November 13, 2000

Chan, Connie S., "Issues of Sexual Identity in an Ethnic Minority: The Case of Chinese American Lesbians, Gay Men and Bisexual People." *Lesbian, Gay and Bisexual Identities Over the Lifespan: Psychological Perspectives*, eds. Anthony R. D'Augelli and Charlotte J. Patterson, New York: Oxford University Press, 1995.

Dang, Alain & Hu, Mandy. "Asian Pacific American Lesbian, Gay, Bisexual and Transgender People: A Community Portrait. A report from New York's Queer Asian Pacific Legacy Conference, 2004." New York: National Gay and Lesbian Task Force Policy Institute, 2005.

Eng, David L., and Hom, Alice Y., eds. *Q & A: Queer in Asian America*. Philadelphia: Temple University Press, 1998.

Family Violence Prevention Fund and Asian Women's Shelter, "The Queer Asian Women's Community, Understanding Same Gender Relationship Violence & Meeting the Needs of All Battered Women," draft, date unknown.

Lim-Hing, Sharon, ed. *The Very Inside: An Anthology of Writing by Asian and Pacific Islander Lesbian and Bisexual Women*. Toronto: Sister Vision Press, 1994.

Hom, Alice Y., "Addressing Differences: A Look at the Asian Pacific Lesbian Network Retreat, Santa Cruz 1989" *Privileging Positions: the Sites of Asian American Studies*, eds. Gary Okihiro, et al. Pullman, WA: Washington State University Press, 1995: 301-308.

Hom, Alice Y., "In Print/In Practice: Linking Images and Politics of Asian American Lesbian/Bisexual Women," *Asian Pacific American Genders and Sexualities*, ed. Thomas K. Nakayama. Conference proceedings. Tempe, AZ: Arizona State University, 1999: 13-27.

Lu, Lynn, Critical Visions, "The Representation and Resistance of Asian Women," published in *Dragon Ladies, Asian American Feminists Breathe Fire*, Sonia Shah, editor, South End Press, 1997.

National Coalition of Anti-Violence Programs, "Lesbian Gay, Transgender and Bisexual (LGBT) Domestic Violence in 1999," 2000 Final Edition.

Pegues, Juliana, "Strategies From the Field, Organizing the Asian American Feminist Movement," published in *Dragon Ladies, Asian American Feminists Breathe Fire*, Sonia Shah, ed., South End Press, 1997.

APPENDIX
List of Interviewees

Chapter 1 Welfare Reform's Impact on Asian American Women

Jane Bai & Eric Tang, Committee Against Anti-Asian Violence (CAAAV), New York, NY

Luz Buitrago, formerly with Center on Poverty Law and Economic Opportunity, Oakland, CA

Rini Chakaborty, formerly with California Immigrant Welfare Collaborative, Sacramento, CA

Christina Chung & Dennis Kao, Asian Pacific American Legal Center, Los Angeles, CA

Gen Fujioka, Asian Law Caucus, San Francisco, CA

Dan Hosang, Grass Roots Organizing for Welfare Leadership (GROWL), Oakland, CA

Pat McManaman, Na Loio No Na Kanaka, Honolulu, HI

Karen Narasaki, Asian American Justice Center (formerly National Asian Pacific American Legal Consortium), Washington, DC

Doris Ng, formerly with Equal Rights Advocates, San Francisco, CA

Amy Taylor, New York Immigrant Coalition, New York, NY

Jim Williams & Naomi Zanderer, National Employment Law Project, New York, NY

Chia Vang, Urban Coalition, Minneapolis/St. Paul, MN

Ka Ying Yang, formerly with Southeast Asia Resource Action Center (SEARAC), Washington DC

Ly Vang, Association for Advancement of Hmong Women, Minneapolis, MN

Naly Yang, formerly with Women's Association of Hmong and Lao, St. Paul, MN

Sung Kyu Yun, National Korean American Services and Education Consortium (NAKASEC), Flushing, NY

Wendy Zimmerman, Urban Institute, Washington DC

Chapter 2 Trafficking in Asian Women

Muneer Ahmad. formerly with Asian Pacific American Legal Center, Los Angeles, CA

Nahar Alam, Andolan, New York, NY

Hae-Jung Cho & Kathryn McMahon, Coalition Against Slavery and Trafficking in Women (CAST), Los Angeles, CA

Helen Choi, Asian Task Force Against Domestic Violence, Boston, MA

Lana Hoang, Asian Women's Shelter, San Francisco, CA

Ken Kimmerling & Chumtoli Huq, American Legal Defense and Education Fund, New York, NY

Ivy Lee, formerly with Asian Law Caucus, San Francisco, CA

Carol Pier, Human Rights Watch, Washington DC

Debra Suh, Center for the Pacific Asian Family, Los Angeles, CA

Joy Zarembka, Campaign for Migrant Domestic Workers Rights c/o Institute for Policy Studies, Washington DC

Chapter 3 Asian American Garment Workers

Rini Chakraborty, Sweatshop Watch, Los Angeles, CA

Jill Esbenshade, California State University, San Diego, Department of Sociology

Margaret Fung & Ken Kimberling, Asian American Legal Defense and Education Fund (AALDEF), New York, NY

Tarry Hum, Department of Urban Studies, Queens College, City University of New York, Flushing, NY

Nan Lafhuay, Asian Immigrant Women Advocates, Oakland, CA

Joanne Lum & Karah Newton, National Mobilization Against Sweat Shops, New York, NY

Hina Shah, formerly with Asian Law Caucus, San Francisco, CA

Betty Yu, Chinese Staff & Workers Association, New York, NY

Chapter 4 Other Low Wage Workers

Domestic Workers

Nahar Alam, Andolan, New York, NY

Jane Bai, Ai Jen Poo & Caroline De Leon, Committee Against Anti-Asian Violence, New York, NY

Lillian Galedo, Filipinos for Affirmative Action, Oakland, CA

Ken Kimmerling & Chumtoli Huq, Asian American Legal Defense and

Education Fund, New York, NY

Homecare Workers

Leon Chow, United Health Care Workers West, San Francisco, CA

Rachele Savola, SEIU Local 616, Oakland, CA

Mila Thomas, SEIU Local 616, Oakland, CA

Chapter 5 Health Care Needs

May Akimine, Kalihi Palama Health Center, Honolulu, HI

Lisa Hasegawa, formerly with Office of the White House Initiative on Asian Americans and Pacific Islanders, Rockville, MD

Allicyn Hikida Tasaka, Hawai'i State Commission on the Status of Women, Honolulu, HI

Afton Hirohama, National Asian Women's Health Organization, San Francisco, CA

Val Kanuha, University of Hawai'i—School of Social Work, Honolulu, HI

Rod Lew & Karen Rezai, Association of Asian and Pacific Islander Community Health Organizations (AAPCHO), Oakland, CA

Eveline Shen & Gina Acebo, Asian Communities for Reproductive Justice (formerly Asians and Pacific Islanders for Reproductive Health), Oakland, CA

Shobha Srinivasan & Tessie Guillermo, Asian & Pacific Islander American Health Forum, San Francisco, CA

Chapter 6 Sexual and Reproductive Freedom

Cindy Choi, formerly with Environmental Justice Fund, Los Angeles, CA

Vanessa Chong, American Civil Liberties Union of Hawai'i, Honolulu, HI

Lisa Ikemoto, Loyola Law School, Los Angeles, CA

Miriam Kuppermann, University of California—San Francisco, San Francisco, CA

Peggy Saika, Oakland, CA

Eveline Shen & Gina Acebo, Asians and Pacific Islanders for Reproductive Health, Oakland, CA

Chapter 7 Domestic Violence

Judy Chen, Washington State Coalition Against Domestic Violence, Seattle, WA

Colleen Ching, Pat McManaman, Jodi Nishioka, Na Loio No Na Kanaka, Honolulu, HI

Chic Dabby, Asian and Pacific Islander Domestic Violence Institute, San Francisco, CA

Justin Fujikawa, API Family and Safety Center, Seattle, Washington

Ivy Lee, formerly with Asian Law Caucus, San Francisco, CA

Pacyinz Lyfoung, formerly with Asian Women United, Minneapolis, St. Paul, MN

Janice Kaguyutan, NOW Legal Defense and Education Fund, Washington DC

Leni Marin and Debbie Lee, Family Violence Prevention Fund, San Francisco, CA

Beckie Masaki, Asian Women's Shelter, San Francisco, CA

Mee Moua, Hmong Bar Association, Roseville, MN

Gail Pendleton, National Immigration Project–National Lawyer's Guild, Boston, MA

Bo Thao, Hmong Women's Action Team, St. Paul, MN

Pradeepta Upadhyay, Chaya, Seattle, Washington

Chapter 8 Hmong Women in the US

Keo Chang, Hmong American Partnership and Professional Hmong Women's Association, St. Paul, MN

May Ying Ly, Hmong Women's Heritage Association, Sacramento, CA

Pacyinz Lyfoung, formerly with Asian Women United, St.Paul/Minneapolis, MN

Kashia Moua, founder, Hmong Women Circle, Madison, WI

Sheng Lee, Hmong Women's Action Team and Professional Hmong Women's Association

Mee Moua, Hmong Bar Association, Roseville, MN

Bo Thao, formerly with Hmong National Development, Inc.

Chia Vang, Urban Coalition, St. Paul/Minneapolis, MN

Chu Vue (Male), Hmong Circle of Peace, St. Paul, MN

Ly Vang, Association for Advancement of Hmong Women, Minneapolis, MN

Naly Yang, formerly with Women's Association of Hmong and Lao, St. Paul, MN

Nou Yang, Hmong Womwn Circle, St. Paul, MN

Chapter 9 Hawai'i

Amy Agbayani, Student Equity Education and Diversity, University of Hawai'i—Student Services. Honolulu, HI

Joyce Chinen, University of Hawai'i-West Oahu, Pearl City, HI

Ku'umealoha Gomes, Kua'ana Student Services, University of Hawai'i—Manoa, Honolulu, HI

Marya Grambs, Honolulu, HI

William Hoshijo, Hawai'i Civil Rights Commission, Honolulu, HI

Chris Iijima, William S. Richardson School of Law, University of Hawai'i—Manoa, Honolulu, HI

Kyle Kajihiro, American Friends Service Committee, Honolulu, HI

Val Kanuha, University of Hawai'i-School of Social Work, Honolulu, HI

Mire Koikari, UH-Manoa-Women's Studies, Honolulu, HI

Ah Quon McElrath, Honolulu, HI

Pat McManaman, Na Loio No Na Kanaka, Honolulu, HI

Leanne Miyasato, Asian Pacific American Women's Leadership Institute, Honolulu, HI

Hermina Morita, Hawai'i State Representative—District 12, Honolulu, HI

Suzanne Chun Oakland, Hawai'i State Senator—District 14, Honolulu, HI

Chapter 10 Asian American LBTs

Dipti Ghosh, Trikone—Bay Area, San Jose CA

Judy Han, Korean Americans for Civil Rights, Los Angeles/Oakland, CA

Alice Hom, Los Angeles, CA

Christina Hwang, formerly with National Center for Lesbian Rights, San Francisco, CA

Val Kanuha, University of Hawai'i—School of Social Work, Honolulu, HI

Christine Lipat, Astrea Lesbian Action Foundation, New York, NY

Trinity Ordona, API-PFLAG Family Project and Institute for Health and Aging, San Francisco, CA

Janet SooHoo & Anne Xuan Clark, Asian Pacific Lesbian Bisexual Queer Transgender Task Force, Seattle, WA

Doreena Wong, Asian Pacific Lesbian Bisexual Network, San Francisco, CA and National Health Law Project, Los Angeles, CA

About the Author

Lora Jo Foo is a labor and community organizer and an attorney. She was born and raised in the San Francisco Chinatown community where she began working as a garment worker in a sweatshop at the age of 11. As a student in the early 1970's at San Francisco State College, she became a feminist and co-taught the college's first Asian American Women's course. From college, she went back into a garment factory to work with Asian, Latina and African American garment workers, this time as a union organizer. She was a leader in the 1980 citywide strike of 6000 San Francisco hotel workers. After graduating from law school in 1985, she worked for private labor law firms representing unions. She was with the Asian Law Caucus in San Francisco California from 1992 to 2000 where she represented Asian American immigrant workers in sweatshop industries in their struggles for decent wages and working conditions. She litigated numerous groundbreaking cases on behalf of these workers. In 1999 she led a statewide coalition of garment worker advocates in passing the California Garment Accountability Bill which holds retailers and apparel firms strictly liable for the minimum wage and overtime violations of their contractors. She co-founded the California-based Sweatshop Watch in 1995 and the National Asian Pacific American Women's Forum ion 1996. Ms. Foo returned to graduate school and in 2002 obtained her Masters in Public Administration from the Kennedy School of Government, Harvard University. She has returned to her roots as a labor organizer and today works as the organizing director for a major union in California. She lives in the San Francisco Bay Area.

978-0-595-45299-6
0-595-45299-X

CPSIA information can be obtained at www.ICGtesting.com
Printed in the USA
LVOW08s1708240616

494010LV00001B/197/P